T0318621

Dwelling, Building, Thinking

TRANSGRESSIONS: CULTURAL STUDIES AND EDUCATION

VOLUME 127

The titles published in this series are listed at *brill.com/tcse*

Dwelling, Building, Thinking

A Post-Constructivist Perspective on Education, Learning, and Development

By

Wolff-Michael Roth

BRILL

SENSE

LEIDEN | BOSTON

All chapters in this book have undergone peer review.

The Library of Congress Cataloging-in-Publication Data is available online at http://catalog.loc.gov

ISSN 2214-9732
ISBN 978-90-04-37691-5 (paperback)
ISBN 978-90-04-37712-7 (hardback)
ISBN 978-90-04-37713-4 (e-book)

This book is printed on acid-free paper and produced in a sustainable manner.

Contents

Preface

Appearing in various guises, constructivism is the dominant epistemology in education today. This epistemology holds that the individual is constructing itself, its identity, its beliefs, and its knowledge – sometimes alone, sometimes in interaction with others. The Self who does the construction is presupposed. Indeed, the term *inter*action is based on the a priori separation of the individuals between whom the actions is said to operate: one acts on the other. In interactions with others, and, as part of the exchange, individuals are said to negotiate and then internalize new forms of knowledge. That is, first the unity of relation is taken apart into elements, the individual, and then the attempt is made to put the broken unity back together again. This is hard and even impossible given that the problem of intersubjectivity poses. Every person acts in the world through the lens of its individual, subjective constructions. The result of theorizing the being of humans is that they appear as ratiocinating individuals, who, engaged in their autopoietic projects, make themselves. There are less important epistemologies – such as enactivism and embodiment theory – that attempt to make thematic the important role of the body in human knowing and behavior. Yet these epistemologies – precisely because of the focus on the individual body – do not get away from the idea of human becoming as an autopoietic project that is anchored in the materiality of that body.

There already exist radical alternatives to constructivism in which there is a primacy of the social and include the material body, endowed with the capacity to suffer – i.e. with *passibility* – as a condition of any knowing and consciousness. Constructivism completely fails to account for the fact that we are affected, subject and subjected to conditions that we nevertheless contribute to making. Moreover, it fails to recognize the world as transactional so that no act can be attributed to an individual (mind) unless some reduction has occurred. Even 'dependency', 'aggressiveness', or 'pride', words normally considered to refer to individual characteristics, 'have their roots in what happens between persons, not in some something-or-other inside a person'.[1] As shown in cases such as having an insight or falling ill, we are as much patients as we are agents in and of life; and as shown in the case of query–reply sequences, from the perspective of a conversation, there are no statements that have the social function of questions unless there are statements that have the function of replies that make and vice versa. Although (phenomenological) philosophers have recognized and articulated these aspects of the human condition, the research community by and large has failed to develop an epistemological position that takes into account how, as teachers and students, we *actually* witness and feel our living of life. This includes how we undergo our own thinking and learning, the feeling of resistance to which we are subjected in regards to our own intentional endeavors, how we come to recognize history in our personal actions, and so on.

In this book, a series of investigations are presented to constitute and exemplify a different epistemology in and for education. This epistemology emphasizes how we always already find ourselves in situations that we live in and through and that much of what we do is not characterized by ratiocination ('interpretation'): we walk without calculating and placing our feet, and we talk without producing phrases or complete, fully articulated ideas in our heads only to spill them like beans. This idea of life – on that goes on and is grounded in our familiar and habitual behavior – is captured in the notion of *dwelling*, which, as suggested here, precedes and is the condition of any building and thinking ('constructing'). This dwelling always is social through and through. Theorizing in this way has the consequence that the derivatives of dwelling, building and thinking, also are social rather than individual. This social nature of humans is the condition for anything that we classify under thinking or mind; and it is the condition for our sense of the Self as distinct from the other, human or material.

In its approach, this book follows particular themes and the rigor that characterized the classical philosophical studies (e.g. Edmund Husserl, Martin Heidegger, Maurice Merleau-Ponty). It pursues these themes through the lens of social (psychological) theory, as articulated in the works of Lev S. Vygotsky, Mikhail M. Bakhtin, George Herbert Mead, and Gregory Bateson. The present book differs from other studies in that it takes a concrete approach by extensively describing actual experiences and scenes from classroom life. In its particular rigor, this volume differs from many texts that currently exist in the field of education, where there frequently is an emphasis on describing the singular (as in phenomeno*graphy*) rather than on describing the general processes that give rise to the phenomena as we experience them (phenomenalization and phenomeno*logy*, the science of phenomena).

In each chapter, examples are used to which readers can easily relate, from everyday life in and outside the classroom. I develop the different, phenomenological way of thinking in and through the careful, slow reading of these everyday examples, thereby never leaving readers in dark – as philosophers sometimes do – about how the concepts relate to and realize themselves in the life we all know so well through common, mundane, and daily living. This daily life is the origin of common sense, and any new and unfamiliar *things, actions*, or *events* that we may encounter will make sense if they fit within one of the many contextures that we are already familiar with – like an unfamiliar word of the English language that has a place in this language, and that makes sense because of the place it has within the contexture that includes all the other words with which we are already familiar. These familiar words in turn are part of the vast ensemble of social activities that we have produced and undergone with others. Any word that I encounter makes as much sense to me as I make sense of it – a statement that foreshadows the different perspective on the subject and subjectivity developed in the course of this book.

This book is the result of ideas and empirical materials that I have accumulated (and that have transformed my thinking) over the course of an extended period of time. The empirical materials appearing in chapters 2 and 5 were collected with the help of grants from the Social Sciences and Humanities Research Council of Canada. Some of the chapters are based on earlier publications, the materials of which are developed to new levels in this book to represent my current ways of understanding the world. Since about 2011, I have suggested that we need to move beyond constructivism, showing where this metaphor of knowing and learning reaches its limits because it fails to account for *possibility* and its role in the constitution of humanity.[2] It fails to account how we really come to know, learn, and develop. At that time, I strongly felt the need to develop a post-constructivist epistemology that also accounted for a range of other phenomenon that do not return us to idealism of which constructivism in fact is only the last reincarnation and a philosophical position that has been discredited for a long time.

My recent engagement with the works of L. S. Vygotsky, G. H. Mead, and Alfred Schütz were decisive in opening up avenues for theorizing knowing and learning in ways that do not reproduce the errors of radical or social constructivism. These earlier works of mine, though I now recognize them as more naïve, nevertheless constituted the ground for overcoming this naïveté – which is one of the themes in this book. Thus, prior to considering the notion of *dwelling*, I had described how the non-moving earth constituted the vary basis and ground upon which all of our thinking capacities are built.[3] This is the ground in which we are rooted and from which we come. Any disregard for this ground will lead to the sense of being uprooted (chapter 3). Under this condition, one has to ask: how can (radically) new (e.g. scientific) knowledge emerge from being rooted in a condition that begins with all the things characteristic of a child's naïveté. I attempted a first answer in an analysis of online videos in the context of which I showed how such videos allow the re-production and re-understanding of the initial overturning from common sense to scientific sense.[4] A video on the heart and circulatory system is compared with the observations of an English doctor, who was the first to describe and theorize the now-accepted view on these phenomena. We often learn when we are struck (passive tense) by something surprising, something that has 'hit' us, which we did not see and which thus was unforeseen. I began to articulate implications of such experiences in an article that describes how a girl in a mathematics class initially felt an object hidden from view to be a cube until, surprisingly, she began to feel it as a rectangular prism.[5] While working on this and similar cases, I treated the having of an insight as a sudden, instantaneous phenomenon – until I later realized that awareness is not instantaneous. There is instead a movement of *becoming aware*.[6] These new ideas have their origin in detailed and meticulous analyses of what people actually see, attend to, and make available to one another

– thus available to the researcher as well; and they have their origin in the detailed and disimpassioned analyses of situations that I have undergone and lived through – such as the noted phenomenalization of awareness. Other significant situations I underwent that led to the position articulated here involve suddenly finding myself struck by a mysterious illness, which, though many different doctors tried to uncover its source, could not be diagnosed.[7] It would not have been appropriate here to reproduce (reprint) these first studies because I am finding myself to have moved on and I am not able to look back on this earlier work from a new phase in my development. But the materials, the phenomena, because of their everydayness, nevertheless are useful and instructive – which is why I have made use of these again.

Notes

[1] Gregory Bateson, *Mind and Nature: A Necessary Unity* (New York: E. P. Dutton, 1979), 133.

[2] Wolff-Michael Roth, *Possibility: At the Limits of the Constructivist Metaphor* (Dordrecht: Springer, 2011).

[3] Wolff-Michael Roth, 'Enracinement or The Earth, the Originary Ark, Does not Move – on the Phenomenological (Historical and Ontogenetic) Origin of Common and Scientific Sense and the Genetic Method of Teaching (for) Understanding', *Cultural Studies of Science Education*, vol. 10 (2015), 469–494.

[4] Wolff-Michael Roth, and Norm Friesen, 'Nacherzeugung, Nachverstehen: a Phenomenological Perspective on How Public Understanding of Science Changes by Engaging with Online Media', *Public Understanding of Science*, vol. 23 (2014), 850–865.

[5] Wolff-Michael Roth, 'On the Pregnance of Bodily Movement and Geometrical Objects: A Post-Constructivist Account of the Origin of Mathematical Knowledge', *Journal of Pedagogy*, vol. 5 (2014), 65–89.

[6] Wolff-Michael Roth, 'Becoming Aware: Towards a Post-constructivist Theory of Learning', *Learning: Research and Practice,* vol. 1 (2015), 38–50.

[7] Wolff-Michael Roth, 'Personal Health – Personalized Science: a New Driver for Science Education?', *International Journal of Science Education*, vol. 36 (2014), 1434–1456.

List of Figures

Consciousness [Bewußtsein] never can be anything else than the conscious Being [bewußte Sein], and the Being of men is their real life process. … It is not consciousness that determines life, but life determines consciousness.[1]

Building and thinking are, each in its own way, inevitable for dwelling. The two, however, also are insufficient for dwelling so long as each busies itself with its own affairs in separation, instead of listening to one another. This they are able to do if both, building and thinking, belong to dwelling, remain within their limits and know that the one as much as the other comes from the workshop of long experience and incessant practice.[2]

Notes

[1] Karl Marx and Friedrich Engels, *Werke Band 3* (Berlin: Dietz, 1978), 26 and 27.
[2] See Martin Heidegger, 'Wohnen, Bauen, Denken', in *Gesamtausgabe. I. Abteilung: Veröffentlichte Schriften 1910–1976. Band 7: Vorträge und Aufsätze* (Frankfurt/M: Vittorio Klostermann, 2000), 163.

1

Toward Post-Constructivist Epistemology

In the epigraph on page 1, there are quotations from the works of two very differ-ent philosophers, each taking *Being* (dwelling) as the condition for consciousness, for example, in the form of building and thinking. The two philosophers – Karl Marx and Martin Heidegger – articulate a position that is opposite to that typical of constructivism, where something is mentally constructed before it *is*. The position is epitomized in the following description how the Self comes to exist for a human subject: 'Just as we construct a *model* of a world, externalize it, and then treat it as thought its existence were independent of our doing, so we construct a model of the entity that we call our "self" and externalize it so that it ends up as a "thing among other things"'.[1] The constructivist scholar thereby literally turns the issue on its head so that people and their relations to each other and the world appear as if they were projected through the pinhole of a camera obscura. We might alterna-tively say that constructivism puts the cart (mind) before the horse (real life). Karl Marx and Friedrich Engels, who specifically critique German ideology also point out that the very existence of these illusory conceptions have to be understood as the consequence of the real conditions and relations of those who pronounce and adhere to such ideologies.[2] They recommend that a more appropriate approach to being exists in theorizing characteristics of human individual and social life with the real conditions, real individuals, and their real actions that are part of the mun-dane life process also producing the life conditions. In this book, the conditions of life, the real life process, is thought of by means of *dwelling*. It is out of dwelling that any building arises; and with building, thinking also becomes possible. When we look at the closest relatives of humans, chimpanzees, we observe that new forms of behavior emerge that are not innate and which new generations learn while participating in collective life. They fashion (build) tools to get at food prior to devouring it. In other instances, young chimpanzees will have been picked up by their mothers many times before they produce a sign to communicate wanting to be picked up (e.g. because she is a distance away from the infant or has not started the

© KONINKLIJKE BRILL NV, LEIDEN, 2018 | DOI 10.1163/9789004377134_001

pickup movement). The chimpanzee infant's sign exists in the form of one part of the movements when it is picked up, which in the infant's behavior comes to be 'frozen' into a posture. The mother *treats* the posture as a *sign* for the infant wanting to be picked up. That is, first there *is* a movement (Being), which then is treated as a sign, and subsequently part of it comes to be a communicative sign and a public manifestation of will or desire. It is only later in evolution – which thereby turns into culture – that the special form of *human* consciousness emerges. This consciousness is not constructed, because the very tools required for the construction emerge at the same time (i.e. with consciousness). In chapter 6, I quote the American philosopher Richard Rorty, who points out that the creators of something new, poets – in Middle English, *poiette*, ultimately deriving from the ancient Greek *poiêtês*, creator – cannot say what they are doing until they have developed the language in which they have arrived at their creation. Something comes to exist *as* a tool only after it has been successfully deployed in such a function. A twig, or a stone, is not a tool. Each can become a tool once chimpanzees successfully extracted a few termites from their mounts or successfully cracked a few nuts with them. Then even chimpanzees come to carry stones for miles *in anticipation* of finding nuts at a different site, where there the stones required for cracking cannot be found.

It should be apparent that we would not be able to 'construct' knowledge or anything else that the (social) constructivist discourses say we are constructing as part of our everyday lives – whether this is at home, at school, or at work – unless we *already* knew beforehand the possible outcomes of our constructive actions. But if we already have to know what we construct before constructing it – like the builders who know (have to have in their head an image of) what they want to build prior to building it, the analogy that both Rorty and Marx / Engels use – then there is no sense in using the metaphor of construction. Learners are not in the position of the construction worker. A more appropriate metaphor for the learner is that of a *creative* artist – a poet in the wider sense – who does not yet know the final outcomes of his or her creative activities. Like painters, who step back from the painting to see and learn what their doing has yielded, learners of all types and in all walks of life will find out what they have learned – are now able to do – after having done the brush strokes. *Creative* persons – those who do that they (or anyone) have never done before – cannot say what they are doing until they have succeeded creating the new. Moreover, they cannot tell whether they are on the right track – they cannot be metacognitive about their doing – because they do not know the right way until they are at a point where they can look back and see the path they have laid in walking for getting to where they are now (and possibly coming to see some alternative ways of getting there). We are thus returning to Marx and Engels or Heidegger: first life, then consciousness; first dwelling, then building and thinking.

Once we are at this point of realization, other pressing questions emerge: What does it mean to learn when we take the perspective of the learner – student, teacher, craftsperson, hobbyist, or academic? How does the sense of the world evolve so that more and more things make sense in that special world of ours? How do we become aware of something that has not existed in our awareness before? How can we look for something that we do not know what it looks, feels, smells, tastes, or sounds like? Who is the subject of the activity that makes us grow? Who is the Self? and How does the Self come about?

Respecting *Common* Sense and First-Person Perspective

Growing up in a world always already populated by others with whom we are in relation before actually recognizing a difference between others and our selves, we develop a sense of how the world works. We do so even before speaking and before having the capacity to conceptualize and theorize. The infant is oriented toward the sense of things and surroundings long before it develops the capacity – with language – to be concerned with 'meaning'.[3] This sense we share with other people: it is common sense. This common sense functions as a common ground upon which we operate and behave in everyday life; and anything that is common sense goes without saying and therefore does not require being thought or talked about – until some such point that a problem arises. Interestingly enough, when we come to school, this common sense and the intuitions related to it often are opposite to what we are asked to learn. For example, for years we see the sun rise in the morning, wander across the sky, and set in the evening (see chapter 3). Then, coming to school, we are told that the sun is not moving at all, that the movement is an illusion. We are also told that the moon, although it moves across the sky in ways very similar to the sun, is not stationary but moves. Its movement across the sky is largely explained by the rotation of the earth whereas the phases of the moon are due to its own movements around the earth. Concerning the movement, I still remember a night nearly sixty years ago when we were returning home from a camping trip. My parents had decided to drive at night because they anticipated that we children would sleep much of the time. I was stunned when I saw the moon first looking through one then through another window and then yet another window. I was struck because I had never seen the moon move that fast – until I realized based on some closer looks that it was the car's movement that was responsible for my observations. A child younger than I was then – having just turned seven – might continue to think about the moon as moving rather quickly and following her. The reconfiguration that occurred for me was based on what I already knew and could do; and it was completed with existing competencies that assisted in the reconfiguration.

Having a common sense means that we are grounded in the same world as others, which we inhabit even before we build (construct materially) and think (construct mentally). We are dwelling in this world together with others. We know our ways around this everyday world, which makes sense because our knowing is based on our senses. That is, dwelling on this earth provides us with a ground. Our grounding on the earth constitutes a horizon of understanding within which the feeling and understanding of objects at rest and in motion comes to emerge. It would be absurd, in looking for a lost toy or a misplaced set of keys, to take into account the earth's rotation (at 1,500 km/h) or its orbit around the sun (30 km/s). The *real* problem, instead, is how the earth can become an object for us at all, when it is always already the ground of all of our sense and understanding. A similar problem exists with respect to our bodies, which, with their senses, constitute the ground and body of common sense.

When later in life we go to school, there is a lot that does not make sense – the specific amount of the non-sense we encounter in part depends on the social class to which we belong. Because the common sense we have developed often conflicts with the sense of what we are supposed to learn, educational and psychological researchers take a deficit perspective on people. I still remember a physics education colleague showing me some system he had set up and asking me to predict its behavior – which I failed. He pointed out that I had a misconception despite my Masters degree in the subject area based on a thesis that was published in a major peer-reviewed journal. The educational system is supposed to fix those deficits, which exist either because children are untutored, have constructed inappropriate cognitive structures (misconceptions), or have acquired from the everyday world wrong conceptions. It is generally accepted that what individuals already know and can do is the basis on which they learn something new and to which the new accretes. Even if children had to 'accommodate' their conceptions so that they can 'assimilate' the new, this accommodation would have to be done with the commonsense tools and on the commonsense ground of what already exists for them.

There are over 8,000 studies that confirm that the initial world children encounter and understand is non-scientific and thus – implicitly or explicitly stated – is a deficient one. Researchers have documented, for example, that what children, high school students, and even teachers say about the human heart is inconsistent with the scientific explanation. Some studies reveal that children talk about the heart as if it were storing and purifying blood or as if it were functionally subordinate to breathing; other studies report students to say that the heart is responsible for transforming food into blood. Adults, too, are characterized in deficit ways when it comes to the facts and theories of science. Many future primary teachers say – when interviewed about the topic – that the beating of the heart simply prolonged life. Most of the secondary biology teachers in another study are said to have misconceptions about (a) the blood flow and blood pressure in the capillaries or (b) about the exchange of nutrients and wastes between the blood and body cells. Fifteen-year-old students often do not exhibit coherent narratives about the circulatory system as a whole, including the heart. Thus, children between the ages of six and nine years tend to draw isolated organs and blood vessels – the heart and the veins; although both are represented, they remain unconnected rather than constituting the closed circuits that science presents. Cross-age studies sometimes show that there is little difference in the way that eight-year olds and undergraduate students describe body systems, with only two percent rendering appropriate depictions of the entire system. Interestingly, the heart is one of those internal organs more frequently talked about and drawn in the right place, a fact that researchers have attributed to its beat, implying that it is more easily felt than other organs, like kidneys or liver. The research thus shows that not only students but also biology teachers talk about the motions of the heart and blood in ways that is incorrect from a scientific perspective. Indeed most of the research suggests that not only the talk is incorrect but also what these participants have in their minds – their mental frameworks or conceptions. The talk is theorized as an externalization of speakers' mental contents.

It is interesting to follow these ideas a little further. If these students (and their teachers) were to move from an everyday commonsense to a scientific understanding, their mundane understanding would necessarily be the ground on which the new understanding is born; their mundane commonsense means of doing and thinking things, as wrong as these are, would constitute the tools with which the revolution to the scientific viewpoint will be reached. In the constructivist position, getting completely rid of what you think and how you think is impossible. The kinds of radical revisions of our conceptual frameworks that some scholars in the field postulate would be impossible because the destruction of the old ways of thinking also would mean a destruction of your thinking tools. The paradox thus is constituted by the fact that the unscientific or pre-scientific is the basis for and the means of attaining something scientific – and this precisely is the phenomenon of interest in the present volume. This phenomenon requires a radical revision of the attitude that educational and psychological research is taking toward our common sense, which is indeed the foundation for everything else we learn to do.

The learning problem or paradox for both adults and children – how to arrive at some standard conception on the basis of non-scientific knowledge and evidence – is exemplified in the case of the earth as an object for the human subject (see chapter 3). The earth *cannot be* an object originally flying around the sun because, for the subject, it is the *ground* in reference to which a sense of fundamental experiences comes about: 'it is this *universal ground of belief in a world* which all praxis presupposes, not only the praxis of life but also the theoretical praxis of cognition. The being of the world in totality is that which is not first the result of an activity of judgment but which forms the presupposition of all judgment. Consciousness of the world is consciousness in the mode of certainty of belief'.[4] In other words, we come to know things as in motion or at rest only with respect to the earth that is ground, as an adjunct to a pre-existing certainty of belief. Both resting and moving occurs against a background experience that itself is *not* made thematic (like our own bodies). Thus, the earth itself, our point of reference in all experience, does not move. It is only in relation to a stationary referent that there are movement and rest.[5] The terms 'protodoxa' and 'urdoxa' refer to these fundamental experiential certainties that are the precondition for cognition and theorization – we might as well say the most fundamental sense that humans have in common – and these are the condition for the possibility of all further elaboration of knowledge and certainty: 'All experience in this concrete sense rests at bottom on the simple pre-giving *protodoxa [Urdoxa]* of ultimate, simply apprehensible substrates. The natural bodies pre-given in this *doxa* are the ultimate substrates for all subsequent determinations, cognitive determinations as well as those which are axiological or practical'.[6]

Infants and toddlers knowledgeably have their ways around the world even before they get to a stage in life that Jean Piaget characterized as being dominated by 'concrete operational thinking'. During that time, they also develop considerable linguistic capabilities. Indeed, knowing their way around the world and knowing their mother tongue are indistinguishable. This ensemble – language *and* the material / social activity to which it belongs – sometimes is referred to as *language-game*. Anything, including language, makes sense that fits into this inhabited world – the world of our dwelling – generally and the concrete activities specifically. This is so because the term *sense* denotes that something has a place within a contexture. The everyday world (activity), including the familiar language that belongs to this world, constitutes a contexture. Anything that stands out is figure against ground; but the figure retreats and becomes part of the ground within ground against which something else becomes figure. Common sense includes those contextures that are so fundamental that they are common to all members of a particular community. Common sense is so powerful and so general that if we were to state something that is common sense – e.g. pointing to a tree saying 'this is a tree' – others would question our sanity or our hidden intentions. On the other hand, in the context of teaching our language to a child or a foreigner, pointing to a tree and saying 'tree' does make complete sense. What has changed is the figure–ground relation of the existing contexture.

The phenomenon of common sense constitutes a bridge from first-person perspectives to the perspectives of others. Common sense is *ours*, thus also mine. That sense begins before there are words. The importance of sense over meaning became important to Lev S. Vygotsky near the end of his life leading him to move away from word-meaning as the dominant concept. Thus, his priority became the role of sense in the dynamics of consciousness: There is a sense-giving field that 'precedes and anticipates any action with a real object, it links impressions and intuitions of the sense of an event or thing to words'.[7] That sense is the result of connections within the field that allows something to make sense or it not to make sense (to the subject). The subject is subject to sense as much as actively seeking connections (i.e. figure–ground relations) that *give* sense to a thing. The sense thus is an aspect of dwelling, which precedes the active building of things and thinking, especially thinking in the form that is apparent to adults.

In common sense, my personal sense and the sense of the generalized other intermingle. Indeed, there could not be (common) sense unless my perspective already implied the perspectives of others. Realizing that I have a perspective implies that I see myself through the lens of another, who, in turn, sees him/herself as through my (or another's) lens. In this theoretical move, we overcome the subjectivism of radical constructivism. Because theorizing begins with a common life and common sense in dwelling, we do not enter the cul-de-sac of social constructivism, which, though it recognizes everything to be social, presupposes the individual. The individual is presupposed, because it does the negotiation or collaboration from which the jointly constructed object emerges that subsequently comes to be internally constructed. But an individual 'does not first ... reach his own identifications, and then compare these with those of others in order to reach a common object'.[8] Instead, the individual does this work by using a language, which is language only because of a common attitude taken with others in the same situation and subject to the common undertaking. If that common world were to disappear, the individual would too. Social constructivism (constructionism) only proposes the social in the weak sense, whereas the entire point of the current volume lies in elaborating the social in a strong sense. Dwelling, on the other hand, is social through and through; and it is only because it is social that *con*sciousness can emerge, and, with it, self-consciousness – literally, a self-together (with others)-knowing. Any individuality and individual characteristic always arises from what a person has in common with others: life, sense and sense, and ground.

On Method

In many journals where empirical data are standard features of articles, there also feature standard sections entitled 'methods', 'methodology', or something of similar ilk. But we may ask this: how can something be relevant in the learning and development of a person that requires a special method to be seen and to make sense? Do not our everyday methods of making (social, psychological) phenomena and making them visible constitute the basis for any scientist to identify those phenomena in the first place? Do not our everyday methods of seeing, making, and communicating the ordered and orderly properties of the social world provide the basis for making sense of the so-called special methods of the sciences? Do not all scientists today develop their special methods on the basis of the commonsense methods that characterize everyday life?

The distinction between everyday (ethno-) methods and scientific methods, the inherent need to specify the latter as something special, and the also inherent qualitative superiority of the latter over the former, is a general, though by-and-large unacknowledged feature of the scholarly literature. Throughout this book, I emphasize perspectives onto the world that make common sense – to us, others and me. I also use first-person approaches to the study of learning. Such an approach is still uncommon in the educational and learning sciences, which are by and large limiting their methodological toolbox to third-person approaches – and they do so even though first-person approaches have gained some currency in the cognitive sciences. The (social) sciences, just as everyday life, are beleaguered by pre-constructions and natural attitudes. Fundamental to a rigorous method is the bracketing of scientific and mundane pre-constructions (presuppositions) alike. This occurs in a process called *epoché*[9], which is designed to make the pre-constructions inoperative. Epoché involves three stages:

– *Suspending* your 'realist' prejudice that what appears to you is truly the state of the world; this is the only way you can change the way you pay attention to your own lived experience; in other words, you must break with the 'natural attitude'.
– *Redirecting* your attention from the 'exterior' to the 'interior'.
– *Letting-go or accepting* your experience.[10]

The method is rigorous because epoché strips anything subjective from the way phenomena are often described. The present approach therefore is unlike those taken by others who claim to be phenomenologically grounded but who really are concerned with personal feelings ending up in woe-me and me-me-me studies. The point of a *rigorous* first-person method as is to generate data and analyses that may serve as the referents for the natural and psychological sciences investigating relevant experiences (e.g. neural correlates of conscious experience).[11]

Another method often employed in this volume is auto/biography and auto/ethnography. The method, akin to apprenticeship as ethnographic method, is designed to study *cultural* and therefore *shared, collective* practices in and through the researcher's participation and learning in common places. The point of the data and analysis is not how I (or any other first-person researcher) feels or felt but to understand the structure of phenomena and the processes of their phenomenalization. In this process, all natural and scientific explanations – which, in fact, are grounded in the former – are ruled out and therefore bracketed: 'I *do not make any use* of their validity … even if they are completely evident'.[12]

Becoming aware (chapter 6) or being subject to an illness (chapter 7) are among those phenomena that we know to be occurring and whereof we have manifestations. But these phenomena eschew in-depth study from a third-person perspective because awareness always is the awareness of someone and of something. However, 'hardline' phenomenological inquiry – a form of inquiry aimed at scientifically rigorous description – produces data that can be correlated with third-person methods. For example, becoming aware and changes in awareness can be studied under controlled conditions and used conjointly with functional magnetic resonance imaging (fMRI) methods. There is no reason why the study of learning phenomena, as these are experienced from within, ought not be an integral part of the methodological toolbox of the educational and learning sciences. Recent work suggests that such 'hardcore' phenomenological approaches arrive no less at generalizations, and sometimes are more generalizable, than experimental and quantitative approaches. By means of first-person investigations, we can actually study what underlies the awareness of one or the other shape. The crucial point in such approaches lies in identifying those aspects of a situation that are general and disregarding other aspects that are incidental.

Rigorous first-person methods are based on within-person variations quickly shifting from one to some other appearance, which allows investigators to recognize the conditions under which they are aware of one or the other shape. For example, there are well-known drawings that allow at least two dominant figures to stand out: old woman vs. young woman, vase vs. two faces, or duck vs. rabbit (Fig 3.2b). When we attempt in such cases to see both images simultaneously – by keeping the lines on the same place on the retina either through training or by using a device that psychologists invented – we come to note that the entire visual field turns into a homogeneous grey. We may turn such findings into instructions for others to experience the same phenomenon, for example, where and how to look to see one rather than another thing. Because of this, these phenomena no longer are to be considered merely subjective; their *instructability* makes them what some cultural psychologists call 'interobjective'. In chapter 6, which investigates the phenomenon of becoming aware (as extended event), I provide some suggestions about how we might create conditions that slow fast phenomena to the point that they become accessible; and training generally is required to ready the researcher for investigating such phenomena. During think-aloud protocol studies involving experts and students/novices, we often observe participants remain silent for some time (i.e. not articulating thinking). Researchers generally address silence by means of directions such as 'say what you are thinking'. Little discussed in the literature on this research method is the fact that participants may not be 'thinking' at all, not in the way we commonly understand this phenomenon: they may be in fact waiting for the arrival of a thought. The method used here would be a prime candidate for exploring this aspect of cognition and instruction.

Looking Ahead

In this book, I provide descriptions of various aspects in the process of our becoming, how we come to know, how we become aware, how we become subject, and how our subjectivity is deleted by the very ways that research is conducted. The series of studies that follows is characterized by its phenomenological orientation even though and precisely because it also draws on intellectual traditions that are very different but that historically have paid attention to creating theories that are viable on evolutionary-historical and ontogenetic grounds. The phenomenon of dwelling that precedes building and thinking is used as the fundamental condition from which our building, thinking, self–other consciousness, and sense of subjectivity arise. All of these studies are grounded in everyday life and analytically reveal phenomena that go unnoticed in other approaches – often because of the blinders that theories come with. In this take, Pierre Bourdieu and Edmund Husserl have been great influences on my ways of working and thinking – it was through my reading their works that I became aware of the pervasive presence of the preconstructed and of epoché and its pursuit of rigor by holding at bay folk as much as scientific theories. All the studies that follow are characterized by a stance that respects the first-time-through and once-occurrent nature of our lives and our perspectives (in the heat of the moment) – as opposed to the usual perspectives of an omniscient entity (researcher, deity) that characterizes the research literature. In the following, I sketch the studies presented in the different chapters.

'Building, Dwelling, Thinking' is the title of a well-known text by Martin Heidegger, in which he meditates on the relationship between thinking and technology. In chapter 2, 'Being is Dwelling', I use the insights that can be gleaned from that text for grounding an alternative theory of learning that overcomes the problems of the conceptual change and constructivist approaches that mark current educational discourses. This alternative is grounded in the phenomenological insight that we always already find ourselves in a familiar world into which we have been thrown and that we inhabit. Hence the subject contemplating a world presupposes the event of dwelling. Dwelling (habiting) immediately grounds this approach to knowing and learning in the environment because sociologically, in*hab-iting* implies not only habitus, habits, inhabitation, and habitat – as Maurice Mer-leau-Ponty and Pierre Bourdieu point out – but also labor, the body, and con-sciousness. That is, dwelling leads us to a practice-theoretical foundation of education.

Dwelling is the beginning of a sequence that grounds human experience. That is, it is not building ('constructing') that starts our lives. Even less so does think-ing, which has to precede and accompany building ('constructing') something. We are always already born (thrown) into a social world; and this world constitutes the very ground from which any sense can emerge and against which sense stands out. It is not surprising, perhaps, that the famous psychologist Lev S. Vygotsky realized near the end of his life that *sense* is much more foundational than signification ('meaning'). This world into which we are thrown, the Earth, does not move be-cause it is the condition for movement to be perceived – including its own. It is in this ground that we are rooted. In chapter 3, 'On Being Rooted', I take up Simone Weil's concepts of rooting [Fr. *enracinement*] and uprooting [Fr. *déracinement*] to theorize the root of this alienation, the confrontation between our familiarity with the world, on the one hand, and the unfamiliar and strange conceptions that we are eventually confronted with, on the other hand. I build on the works of the phenom-enological philosopher Edmund Husserl to make a case for the rooting function of original and originary experiences and the genetic method to teaching abstract sub-jects. The genetic approach to education allows students to retain their foundation-al familiarity with the world in which they are rooted all the while evolving other (more scientific) ways of explaining natural phenomena.

Dwelling in a world that always already exists and has formed us constitutes the basis of our becoming. It is widely acknowledged that our mundane understand-ings are generally inconsistent with the scientific views on the matter: 'heartache' has little to do with cardiopulmonary matters, and a rising or setting sun actually reflects the movements of the earth. How then does an everyday person, who in many areas of science is characterized as 'illiterate' and 'non-scientific', come to regard something scientifically? Moreover, how do mundane but generally unsci-entific views continue their lives, even many centuries after scientists have over-thrown them in what are termed scientific revolutions? In chapter 4 ('Cultivating Culture'), I develop a phenomenological perspective, using the Edmund Husserl's categories of *Nacherzeugung* (literally re-production) and *Nachverstehen* (literally re-understanding). I build on the philosopher's insight that the original sense-giving act is reproduced each and every time the relevant aspect of culture is per-formed. Each person can produce phenomena again (and again) and, thereby, pro-duce again understandings and changes therein that others historically have pro-duced before. The German preposition *nach* not only translates 'again' but also 'according to', so that *Nacherzeugung* and *Nachverstehen* also mean producing and understanding *in the manner of* those (scientists) doing so before. Cultivating culture does means cultivating the soil in which common sense fundamentally is rooted. It is in the individual production that historical understandings and discov-eries come to life and live again. To concretize these phenomena, a case study is presented of how we may learn from online video concerning the motions of the heart and blood.

In chapter 3, I make a case for the constitutive nature of the unmoving ground from which any image (self, knowledge, identity) emerges and against which the image is seen. Chapter 5 ('Emergence of the Image') focuses on movement relative to the unmoving earth as the site and phenomenon for the birth of knowledge. The chapter provides a phenomenological account of the *naissance* (birth) of *knowledge*, two words that both have their etymological origin in the same, homonymic Proto-Indo-European syllable ĝen-, ĝenə-, ĝnē-, ĝnō-. Accordingly, the things of the world and the bodily movements they shape, following Maurice Merleau-Ponty, are pregnant with new knowledge that cannot foresee itself and that the existing knowledge cannot anticipate. I draw on a study of learning in a second-grade mathematics classroom, where children learn geometry by classifying and modeling three-dimensional objects. The data clearly show that the children do not foresee, and therefore intentionally construct, the knowledge that emerges from the movements of their hands, arms, and bodies that comply with the forms of things. The chapter therefore provides a radical alternative to traditional (e.g. constructivist) accounts of knowledge, which are blind to the fact that learners cannot orient toward this knowledge-to-be as an object to be constructed precisely because they do not know the knowledge to be acquired.

Movement alone, as described in chapter 5, does not make knowing – at least not the explicit kind that is valued in and required by the different cultural contexts that constitute our everyday lives. We actually have to become aware. But how do we become aware of something that we could not have been aware of precisely because we did not know it? How can we orient toward seeing the unseen and therefore unforeseen? The dominant paradigms conceive of such learning as the construction of something (e.g. 'meaning', 'knowledge', 'conceptions', or 'conceptual frameworks'). Learners cannot intentionally orient towards what is to be known after a curricular event precisely because the object that directs such an orientation (e.g. future knowledge) does not yet exist. In chapter 6 ('Becoming Aware'), I describe and theorize the phenomenon of *becoming aware* and suggest the underlying movement as a more appropriate way of thinking about learning: becoming aware may serve as an analogy or metaphor for learning more appropriate than construction. I use the careful description of how we become aware of something in our environment that we had not been aware of before to articulate the structure of the movement that takes us from the unseen thus unforeseen to the seen and grasped ('I see!').

Personal health is not something abstract but goes to the heart of who we are. It is here that the nature of human being comes to express itself in the most explicit way: *possibility*. This notion highlights that we are subject and subjected to pain, illness, mood, and emotion; we *live* these aspects of life rather than 'constructing them in our minds'. Possibility, the capacity to suffer, thus constitutes an alternative grounding of dwelling, building, and becoming. But possibility remains the great unseen in research studies. Indeed, possibility requires us to consider the body as alive, and it is its life, its living and change, that are invisible. It is not surprising that many phenomenological investigations – e.g. on the part of Jean-Luc Nancy and Francisco Varela – were born in the experiences of undergoing (having to undergo) a transplant. Even Immanuel Kant had reached and experienced the limits of his theoretical work on knowing when confronted with health issues. Drawing on my confrontation with illness, chapter 7 ('The Invisible Body') presents a phenomenological investigation as the basis for suggesting why and under which condition health and environment may constitute suitable contexts for (also) education. I conclude that more than content and approach, educators need to reconsider the very structure of schooling, which may be the real problem in making learning an authentic endeavor.

In the opening statements of this chapter, I note that in everyday life, we do not do what (social) constructivists say we do. We do not first cogitate – 'think', 'interpret', or 'construct' – and then act; we do not say aloud what is already figured in our conceptual framework; and we do not 'construct' knowledge with others that we then take from the public arena and incorporate it into our own minds.[13] Attributing to people 'constructions' that they do not see and feel themselves produce simultaneously makes the real living people disappear from the accounts of student and teacher learning, teacher professional development, and all the other topics currently in fashion in the academic arena. Theory does not apply to practice because the theory is not about how we live – undergoing as much as affecting our mundane lives – and how we live in the consciousness of others we make everyday situations and make their structures visible to one another. In chapter 8 ('Disappearance of the Subject'), I show how the living human subject comes to disappear in and because of research. I draw on an extensive analysis of materials from an email exchange with a student whom I had taught over thirty years earlier and who wrote that I had a tremendous impact on his life – even he, as much as I, was told before that taking the course that I was teaching would inevitably lead to a clash. I work out the difference between experience, as described after the fact ('*an* experience'), and the ways in which we sense, feel, and witness particular times of our lives that we grasp only after the fact. *Events** (with asterisk) are in the making as long as things are happening; and they become definitive events with beginnings and endings only after some form of closure has been achieved. Some readers may recall the phrase attributed to the baseball umpire Bill Klem: 'it is nothing until I call it [a ball or strike]', where the call constitutes the closure (of the debate). Only when closure has been achieved can we grasp something to which beginnings and endings, causes and effects, and significant actors and objects are attributed.

In chapter 8, the open-endedness of life is said to distinguish our concurrent awareness and feelings from the awareness that is encapsulated in the narrative account of '*an* experience'. If an *event** is inherently open, if we cannot speak of 'an event' (a ball, a strike) until after closure has been achieved, we cannot therefore conceive of the specific role of those individuals and groups who are constitutive parts. Chapter 9 ('The Subject*-in-the-Making') shows why it does not make sense to conceive of a determinate subject – on both evolutionary-cultural historical and ontogenetic grounds – because it can exist as such only after the fact. The subject is a subject-in-the-making (or subject*), where the what of the making is not given beforehand – for the same reasons that are articulated concerning the poets at the beginning of this chapter (see also chapter 6). To mark this unavailability of the subject in the ongoing *event**, both known as such only ex post facto, I mark the 'subject' by means of an asterisk ('*').

Every chapter exhibits phenomena that are inconsistent with and contradict constructivism – that of the radical as much as that of the social kind. This is so because the human capacities to suffer and to be affected are unaddressed in this theory. In other words, *possibility* exhibits the limits of the constructivist metaphor.[14] Possibility is a condition for anything like mind to emerge – we have to explain the emergence of consciousness from life rather than use consciousness to explain life. The book thus presents a very different perspective on how we know, learn, develop, become subjects, come to live in subjectivity, undergo happenings that only after the fact we can grasp as definitive events, and so on. In chapter 10, 'There is (a) Life after Constructivism', I provide the glimpse of a perspective on life after constructivism. It is but an ideology of a particular way of life – the modernist ideology of the 'self-made hu/man'.

Notes

[1] Ernst von Glasersfeld, 'Facts and the Self from a Constructivist Point of View', *Poetics*, vol. 18 (1989), 445–446.

[2] Karl Marx and Friedrich Engels, *Werke Band 3* (Berlin: Dietz, 1978), 26.

[3] This is the position that Lev S. Vygotsky developed near the end of his life, thereby overturning the emphasis on 'meaning' [Rus. *znachenie*] that dominated his earlier work in favor of the phenomenon of sense [Rus. *smysl*].

[4] Edmund Husserl, *Husserliana Gesammelte Work Band XVI: Ding und Raum* (The Hague: Martinus Nijhoff, 1973), 30.

[5] The same point is made in George Herbert Mead, *Philosophy of the Act* (Chicago: University of Chicago Press, 1938).

[6] Husserl, *Ding und Raum*, 59.

[7] Ekaterina Iu. Zavershneva, '"The way to Freedom": On the Publication of Documents from the Family Archive of Lev Vygotsky', *Journal of Russian and East European Psychology*, vol. 48 no. 1 (2010), 63.

[8] Mead, *Philosophy of the Act*, 142.

[9] The term is from Greek, ἐποχή, which sometimes is transliterated as *epokhè* or *epoche*.

[10] Natalie Depraz, Francisco Varela, and Pierre Vermersch, *On Becoming Aware: Steps to a Phenomenological Pragmatics* (Amsterdam: Benjamins, 2002), 25.

[11] See, for example, Wolff-Michael Roth, *Rigorous Data Analysis: Beyond Anything Goes* (Rotterdam: Sense Publishers, 2015).

[12] Edmund Husserl, *Ideen zu einer reinen Phänomenologie und phänomenologische Philosophie. Erstes Buch. Allgemeine Einführung in die reine Phänomenologie* (The Hague: Martinus Nijhoff, 1976), 65.

[13] A student of mine, Pei-Ling Hsu, once began a chapter with the description of a situation where I told her what I had done during the morning only to stop, pull out a notebook, and write down an idea that I had just articulated without every having thought it before. I have also written about research participants telling me that they had never thought about the topic before – thus never constructed a conceptual framework – and then nevertheless provided an answer on the fly, and without a priori consideration.

[14] Wolff-Michael Roth, *Possibility: At the Limits of the Constructivist Metaphor* (Dordrecht: Springer, 2011).

2

Being is Dwelling

The dominant paradigm of knowing and learning is based on the metaphor of construction: the builder, who, prior to beginning the world, already envisions the end result of the activity and who is thus capable of monitoring the stages of getting there (as in metacognition). In some versions of constructivism, including those that go under the banner of enactivism and embodiment, the individual constructs its own mind and mental frameworks. In other versions, individuals get together in groups (organizations, societies) that in some public space construct together whatever there is to be constructed; and the individual then somehow picks up the results in that public space to internalize them through individual construction. At the heart of such a constructive process is the individual, who alone or in coordination with others, constructs knowledge about the world; and this knowledge is used in all interpretive endeavors, those concerning the things of the natural world and those concerning entities of the social world (e.g. texts, signs, inscriptions, or representations). The result of such approaches is a mentalist vision of human beings, who intentionally construct their knowledge, identities, affects, and so on. However, well-known philosophers and social psychologists – not in the least Karl Marx, George Herbert Mead, Martin Heidegger, and the later Lev S. Vygotsky – have denounced such a vision. All emphasize that anything appearing in our conscious experience is the result of and follows Being – in a world that is both natural and social. Being means *dwelling* in a world. There is no world apart from our dwelling. Our Selves are consequences of such relations with others not the necessary antecedents responsible for constructing everything there is. Our building and thinking, too, are consequences of our dwelling, a point that Martin Heidegger articulates in a text that was at the heart of a lecture from 1951 and that bears a title that I have recomposed to make the title of this book.[1] Heidegger's fundamental point in the lecture is that dwelling is the condition for any building (constructing) and thinking.

Conditioning building (constructing) and thinking (interpreting) on dwelling is a radical alternative to constructivist epistemology. It is a post-constructivist episte-

© KONINKLIJKE BRILL NV, LEIDEN, 2018 | DOI 10.1163/9789004377134_002

mology grounded in the way we live our everyday lives, on the one hand, and in philosophical approaches that emphasize the primacy of the social in the human condition, on the other hand. The alternative is grounded in the phenomenological insight that we always already find ourselves in a familiar world that we inhabit and wherein we dwell. We are not thrown into an empty world but are part of relations with others, first and foremost our mothers and then our fathers. Actually, the idea of a constructivist 'subject contemplating a world *presupposes* the event of dwelling'.[2] Research as well as personal experiences are showing us that we know what an instruction is saying only after having been successful in doing what the instruction is intended to tell us. *Dwelling* (in/habiting) immediately grounds this approach to knowing and learning in the environment because sociologically, the now archaic term habiting (dwelling, abiding, residing, and sojourning) not only implies *habitus* (structured, structuring dispositions), habits, inhabitation, and habitat but also labor, the body, and consciousness. That is, dwelling leads us to a practical foundation of being and becoming, where building and thinking are shaped by an ex post facto awareness of dwelling. Karl Marx and Friedrich Engels, in their eleventh thesis on Feuerbach, suggest that philosophers only looked at and interpreted the world when the real point is to change it and therefore to change the conditions to which we are subject and subjected. Indeed, the unity of the intended act – an act oriented to achieve an outcome that does not yet exist – implies both the change in the world brought about in acting and the social required for the ability to link actions and consequences. It is therefore not surprising that Marx and Engels underscored the capacity of humans to transform the world that they inhabit. This makes their work appealing, which, 'despite all of its defects and defaults, is attractive to participative consciousness because of its effort to build its world in such a way as to provide a place in it for the performance of determinate, concretely historical actual deeds'.[3]

It turns out that at least some indigenous peoples have conceptions of the world that are close to that of *dwelling*. The W̱SÁNEĆ – pronounced /xʷsenəč/, the Saanich in our Western language – are a First Nation who, for hundreds of years, inhabited the geographical area where I live today. Many of their place names and things are associated with activities – sometimes even the materials that make the things – important in their life process. The W̱SÁNEĆ, as shown below, do not consider themselves as owners of places. Instead, they belong to specific places; and they understand themselves as caretakers thereof. They first are dwellers; and it is their dwelling that comes with gifts, such as that of the annual fishing harvest bequeathed to them.

In constructivist approaches to education, the environment is but another aspect represented in the mind and therefore constitutes just an external factor that 'mediates' cognition. The notions *sense of place* and *chronotope* – literally time-space – are alternatives to provide an education that emphasizes the everyday encounters that learners have and have had with their environment. However, both concepts presuppose the existence of place (space) and therefore cannot, from a phenomenological perspective, constitute the ground from which emerge our encounters of, in, and with the environment. To ground and exemplify an alternative theory of learning that overcomes the problems of constructivist approaches and their more recent alternatives, I draw on research that I conducted over the course of more than a decade within the municipality where I live. The research project was concerned with the relationship of science, public understanding of science, and the environment in the municipality as a whole. In particular, the research also involved environmental activists and members from the First Nation's community (reserve) that lies within the boundaries of the municipality.

Dwelling Grounds Building and Thinking

Dwelling and the W̱SÁNEĆ ways of understanding the world can assist us in re-thinking the relation of education and the environment. The idea of environmental education that focuses on dwelling can bring us closer to the idea of how the familiar world (our practical understanding) is the *necessary* condition for any theoretical and conceptual understanding that we do and aspire to develop. One of my projects on learning science arose from my concern that there is no apparent reason for students to acquire scientific knowledge (despite all the science education rhetoric to the contrary). Already in the 1990s, I began to argue that we needed to dislocate science education, to take it from school to the community and thereby to de-institutionalize it. This is what has been done with psychiatric institutions that have been dismantled in favor of homes in the community inhabited by small groups of people. Former inmates thereby have been made an integral part of everyday communal life activity. We can do the same for children and students, by providing opportunities for participating in existing community-based, collective activities. The middle school student in the following account, Graham, participated together with others, in a community-based environmentalist movement that intended to increase the environmental health of the watershed in which much of our semi-rural municipality lies. The idea of the unit I taught was to allow students to ground any learning in what they already know and are interested in, and to allow them to expand their action potential in the course of pursuing self-stated goals to help the environment.

Based on the fact that Graham lives in a pristine and largely rural part of the world also much appreciated by many tourists who visit this area (Fig 2.1), he decided to investigate the Hagan Creek / ḴENES (/qʷənəs/) watershed system, which covers and circumscribes much of the municipality where he went to middle and high school.[4] In the W̱SÁNEĆ's SENĆOŦEN (/sənčaθən/) language, the name of the creek is another example of the irreducibility of the language and the W̱SÁNEĆ way of life. Thus, ḴENES is the whale and the name of the creek, particularly its mouth, that is, the place of the whales that used to feed here. The farms along the creek depend on it for water. But by this very dependence on the creek, farmers

Fig 2.1 The municipality, apart from two higher density agglomerations, is largely rural and, as stated in its official community plan, intends to preserve the area like this. It lies on the tribal lands that belonged to the W̱SÁNEĆ prior to the arrival of the Europeans and still is home to their reserve. The forested areas in the center and left of the photograph are part of the reserve.

have altered its state tremendously so that much of it was no longer suitable as habitat for the once – i.e. pre-colonization – abundant trout. Although the creek had been an integral part of the cleansing routines and spiritual practices of the W̱SÁNEĆ before colonization, today high levels of all sorts of biological and chemical contaminants, but especially of coliform, no longer allow consumption or even bathing in its waters.

Graham's learning began *right at home*, with what and whom he knew. Among his first contact persons was the director of the environmentalist group concerned with human and environmental health of the Hagan Creek / K̲ENES watershed. (Different stewardship groups focused on the watersheds in the area until all of them joined into the Peninsula Streams Society looking after fifteen creeks and supporting thirteen stewardship groups.) In an interview, he describes: 'She was the first person that I talked to and she gave me a lot of the background information that they knew at the time about the creek. And I guess that was the most useful stuff at the time to get me going because I knew some things about the creek, like where it started. At one point she didn't know where it started … and, I guess just some background information about the wildlife surrounding the areas and specific places where they've taken tests before so that I wouldn't be just going into someone's backyard that I didn't know about'. In this interview excerpt, Graham remembers that he had known some things about the creek when he got started; but he had not known enough to be able to do his science project on his own. He turned to the executive director of an environmental activist group, an acquaintance of his mother; and she gave him information developed through the labor of her organization. At one time, as Graham suggests, the environmentalists did not know much themselves, as evidenced by the fact that they did not know the location of the source of the creek. Other information articulated in their conversation included wildlife and 'specific places' where the environmentalists had sampled the creek for a variety of biological and chemical contaminants.

Graham also talked to another environmentalist, who sometimes served as the director-designate of the environmentalist group and who was a trained (MSc) biochemist working on a doctoral degree on the topic of environmental stewardship. During the interview, Graham recalls: 'He was talking about fecal coliform and I had no idea what that was at that point. So I read some papers that I didn't fully understand and then again, and then again, and then again. It sunk in eventually: lots of science. So, we proceeded with the work and we took samples from five locations'. In this instance, the interactions with the environmentalist and biochemist opened up new opportunities for Graham to learn, here about a form of organism that he had not known about. Graham then began to read papers, not because he was made to or because some official government-specified curriculum document stated it, but because he became interested in the role fecal coliform played in the watershed and its role in human and animal well-being. Oriented toward the object / motive of environmentalism, he went through this learning loop not as an end in itself but as a means to open up his power to act and his control over his current condition. This opening enabled him to do what he subscribed to be doing by participating in environmentalism. That is, by participating in environmentalism he subscribed to the collective object / motive of this activity and, when he recognized limitations in his power to act, he engaged in learning that enlarged his agency (room to maneuver). This was *expansive* learning, providing him with greater control over the situation and increasing what he could do. But everything began in his world and the things and the people that he was familiar with.

In the course of his project, all of Graham's work took place in the municipality, which both situated what he was doing and allowed him to discover aspects he had not known before. This includes the place of the source of the Hagan / ḰENES Creek watershed system. Here he would take one of his first water samples: 'We took one sample from a farm that was right below the one starting point. It was along Kildeer Road, which is off Old West Saanich Road. There are four ponds that connect to one another and the creek starts at that point. We took a sample right below where there was a chicken farm. We didn't really link that at first. But then after we got the samples back I think it was the second highest point of coliform that we found among the five sites'. In the situation described, what Graham learns about science is integrally related to the village that he inhabits. His samples, the analytic results of which he ultimately makes sense of, are not abstract data points concerning a phenomenon that he might have a hard time to grasp – in

Fig 2.2   Graham presenting during the open-house event of the environmentalist group subsequently reported on by the local news media and on websites featuring the Hagan Creek / K̄ENES project.

the way this tends to happen in school science. Instead, his data derive from locations he knows well or is coming to know, where he has been. Everything he does makes sense because it contributes to realizing his goal: to contribute to realizing the object / motive of the environmentalist movement. This includes the sampling location just downstream from a chicken farm. Later, once he had analyzed the samples with the help of the people in a university microbiology laboratory, he was able to ground the results in the place he knew so well: 'I found out where Hagan / K̄ENES Creek started. Everything I know now, just its vicinity, its directions, where it goes, the land around it, how its used in some places, how it is unnaturally directed in many areas. And then, in some other areas, it is all natural: the top of Centennial Park was still really unaffected. I know the part through Wallace Drive: it all has been ditched. Then there was the one site where the creek crosses West Saanich Road, put under in the pipe, and it just runs out through the ditch and into the pipe. And someone has used it as a nice little stream running through their backyard with rocks around it by the gravel, right across from West Saanich Road'. As his mother would long after suggest, Graham learned a lot about the political and social realities that come with doing research in the community. In fact, Graham reported his results during an open-house event of the environmentalist group and named the two farms down-creek of which he found highly elevated coliform counts (Fig 2.2). Perhaps not surprisingly, he, as other middle school students, was not allowed to return onto the land of the farms where he had taken samples.

At the beginning of all of Graham's work was his familiarity with the community in which he dwelled. From this basis, his knowing expanded as he investigated areas not yet known to him. Thus, all of this (expanding) familiarity with the watershed in which the municipality lies situated what and how he learned from a purely scientific perspective on the work Graham has done. For Graham, living through this attempt to better understand some ecological issues also led to the learning of some science, which he, when specifically asked for, talked about: 'We didn't learn any scientific procedure in school. I've done more this year than I have since I was in Kindergarten. Like, this year I've done– I've learned a lot of the stuff that we've done not as advanced but I guess that was really helpful for what I've been doing this year'. Although most teachers and perhaps many educators have not seriously considered 'open-inquiry' as a context because it does not follow a set of concepts outlined in a hierarchically organized curriculum – e.g., the scope and sequence of the normally specified curriculum – Graham has learned a tremendous amount. But everything was organized according to his needs. In fact, what he learned by far exceeded the official curriculum plan for his year. In the preceding quotation he suggests having learned more than in the (eight) preceding years about scientific procedures. Asked for an example of what he learned about doing microbiology, he said, 'I guess just a lot of the procedure about how sterile everything has to be, about how precise to be. I always knew you had to get it all perfect, I guess it was actually just doing it and getting the specifics. And, I didn't know about the incubation, I always thought that if you wanted to do microorganisms you've got the microscope. But I guess that didn't work out'.

In the end, Graham learned a lot about the interconnected nature of the environment in which he lived, many aspects of which he had not known before. His familiarity with the municipality constituted the very ground on which his new understanding emerged. The science he learned was occasioned when in the pursuit of the environmentalist object / motive – knowing more about the state of the creek to establish a baseline against which to measure future changes – he expanded the levels of his agency and control over extant conditions in loops of expansive learning. Asked about what he had learned in and through his engagement in environmentalism, Graham suggested: 'How everything relates to one another and how they're getting the program trying to get everything to get cleaned up and how, I guess it needs to be a community effort for everything to be put back in its place. There are a lot of areas that could get fixed up. The creek not made to run in a ditch – although then it would need to be moved because the road obstructs its path. I'm not sure it goes across West Saanich road once, and then through the trees in a loop and then goes back across and through the trees. It is natural. It is probably going straight across the road and then across Maber Flats (Fig 2.3), which was a swamp area that is no longer'.

We notice that in these excerpts Graham does not talk much about the science he learned, which, from his perspective, is but a means to an end. It is in the pursuit of the environment-related activity that he learned what he required to expand his control. His learning was motivated by expansion rather than constituting defensive learning, the kind of which students generally do in schools to avoid punish-

Fig 2.3 Before colonization, Maber Flats were marshland that provided for rich hunting grounds to the local First Nations. White farmers created ditches to drain the wetlands and, in so doing, threatened many local and migrating bird populations.

ment and negative repercussions. That is, Graham is learning the kinds of lessons that the W̱SÁNEĆ – who inhabited this area for hundreds of years – now teach again to their own children. This includes the recognition that 'everything relates to one another' and that there is a collective interest that the environmentalists realize. Graham also learned about the fact that the community needs to address the environmental issues *collectively* for 'everything has to be put back in its place'. The locations he is talking about during the interview concern the ditched areas of the creek system, which the farmers had created to increase the water flow from the marshes (i.e. Maber Flats, Fig 2.3). These marshes had been W̱SÁNEĆ hunting grounds. The effects of ditching were detrimental to the whole valley, for not only the birds and mammals disappeared, but so did the fish. Perhaps more importantly, the water no longer is retained to fill the aquifers so that many farmers now depend for irrigation on the costly drinking water piped in from distant reservoirs. Today, some fifteen years after Graham's research (i.e. in 2017), Maber Flats are on the district's community green map as unprotected *significant* habitat. The flats are described as one of the zones where wildlife habitat – including that of peregrine falcons, bald eagles, northern harriers and short-eared owls – would be endangered were subdivision and development to occur.

The Foundation of *Dwelling*

The philosophical concept of *dwelling* can do a lot to assist us, Westerners in the Greco-Roman tradition, in our efforts of rethinking our relationship between the environment and ourselves. In the history of philosophy and psychology, there have been concepts that emphasize the unity / identity of person and environment. The American philosopher John Dewey offered *experience* as one such concept – though, as shown in chapter 8, there are some problems with his notion; and the Russian psychologist Lev S. Vygotsky proposed *perezhivanie*, which he considered to be an equivalent of the German *Erleben / Erlebnis* and the French *le vécu*, both denoting life as we actually live, feel, and suffer it. English does not have its own word for this German and Russian concept. This makes *dwelling* a suitable term. It emphasizes being in and inhabiting a world that is not distinct from us. In our search for ways of thinking about ways of being that constitute the foundation for building and thinking, we can also learn from indigenous peoples. These, too, have concepts that teach us about our situation on this earth characterized by dwelling. Thus, among the indigenous peoples generally and the First Nations of Canada specifically, there is an awareness of the fact that we inhabit this earth, an earth which we do not own like a piece of property. In their discourse, the First Peoples privilege concepts that focus on the places that we live in, inhabit, and that we are caretakers of. They focus on respect for the land that has been given to them and which they inhabit, which they do not inherit from their parents but which they *borrow from their children*. This requires autochthonic peoples to take care of the land so that it will take care of them. In the following, I sketch the phenomenological and indigenous approaches for constituting dwelling as a category. I begin with explicating the notion of *trans*action, which is not simply another form of *inter*action because it names the simultaneous and mutual influence of person and environment or person and person. A *trans*action always is action in two directions involving different agents. The notion of dwelling and the indigenous praxis of Being are based on transactional perspectives.

A Transactional Perspective

Our sense of everyday life is one of integral connection with the environment. We act without having to think and interpret: we walk, talk, sit, lounge, or lay down without a single reflection concerning the earth, chairs, or beds. But we are never in complete control of what we do. Indeed, we do not just act and perceive but act-perceive. It is the object of the perception part that lies to a considerable part outside of our control. Although constructivists tell us that everything is the construction of our minds, this is not so because we cannot construct something that we do not already know (have a plan of). For example, we have listened for a while to another speaking before knowing that we have been and feel insulted. We receive

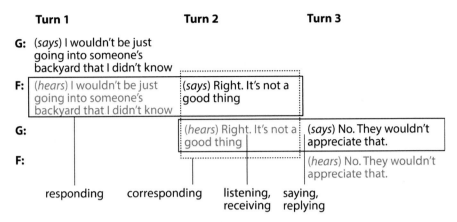

Fig 2.4 A transactional (translocutional) model of conversing.

the new and unseen, therefore unforeseen, as a gift. Ideas *come to us*: we receive and then have sudden insights without any apparent cogitation. This orients us toward the passions (e.g. emotions, and pain), which are given to us; and we are confronted with them because we could not foresee them. When we listen to others, we do not know what they are going to say and what we are therefore given. When we listen, we may indeed be hurt, which we would not have to be if we were merely engaged in the mental construction of the world. We are hurt by something else rather than construct the hurt. Such ideas, grounded in our capacity to suffer – i.e. *passibility* – challenge the very foundation of constructivist thought. Both agency and passivity (suffering) are required to understand the specifically human nature of the reality we live.[5] We therefore need a new and different metaphor about what it means to know and how it is grounded in our ways of being, including at a moment when we do not yet have language and related tools for constructing the world as it is known to adults.

A transactional perspective on life may be exemplified by means of a few turns from a conversation. Consider a brief exchange between our middle school student Graham and an interviewer (Fran) talking to him about his contributions to the communal understanding about the creek traversing the municipality in which he lived (Fig 2.4). Traditionally, a conversation is thought about in terms of the contributions that each participating individual makes. This has its equivalence in the transcription, where a turn is attributed to the speaker. But, as can be seen in the transactional model (Fig 2.4), the listener also acts while the speaker is speaking. To have any hope of a *reply*, the recipient has to actively listen. In so doing, we *receive* the words as a gift. The words simultaneously exist in the resonating vocal cords of the speaker and in the resonating eardrums of listener. That is, the words belong to both, or the sounds are not communicating at all. In the diagram, this co-belonging of words to speaker and listener is indicated by a dotted rectangle. The rectangle marks the event of *corresponding*. This is a transactional event, because it is comprised of two directionalities, from speaker to listener (saying, giving) and from listener to speaker (attending to, receiving). The result of such corresponding in the sense of communicating is a corresponding in the sense of being a little more alike: we share something with someone else. For a listener, the speaker is part of the environment. In corresponding, we have a unity / identity of person and environment. In the particular case of another person being that environment, the unity / identity of person and environment is apparent: the word is part of both, the vocal cords of one and the inner ear of the other. Resonance holds speaker and listener together. The double vision (hearing) not only is their relation but also the condition for consciousness and mind – they arise in a manner as depth (stereoscopic vision) arises from the cooperation of two human eyes.[6] I return to these issues in chapter 8.

There is a second event related to the first: *responding*. This event reaches from actively attending to and receiving words, on the one hand, through the act of replying, on the other hand. The reply grows out of the gift received. It is therefore inconceivable without the gift. Responding also is a transactional event that requires the cooperation of two or more people, for it involves actively listening / receiving *from* and saying / replying *to* someone, the latter of which is specifically designed for *this* recipient. The reply therefore cannot be attributed to the listener or respondent. It has grown out of the word received from the initial speaker, and, thus, has characteristics of both the giver and the recipient, who now replies. Having the characteristic of both means that there is a unity / identity of environment (giver) and replying recipient. Moreover, the recipient speaks *to* the other, *for* her benefit, thus returning a gift. That gift, as before, has characteristics of the giver and the recipient *for whom* it is designed.

These considerations show that we cannot think about a conversation other than in translocutional terms. Any turn belongs to two people, and any statement arises from and is designed for the other – thus having characteristics of both. Each turn simultaneously is a coming and going constitutive of any boundary of Self and other. The phenomenon of dwelling always involves the person and her environment; and both shape and are shaped by the respective other. There is a continual toing and froing. This is what makes the word *dwelling* a suitable category for thinking about our ways of being in the world. These ways constitute the foundation for theorizing thinking and everything else of interest to educators. Karl Marx and Friedrich Engels captured this in the statement that consciousness [*Bewußtsein*] cannot ever be anything else than conscious Being [*bewußtes Sein*]; and the Being, in the case of humans, is their real life-process.[7] Our (human) fundamental mode of Being is that of dwelling, which always already occurs in a world given to us; and any consciousness is the result of becoming conscious of aspects of this dwelling. To paraphrase Marx and Engels, individuals are what and how they express their lives. There is a unity / identity of individuals, their productive processes, their products, and the material conditions that make production possible. Most importantly, perhaps, is the contention that the behavior of humans toward nature (environment) conditions their behavior toward one another, and their behavior toward one another conditions their behavior toward nature (environment).

Dwelling as a Mode of Being

In the phenomenological literature, *dwelling* has been developed as a fundamental concept for thinking Being and its relation to knowledge and representation. Making the past or the future appear in the present is possible only because we already dwell. But we do not just dwell in natural and human-made environments but also in language – which tells us about the nature of a thing provided that we respect it as presenting itself to us from itself. *Dwelling* is the present participle of the verb 'to dwell', a mode of living, and a noun, a (type of) building. The word building can be tracked to the Old English and High German word *buan*, which had the sense of 'to dwell'. The etymology of the verb buan, to build, includes 'taking up one's abode, to dwell'. In fact, 'to build' derives from an even older Proto-Indo-European root bheu-, bheu̯ə (bhu̯ā, bhu̯ē), which made it into many languages as (a) verbs with the sense of to be (and various tenses thereof), exist, propose, become, dwell, prosper, plant, and flourish and (b) nouns with the senses house, dwelling, abode, residence, welfare, good condition, household, and things belonging to a household. The root also means 'to cherish and protect, to preserve and care for, specifically to till the soil, and cultivate the vine'.[8] *Dwelling* therefore captures many characteristics of the human form of being. In our everyday experience, that is, in what we live and live through, building and thinking, as dwelling, are habitual and arise from the fact that we inhabit the earth. This earth is the reference point for who we are and what we think: it is the reference point for our animate bodies and living things so that we may recognize one another as different from thing-bodies; the earth given to (not constructed by) all of us in the same mode, therefore, is the ground for solidarity. The places we inhabit lead to habits, habitual practices, and *habitus*, sets of structured structuring dispositions that ground the homology between human ways of being and their natural and social environments. Habitus fits us like the habits we wear.

As with words generally, the old senses of the word *buan* have fallen into oblivion with the new senses that have evolved over time; and with it, the real sense of building as dwelling has been lost. This means that *dwelling* no longer is thought as the Being of humans, that is, as a fundamental character of human existence. There are three dimensions that we can hear in 'building': building is dwelling because we build only because we always already dwell. Thinking, as Marx and Engels show, always follows and therefore is grounded in practice. Thus, dwelling unfolds into building, which unfolds into thinking, and building and thinking unfold into growing and cultivating things. Growing and cultivating imply rooting, a concept that is developed further in chapter 3. *To dwell* means to stay, to remaining, to be and remain in peace. Dwelling, thought as cultivating things, also un-folds into sparing and preserving: the harvest is stored and preserved to provide for human needs when food is scarce. In cultivating, humans work the earth. The earth we inhabit is central to our thinking, a point that I also develop further in chapter 3. That is, this line of thought beginning with dwelling that unfolds into building – our immediate (e.g. houses) and more extended environments – leads us to envi-ronmentalism. We thus dwell to the extent that we preserve the local places we inhabit specifically and the global place (the earth) more generally. This world therefore deserves preserving. Dwelling is precisely the way to think Being, and thus our being in the world – for dwelling, as preserving, keeps the characteristic order in and of human concerns. Things, standing out in our thinking, only exist because they are distant or absent objects anticipated in our behavior. They are what they are because actions have consequences, and when these consequences are foreseen – which we learn in relation to other persons – then there necessarily is consciousness of things.[9]

The concept of dwelling allows us to think and theorize knowing and learning generally and, because of its decidedly environmental grounding, for environmen-tal education more specifically. This is so because thinking is one of the ways in which dwelling manifests itself. The objective world is a consequence of our dwelling (being) in the world. The event of dwelling 'exceeds the knowing, the thought, and the idea in which, after the event, the subject will want to contain what is incommensurable with a knowing'.[10] The consciousness of the world is consciousness enabled by this world and the society of human beings inhabiting it. I already note above Levinas' position that the idea of a subject contemplating the world – in the way Marx and Engels characterized the philosophical attitude – ac-tually presupposes the event of dwelling. The philosophical (scientific) attitude constitutes a withdrawal from the worldly things into the recollection of the world in the intimacy of one's thoughts. Without already dwelling, intimately and com-fortably, we would not be able to think or build. Dwelling makes labor and repre-sentation (which completes the separation of Being and thinking) possible. This also makes possible the thought of property, which is a dimension in which the thinking and being of many indigenous peoples around the world differ from Westerners. Indigenous peoples do not think of property in the same way, at least not the W̱SÁNEĆ peoples whose ancestors have inhabited the land where I live today. It is to their ways of thinking and being that I now turn.

Dwelling as an Indigenous Praxis of Being

Heidegger and Levinas both attribute the separation between Being and thinking to language – they both may have been thinking about (and in terms of) their own languages (German, French) and in terms of the metaphysical traditions that are embedded in these languages. Property, so central to Western thinking, appears differently in many indigenous languages that do not have the same concept of ownership. For example, in the thought of the W̱SÁNEĆ – an indigenous group that inhabited the peninsula where I live and where some of their remaining members of which still live on a reserve in my municipality – it is a place that owns the family rather than the other way around. Levinas does think in that direction when he says that the house (the dwelling) is possessed because it is already hospitable to / for its proprietor. Dwelling is a concept that the First Nations should be able to identify with easily, for it, too, stresses the relation to the world as it is lived, implying every material and ideal thing.

Dwelling and the world that derives from it are characteristic of the thinking of indigenous peoples. Thus, the First Nations not only inhabited the land but also, and precisely because of it, they knew the habits of the creatures with which they shared the land. For example, the W̱SÁNEĆ developed a particular technique of fishing with the SX̱OLE (/sx̱ʷalə/) or reef net, which is especially suited to the capture of schools of sockeye salmon. The practice seemed to have been lost, but in 2014, a Youtube surfaced showing Nick (XEMŦOLTW̱) Claxton, a graduate student at the University of Victoria, and members of the W̱SÁNEĆ Nation reclaiming and revitalizing this historical approach to fishing. Geographically not far away, members of the Lummi First Nation in the State of Washington also continue to practice this form of fishery.

Being the gift of the salmon spirit, the SX̱OLE not only refers to the technique but also to the material that goes into the construction of the net. Fishing with the SX̱OLE is based on an in-depth knowledge of the habits and travel routes of the salmon, a main staple of the W̱SÁNEĆ. Because the SX̱OLE is stationary, the salmon has to come to where it is, in contrast to commercial fishing that follows the fish and catch it anywhere. Moreover, the SX̱OLE net has to be pulled when the fish is present rather than functioning like a gill net that captures the fish at the gills and thereby drowns it. Because in SX̱OLE the fish is still alive upon hauling of the net, any by-catch can be returned to the ocean alive. There is therefore a close relation between habitat and the habits of the inhabitants – those of the humans and their food habits and those of the animals that humans have hunted and fished to sustain themselves. Their whole ways of looking at the world that contains them, their structured structuring dispositions (i.e. their habitus), are consistent with the philosophical concept of *dwelling*. Their intimate knowledge of the habits of the salmon and other aquatic species was not for the purpose of fishing *more* but to fish sustainably.

Among the W̱SÁNEĆ, a family was tied to a fishing location: they did not own the place but belonged to the SX̱OLE fishing location, called SW̱ÁLET (/swalət/) in the SENĆOŦEN language. The knowledge passed from the elder of the family, who was also the captain of the fishing crew, to the younger. It was the responsibility of the elder to pass on the knowledge, because future generation depended on it for their sustenance. Dwelling means living in a place. For the W̱SÁNEĆ, a fundamental belief is related to dwelling. Their word is ÍY̱,NEUEL (/aiya ne.u.el/]), which translates into English as 'living in harmony with others, with one another, or being good to others'. The SX̲OLE fishery was not just a technique but was especially a way of life suited to the W̲SÁNEĆ and other First Nations making use of reef net fishery. It has allowed them to live in their lands in prosperity for many generations. The SX̲OLE is part of the stories of their origins. For these indigenous peoples, it is a form of governance consistent with Marx and Engels' diction that what and who we are coincides with what we produce and how we produce it. The respect that is embodied in SX̲OLE is the same form of respect that governs the relations between people. Again, it was Marx and Engels who also noted that the relation between people and nature determines (presupposes) the relations between people, and the relation between people determines (presupposes) their relation with nature. In SX̲OLE fishery, respect toward nature expresses itself, for example, in the practice of weaving a ring into the end of the net so that some salmon could escape from each school of fish. In the Lummi First Nation, the hole was referred to as 'the vagina', which guaranteed the continuation of life through the escaping salmon despite the death coming with the fishing practices. SX̲OLE fishing guarantees this fish lineage, which is always tied to a particular river (salmon predominantly return to, spawn, and die in the river where they originally hatched). It is mutual respect and commitment to dialogue. The W̲SÁNEĆ, as other First Nations in the area, understand the salmon and all other living things as gifts, much in the way that phenomenology conceptualizes Being and beings as *given* and as *gift*. The idea of Being and beings (things) as gifts suggests that our very presence has to be thought as such. *Dwelling* is given to us, as it pre-dates and is a condition of our knowing that we dwell.

From Epistemology to Environmental Ethics

Dwelling here is presented as a core concept for a different epistemology to organize our thinking about education in terms of a more expansive relation between environment and the inherently social person. The link between environment and person, on the one hand, and education, on the other hand, is inherent to this category, for dwelling encompasses a person and her environment. Dwelling means being at home, and all the affects that come with a situation where we have a home and everything available to meet our needs. The example from my research shows how the familiar world surrounding Graham firmly grounded his knowing and his subsequent learning, providing both a purpose for expanding his knowledge and a way of contextualizing both the purpose and the learning process. The familiar world – familiar in both literal and figurative senses – is the ground in which he is rooted and upon which he builds. He learned science for the purpose of advancing his goals concerning environmental activism; and this science, unlike what we see happening all too often, did not uproot him. Thus, *dwelling* is the condition and ground for all abstract forms of representation and knowledge. This theme of the earth as the ground in which we are rooted and the contrast to an education that is felt to be uprooting is further developed in chapter 3.

Dwelling also comes with a moral responsibility that is not captured in theoretical approaches to ethics that have been developed within the constructivist approach since Kant. In fact, the constructivist and conceptual change approaches to education do not even have ethics as an integral part of knowing – in contrast to what I have suggested as being implied by a cultural-historical activity theoretic approach.[11] But dwelling implies cherishing, protecting, preserving, and caring for. In cherishing, protecting, preserving, and caring for the environment, we are also cherishing, protecting, preserving, and caring for ourselves because of the intimate and constitutive unity / identity of person and environment. Kant, who emphasizes the rational mind, needs a *moral imperative* as his ethical principle, a dictate of pure reason. As soon was we think Being in terms of dwelling, what we do onto others we always already do onto ourselves.

The theoretical, decontextualized approach of constructivism to knowing and learning does not work. We must not think thinking in theoretical terms, for this would lead us to conclude that 'the detached content of the cognitional act comes to be governed by its own laws, according to which it then develops as if it had a will of its own'.[12] A different way is to think thinking through its subordination to dwelling. This is so because building and thinking are, each in its own way, necessary for the forms of dwelling typical of humans. The two, however, are also insufficient for dwelling so long as each busies itself with its own affairs in separation instead of listening to the other. We have to go further and allow building and thinking to listen to each other because both belong to and derive from dwelling. In the process, both 'remain within their limits and know that each one comes from the workshop of long experience and incessant practice'.[13] Practice involves thinking and doing, and each thought is an integral part of every concrete act or deed that I perform; our whole lives are uninterrupted performances of concrete acts. Thought does not exist separate from act but constitutes an integral part. As seen in the transactional model (Fig 2.4), the thought concerning a particular phrase accompanies our actively attending and receiving the speech of the other, continues on while we reply, and ends with our monitoring the effect of the speech on the other. Indeed, we learn to anticipate the outcomes of our own actions from the ways in which others reply to what we have done. With the ability to anticipate the outcome of an act, that is, with the ability to have a goal, also emerges the existence of a Self in its relation to the (generalized) other. On the other hand, a formal, constructivist approach grounded in the individual subject that exists prior to the social world cannot provide an ethics for the living act that is actually performed in the world of our everyday lives.

The agriculture-related environmental degradation of the Hagan / K̲ENES Creek watershed and the surrounding oceans, increases in heavy metals that make the traditional shellfish food of the W̱SÁNEĆ unusable, and overfishing on the part of commercial and sports fisheries of the waters that has nourished them for centuries give us much to think about the lack of ethics and responsibility. At a time when scientists produce new, genetically modified organisms, new chemical fertilizers, new pharmaceutical products, agents of warfare, and so on without the eventual consequences that (as history has shown) turn out to have deleterious effects not only on individuals but on the collective as well, there is a need for thinking education in new ways. I suggest thinking in terms of *dwelling*: both as a category for analysis and as a way of rethinking and reorganizing school science. Dwelling means thinking, but a form of thinking that is aware of its answerability (see chapter 9). The concept allows us to understand that we are not just exploiting the natural world, but that we are exploiting humanity as a whole, and, because we are human, we are exploiting ourselves.

Dwelling can lead us to think more about the times and places where relating, knowing, and learning take place. That is, times and places (i.e. chronotopes) constitute important ways for understanding ourselves. Many words of the W̱SÁNEĆ's SENĆOŦEN language are in fact chronotopes – ḰENES, the place where whales come to feed during certain times of the year; SṈITȻEŁ (/snitxwets/), home of the blue grouse where hunting, fishing, teaching, and other cultural practices of the W̱SÁNEĆ culture took place; or ḰELSET, literally bailing out (of the canoe), Reay Creek, where one would get out of the canoe to begin a portage. In their very essence, therefore, these words are radically different from the decontextualized and decontextualizing ways in which we – children of the Greco-Roman tradition – conceive of the world. Grounded in familiar places, education becomes memorable determining the chronotopes of the auto/biographical genres that students use to tell their lives. These particular chronotopes shape the way students envision their future. A chronotope may be an abstract notion, but my actual, concrete dwelling in this place and in this time is not abstract but always has consequences. Thinking education from the perspective of dwelling and its inherent connection to the environment gives us a suitable direction for grounding our own answerable actions as (organic) intellectuals.

There is a lot that the W̱SÁNEĆ can teach us about how to go about (science) education embedded in and occasioned by environmental education. Their teaching can be understood in terms of the phenomenological category *dwelling*; their teaching is grounded phenomenologically in the world just as they know it. Grounded in their culture, the W̱SÁNEĆ attempt to teach their own by integrating traditional ecological knowledge and Western science, as their elders told my research team, in the attempt to create restoration or conservation programs for people of all sorts of background and age. The W̱SÁNEĆ are (rationally) grounded in their irreducible connectedness within a complex system. They do so for the purpose of keeping their 'natural environment as a sustainable place to live in and preserve for future generations'. They teach respect for all living beings that inhabit this region of the earth with them and they recognize that their actions have consequences that can affect the local ecosystems generally and their watershed specifically. Their goal is to take care of the land so that it will take care of them. In this, they do not reject the means of Western (scientific) culture. Instead, they are aware of and actively draw upon the results of science – e.g. of electronic spectroscopy that tells them the levels of certain metals (including arsenic, copper, lead, and mercury) in their local water supplies. *Dwelling* is a suitable category for denoting this spirit of ẈSÁNEĆ within a Western cultural history.

Response to a World in Crisis

In this chapter, I develop an epistemology that is grounded not in the primacy of the individual mind but in dwelling. This term names a phenomenon and category, and, for analytic purposes, constitutes a unit / identity of person and environment. But this chapter goes beyond the epistemological dimensions, for it also implies a form of concrete ethics. In many languages, there are proverbs about the bird that fouls its own nest. Regarding the environment, it turns out that humans are precisely that – just think about the coal-fired power plants in the major industrial nations, including China, the US, and Germany. The very ways in which Western cultures have come to think about themselves and the world detaches them from the transactional relations that make our lives. Transactional means that there is a unity / identity of person and environment because there is a constant coming and going from person to environment and environment to person (Fig 2.4). But if this is so, then we humans are never outside of the environment: we are in the environment and the environment is in us. We are relational beings with respect to the natural and social worlds. These are not separate from us: we are integral and constitutive parts. In this chapter, I introduce such a route of thinking, developing *dwelling*. As a category, *dwelling* captures humans' fundamental mode of being, including the irreducible relation of person and environment. Building, as thinking, is possible only because we always already dwell. We are not detached thinkers in the way constructivists make us look to be, ratiocinating about the world that we consider separate from ourselves.

This chapter is particularly relevant in the context of the current debates whether to allow the use of glyphosate, which is not only something that farmers spray on their fields in the form of glyphosate-containing Roundup™ but also something that is now found in high concentration in the bodies of many people. This is precisely my point: we are part of the environment, and it is in us, with considerable consequences for our health. For me as a beekeeper, this is particularly relevant in the context of the debate of neonicotinoids, a class of insecticides similar to nicotine that affect the neural systems of the insects (as well as birds) and that demonstrably have wreaked havoc on apiculture. For me it was indeed an interesting and revealing experience when I found out that a fellow traveler on a plane – after having listened for a while to his stories about eating only organic food – that he was a Monsanto scientist.

The world is in a crisis. There is hardly a day when the various news media do not carry a feature that deals with human-induced global warming, climatic changes, threatening of animal and plant species, or endangerments of human health (lead in toys, obesity, environmentally caused cancers, food allergies). Humans do have the capacity to change the world to satisfy their needs – as K. Marx and F. Engels write in their theses on Feuerbach – but nature, of which we are part, reflexively controls itself. We, a form of life, thus not only affect the environment with our activities but also endanger this very life. This is so even though the current president of the US denies it. But we all are humans. It is not just this or that chemical company, not just this or that oil multi-national that changes the world. As members of society, through our politicians, we make all sorts of action possible that change the environment. Thus, collectively, we *can* halt and reverse the current trend – if there is a *collective will* to act in the *collective, common interest rather than in the special interests of some groups*. At this point in history, a lot of the environmental change is caused by some (e.g. multi-nationals and their investors) but the costs are born by others, a fact that has led to the concept of environmental justice. The research on environmental justice and resilience in the municipality where I reside convinced me that we have to change our thinking about thinking, and, therefore, about knowing and learning to begin addressing how we, as a society, come to deal with the environmental crisis (one of the main 'wicked problems' facing humanity). We have to do so because we are building the world we inhabit and wherein we are dwelling. We build, and we think. But we can think a world different from the one in which we poison ourselves by poisoning the environment. To think and build a different world, we have to become aware of our dwelling. To think and build differently, we require a form of education that allows children and students to recognize our intimate relation with others and the natural environment.

In modern societies, learning is relegated to schooling. In the history of the human division of labor, whereby older forms of collectively motivated activities split to form new activities that serve the collective need, schooling also has emerged as a form of societally reproducing society generally and reproducing its cultural practices (i.e. knowledge) specifically. In the activity of schooling, society ideally has created a formal means of culturing culture (see chapter 4). Culture allows members of new generations to become conscious and to act, despite their young age, to contribute to make this a better world, to change the world to avert that it becomes a threatened habitat for a threatened human species. (Though schools may actually be an integral part of the problem, as I have argued in the past, rather than part of the solution.) An environmental focus in education, therefore, may be a necessary: not just for science education and not merely for elementary or high school. Indeed, an environmental education may be integral to lifelong learning. Having begun a year-round permaculture garden some twenty years ago, I have learned tremendously about the environment, and seen changes in the animal and plant (including weed) life that have occurred over his time. Our garden has become habitat to animals that did not exist there before: the doves that find shade under the kiwi trees, the many different (bumble) bee species enjoying the flowers on the kale plants that we leave for them, the lizards that find warm spots and insects to thrive. The obstacle to changing our ways of being may lie in the epistemology for thinking about knowing and learning and therefore for thinking about how we teach. It may be precisely these ways – which decontextualize knowledge from the environment, economy, and our human lives – that lead to the destructive forms of collective behavior.

Notes

[1] Martin Heidegger, 'Bauen Wohnen Denken', in *Gesamtausgabe I. Abteilung: Veröffentlichte Schriften 1910–1976. Band 7: Voträge und Aufsätze* (Frankfurt/M: Vittorio Klostermann, 2000).

[2] Emphases added. Emanuel Levinas, *Totalité et infini: Essai sur l'extériorité* (La Haye: Martinus Nijhoff, 1971), 127.

[3] Mikhail Bakhtin, *Philosophy of the Act* (Austin: University of Texas Press, 1993), 20.

[4] Out of respect for the indigenous peoples who lived before the white people arrived in this part of the world, I use their indigenous names and words in the SENĆOŦEN (/Sənčaθən/) language for which I provide the pronunciation when they are first used.

[5] Karl Marx and Friedrich Engels, *Werke Band 40* (Berlin: Dietz, 1968), 540.

[6] Gregory Bateson, *Mind and Nature: A Necessary Unity* (New York: E. P. Dutton, 1979), 133.

[7] Karl Marx and Friedrich Engels, *Werke Band 3* (Berlin: Dietz, 1978), 26.

[8] Heidegger, 'Wohnen', 149.

[9] See George Herbert Mead, *Philosophy of the Act* (Chicago: University of Chicago Press, 1938), 426–432.

[10] Levinas, *Totalité,* 126.

[11] Wolff-Michael Roth, 'The Ethico-moral Nature of Identity: Prolegomena to the Development of Third-generation Cultural-historical Activity Theory', *International Journal of Educational Research*, vol. 46 (2007), 83–93.

[12] Bakhtin, *Act,* 7.

[13] Heidegger, 'Bauen', 163.

3

On Being Rooted

Constructivist ideology always presupposes and uses as explanatory resource what really ought to be explained. For example, underlying the constructivist epistemology is the idea that human subjects construct their knowledge. But construction requires tools, the dominant one being verbal language. In the constructivist discourse, however, we never find any account of how language first has come about as an early accomplishment in human history, and how it could have been constructed in the absence of the tool for constructing the tool. Similarly, the constructivist epistemology maintains a focus on the figurative aspects of facts and concepts without asking questions about the ground that makes any figurative image possible. There is no figure without ground; there is no motion without rest against which movement takes place. Where does the ground come from? It is from our everyday ways around the world: as we see in chapter 2, *dwelling* is the condition for building and thinking. Our knowledgeable ways of getting around the world constitute the ground for learning anything else (e.g. in schools). Yet these forms of knowing our way around the world often are discredited – such as when our natural ways of talking about the physical world are said to be wrong and constituting 'misconceptions'. In this chapter I make a case for the ground – however inappropriate it may be and however much it fails to correspond to adult and scientific conceptions – that is the condition for new figures (concepts, knowing) to appear. Once appropriately acknowledged, the ground becomes a fertile soil in which further (school) learning may be rooted. Unfortunately, too much of school experience constitutes an uprooting and a loss and rejection of the very ground that anchors us in the world. This uprooting is the opposite of dwelling or an upsetting form of dwelling.

Eppur si muove [still it (the earth) moves ([by] itself)] Galileo is said to have stated under his breath – historians are certain that he never actually said it, though he might well have said it to himself. Galileo was doing so while leaving the room where the Holy Inquisition had summoned him. There he had recanted the claims made in his recently published book in favor of the Copernican view that the earth rotates and the sun rests rather than the opposite that was the going dogma of the

© KONINKLIJKE BRILL NV, LEIDEN, 2018 | DOI 10.1163/9789004377134_003

Roman Catholic Church. In the course of time, the Copernican description of an earth that moves around the sun asserted itself, as scientists found themselves speaking in the new, Copernican way after something of the order of one hundred years of conceptually confused, muddled talk. Today it is *the* view, that is, the scientific view and, like Galileo in the eyes of the Inquisition, anyone who claims today the opposite to the scientific view is a heretic or denier. Yet, as the following fragment and accompanying analysis shows, today – that is, just about 400 years later – some adults still talk about the sun as moving around the earth when asked for explanations of day and night. Even more stunning, perhaps, the phenomenological philosopher Edmund Husserl restates the supposition that the earth really does not move: '*Die Erde* bewegt sich nicht'.[1] He does so in the context of an argument that no scientific conception, such as the one propagated by and since Copernicus and Galileo, would be possible unless there had been a stable ground on and against which we, in our own cognitive development, experience ourselves and other things move. At about the same time, George Herbert Mead, an American pragmatist philosopher, says something similar: 'There is no permanent space and, hence, no motion, until relation to a percipient or prehensive event gives rise to a consentient set, or a perspective'.[2] That is, there is no permanent space (or time) as the philosopher Immanuel Kant had claimed. In contrast, Mead describes a field of rest, arising from an orientation in reference to a goal of (future) action; and it is only in this field that motion takes place. As Husserl, Mead lets the inhabited and dwelled-in earth to be that reference: 'our action fixes the earth as stable and the sun as moving'.[3] The scientific view of a moving earth and a stable sun is the consequence of a relativistic approach that is inherent in sociality, where through moving about we actually live the different perspectives others have on our own actions.

The alternative approach to the earth as moving or resting can be taken from Husserl's inscription on the envelope in which he had gathered his manuscript: 'Overthrow of the Copernican theory in the usual interpretation of a world view. The originary ark, earth, does not move. Foundational investigations of the phenomenological origin of the corporeality of the spatiality pertaining to nature in the first sense of the natural sciences'.[4] Even though our subsequent understandings may overturn the fundamental sense of the earth as ground and may make it but a thing among things, this overturning is possible only on the ground of an unmoving earth – a point that both Husserl and Mead make in their considerations of how we come to know science and how science further develops. In the shift to a Copernican worldview, this unmoving earth has not disappeared but has become sedimented into our understanding as the fundamental condition for conceiving of anything such as relative motion. In a strong sense, therefore, even though we (some of us) eventually come to understand the earth as a thing moving among things, the unmoving earth is the condition that makes any subsequent understanding possible.

Education, despite considerable amounts of funding that has been poured into developing programs and doing research on learning and instruction, has not been able to increase (significantly) the number of graduates with science degrees. Thus, for example, the number of graduates with science degrees has remained more or less constant over the past twenty-five years, whereas the total number of students has increased by about fifty percent and the total number of computer science graduates has dropped over the same period of time. At the University of Wisconsin researchers have received over US$ 4.3 million to study why so many students are finding science hard and are dropping out rather than engaging in science, technology, engineering, and mathematics degrees. One of the reasons may lie in the fact that despite all efforts spent since the 1950s, little has changed since the Russian spacecraft Sputnik 1 triggered frenzied efforts to advance American science through improvements in science education. In those days, the French philosopher Simone Weil, characterized by her a remarkable compassion for the suffering of others, wrote about education: 'What today is called instructing the masses is taking this modern culture, elaborated in a milieu so closed, so imperfect, so indifferent to truth, to lift everything that it still could contain of pure gold, an operation that one calls vulgarization, and shovel the residue as is into the memory of the unfortunate desiring to learn, as one gives a beakful to birds'.[5]

The problems arise from education because concept words are taught too early, with too great of an insistence, addressing only the intellect with a complete disregard of common sense and children's existing competencies of navigating their worlds. In this manner, students come to a rational 'understanding', an expression by means of which he refers to students who repeat standard phrases in formulaic ways, but who loose their familiar worlds that are home and become estranged. Estrangement, or alienation, for many is a fundamental feeling associated with going to school. This can be seen from the fact that one quarter of the students graduating from the German upper-level schools believed the phases of the moon to be caused by the shadow of the earth. All that suffices is to look at the relative position of the moon and sun in the morning (decreasing crescent) or evening (increasing crescent) to understand that the earth *cannot be* between the two heavenly bodies. The damage thereby caused is greater than the benefits that instruction actually accrues. Education not only pays lip service to children's ideas but also fails to ground every new acquisition in their world in the manner that the concept of *dwelling* suggests (see chapter 2). The speed with which concept words are presented to students during their school years is in contradiction with the recommendation to limit the frequency of ideas when the purpose is to get people to think rather than to besot them. Learned concept words often are used inappropriately, as research in the 1980s shows: Youths struggle matching dictionary definitions and real, everyday situations in which these words have their rightful place. Learned concept words are mere instructions for a particular proven, confirmative intuition rather than something that has arisen from a truly intuitive sense of how the world works. It is when we take these instructions as occasions to travel back that we (historians of science) get to the originary undergoing of a conceptual overturning; and it is when we start with the originary sense that a genetic approach to education moves forward to and through the first idealizations that have led to the initial scientific formulations and that have everything that is characteristic of science and led to its cultural history. The genetic approach to education is built on and emphasizes dwelling and our being rooted in the everyday world.

In this chapter, I show why and in which way it makes sense to say that the earth does not move; and I articulate the implications for education not only with respect to the theories of the solar system but with respect to the relationship between every kind of observation and the scientific way of explaining them. I use examples from astronomy, for it already is part of the elementary curriculum in many jurisdictions around the world. That is, all the while drawing on the linguistic repertoire afforded by the astronomical discussion, this chapter is not about astronomy and the question whether or not the earth moves. Instead it is about the fundamental rooting that we have in the earliest forms of inhabiting this world, which in every place and at any time also goes with some form of language the knowing of which is indistinguishable from knowing one's way around the world.

The Earth Does not Move – Literally

'*From this it is evident that the earth necessarily is located in the center of the world and* immobile', Aristotle wrote.[6] Today, many people, as many as ninety-five percent and including most college students, are said to hold misconceptions about astronomical facts and events such as what brings about the seasons. From a cultural-historical perspective we may better say that such people use language to talk about frequently unknown situations in ways that make intuitive sense and do not inherently lead to contradictory statements. We observe this to be the case in the following fragment, where a graduate student interviewer (I), as part of a project about scientific and common sense concepts in astronomy, interviews Mary, a Taiwanese graduate student working on a PhD in language and literacy education. Mary already has said repeatedly that she is being asked questions about phenomena that she has not thought about before. This particular fragment comes from that part of the interview in which the two talk about day and night. The fragment picks up with a turn sequence about the position of the sun in the sky, which is completed with the statement that the sun should be in the east in the morning. The statement is questioned: why? (turn 10). In the turn pairs that follow, the conversation establishes the sun as moving from east to west, which is elaborated into a movement from east to north to west (turn 17), followed by a movement to the south and east again (turn 19).

Fragment 3.1
07 M: so the sun is in the position of that a sky ((*hand gesture*)) position- ((*looks at interviewer*))
        (0.2)
08 I: yea (0.9) a:nd which? direction. maybe east or north or?
09 M: uh:: ((*hand moves up to the chin, eyes move upward, pensive*)) in the morning it should be in the east
10 I: yea. why.

11 M: why:: uh: i never think about that. () i th*ink* i:ts becau:se of the movement
        of the sun,
12 I: ⌈uh hm
          ⌊((*begins to nod*))⌉
13 M: the sun is moving⌉
14 I: so which? ⌈direction the sun will moving?
                    │((*hand moves back and forth*))
          from? () you know, where to⌉ where?
          as in pendulum motion))   ⌉
15 M: from east to west
16 I: uh hm
17 M: ea:st ta ((*gesture in the air, to upper legs to make "drawing"*)) (0.5)
        u:::m:: () east north ⌈() in⌉ the west an
18 I: ⌊yea⌋

19 M: and the ⌈south and [east again
                ⌊((*finger in the "south" position closer to Mary's body*))
                          [((*finger back in "east" position
20   ()
21 I: so you say *ea*st and moving to?
22 M: north ((*gestures*))

23 I: north () and then moving to
24 M: east
25   ()
26 I: east=
27 M: =okay from () from east to north and to west

The common way of analyzing data in education or the learning sciences would
attribute a misconception to Mary. She articulates phrases that say something of
the same ilk as that which made the Harvard graduates featured in a documentary
the laughing stock of the science education community. In fact, conceptions and
conceptual change research has shown that this is a common way of talking about
these phenomena among Taiwanese elementary students. Mary would be said to
think – holding a conception that she has constructed in her mind during previous
experiences – that the sun moves from east to north to west to south. We hear a

statement that explains night in terms of a sun that makes it day in the south. The second misconception that educational researchers would attribute to Mary is the fact that in the statements the sun is the entity that moves around the earth rather than the earth rotating around its axis. Such misconceptions are theorized as mental structures that are organized like concept maps on paper. Those teachers working from that same research tradition to science education – i.e. a conceptual change orientation within constructivism – intend to assist students in constructing a scientific conception, restructuring the concepts in their mind to produce new hierarchical relations between concepts that more closely correspond to the way in which scientists explain the phenomena. Although conceptual change may be 'nonradical', in those cases that correspond to scientific revolutions – such as the changes students undergo from Aristotelian to Galilean conceptions of movement, from Aristotelian (Ptolemaic) to the Copernican worldview, or the change from ancient to modern understandings of the motions of the heart and the circulatory system – the changes are radical, that is, literally from the root up (Lat. *radic(x)-*, root). Thus, educators working from this perspective sometimes talk about eradicating children's and even college students' misconceptions, that is, literally uproot – eradicate, from Lat., *e(x)-*, out + *rādix,* root – the ways in which they (have come to) understand the world. Education, then, becomes an uprooting experience: students come to be uprooted or *déraciné,* to use an adjective and noun that the English language has borrowed from the French.

The eradication of ideas, however, appears to be a work of king Sisyphus, who, as Greek mythology goes, had to roll a boulder uphill only to see it roll down again so that he had to do the same kind of work all over again. To understand this framing of the problematic, consider this. The interview with Mary was conducted not too long ago, nearly five centuries after Copernicus published *De Revolutionibus Orbium Celestium*[7], which ninety years later was followed by Galileo's publication of the *Dialogue* and his renunciation of the Copernican view before the Inquisition in 1633. It may therefore be surprising why, although the scientific revolution has changed the description of the relative movements of the sun and earth centuries ago, (some) children and adults alike continue to explain the sequence of day and night in terms of a moving sun rather than a rotating earth. Why, at a cultural level, has the scientific conception not replaced the Aristotelian (Ptolemaic) conception long ago? Why is it still intelligible to talk about the sun as moving around the earth rather than having a consistent discourse that makes the earth rotating its axis, which makes the sun appear and disappear in the sky?

Of course, scientists themselves continue to marvel at a beautiful sun*rise* or sun*set*. I would surely receive strange looks if I were to talk about the rotation of the earth while standing with a colleague on the shores of the Straits of Georgia near Vancouver (Canada) marveling at the sun 'setting' behind clouds and mountains (Fig 3.1). That is, in our language – as in other languages, such as French, where the sun '*se couche* [goes to bed]' or German, where it 'geht unter [drowns]' – it is the sun that moves relative to a fixed ground on which we stand and that always already reaches right toward the visible horizon. This aspect of our language, though more consistent with the Aristotelian (Ptolemaic) way of talking

Fig 3.1 A beautiful sun*set* at the Straight of Georgia near Vancouver (Canada).

about the world than with the Copernican / Galilean way, is deeply rooted in our daily, intuitive, and commonsense way of dwelling in and knowing our ways around the world.

Instead of thinking about the issue in deficit terms, we may take a cultural and phenomenological approach to language. In such an approach, the exchange between the interviewer and Mary is understood in a tradition that considers words as not belonging to individuals but always to speaker and recipient, author and reader. That is, we analyze the exchange at the level of language, which never is our own but always already comes from the Other to which it returns. Language makes us live in and relive the thoughts of others. What we then hear are statements about the sun moving around the earth in a particular way (north is above, south below and on the opposite side of the earth) that are enabled by the very existence of language, its genres, and its ways of producing explanations. The very fact that our language enables us to intelligibly talk about a beautiful sunrise or sunset allows a person unfamiliar with models of the solar system – e.g. a child – to infer that the sun is moving across the sky, rising in the morning and setting in the evening. However, from a pragmatic perspective, knowing a language and knowing one's ways around the world are indistinguishable, which makes it intelligible why our descriptions are so deeply rooted in our *dwelling*. An English adjective denoting the fact that we are rooted is *enraced*. We could further borrow from the French and use *enraciné* (being rooted, having roots) and *enracinement* (rooting, the fact to be rooted). These words have a history in the philosophical discourse, pointing to the fact that we are deeply rooted in our everyday lives, language, and experience. Any form of education that attempts to replace this deep rooting will lead to a sense of uprooting [*déracinement*].

In the preceding interview fragment, Mary talks to the interviewer using words and statements that are deeply rooted in her experiences in the world, where the sun rises in the morning, moves across the skies, and sets in the evening. These are also words that root her in these experiences and phenomena. There is nothing in language that prohibits or makes unintelligible what she is saying. In the very fact that she is using particular expressions to talk to the interviewer, we can see evidence that such talk makes sense and thus is implicitly intelligible. It is not Mary's language; it is the language she shares with the interviewer. In fact, for a researcher to state that Mary *has* a misconception, the statements that come from her mouth already have to be intelligible to the researcher as well. It is only then that the researcher can say that what Mary has said is incommensurable with what scientists say about the earth and sun. Simply replacing this talk with other talk – or, in conceptual change language, to replace the misconception with a scientifically correct conception – may lead to a sense of uprooting. Today, much of education, as science itself, is fundamentally alienating, because it robs children of what they have lived and learned in the past.

In our considerations of education as uprooting, we may return to a work entitled *L'enracinement* [Rooting], where we can read about the effect of education in precisely this case of the sun and earth: 'One commonly believes that a little country boy today, student in primary school, knows more than Pythagoras, because he repeats in docile manner that the earth turns around the sun. But in fact, he does not look at the stars. This sun that one talks about in class has no relation for him with the one he sees. One tears him out of the universe that surrounds him, as one extracts the little Polynesians are torn out of their history by forcing them to repeat: "Our ancestors, the Gauls, had blond hair"'.[8] Being able to talk about the universe in the way we have learned from Copernicus is insufficient. Thus, for example, in the case of the lunar eclipse, the acquired discourses intervene and eclipse the moon a second time so that it can no longer be lived in the intuitive ways that a child may originally live it. Children, as Weil notes, repeat the words in a docile manner without really understanding, comprehending from their roots up, what they are saying. The words do not make sense, but children learn to repeat them nevertheless – at least for the purposes of the next test. In this way, they become uprooted, no longer able to hold on to their old beliefs, and unable to hold onto the ones they are forced to acquire to maintain good standing at school. They are alienated from their roots. We therefore may come to the conclusion that it is not sufficient to teach statements like 'the earth moves about the sun'; and it also is insufficient to illustrate them with sentences from the everyday world by saying something as 'like this apple around the lamp'.

What might it mean to teach (for) understanding? To me it means connecting to the fundamental sense of being- and becoming-in-the-world, which arises even before we have words and indeed since we are born. It means connecting to our

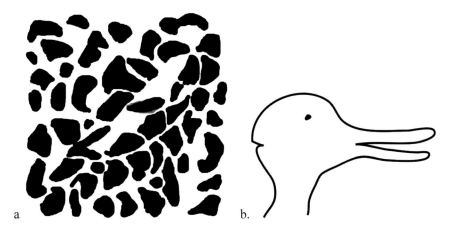

Fig 3.2 A contexture may split into figure and ground – in various ways.

common sense and our commonsense understandings of how the world works. From living in this world with our senses comes our sense of the world. This world is still mysterious and is populated with phenomena that later disappear with and because of instruction. But in some instances, and with some phenomena, those connections with the original and originary sense are never broken. This allows us to understand the responses of Harvard graduates, who suggest that it is warmer in the summer because the sun is closer to the earth – where they talk from the grounded experience of feeling warmer the closer we are to a source of heat. What the graduates said makes sense; it is common sense, tied to what anyone can feel with their senses. Common sense is the ground upon which anything else (figure) may be learned; and it is the ground in which our knowing is rooted.

The Ground of the Image

In the mundane attitude, things are taken as given, independent of their context and the organism for which they exist. A simple experiment, however, shows that the thing, a figure, exists as a figure against a ground, as a text against context. Consider a contexture of white and black blotches (Fig 3.2a). When you begin moving about it with your eyes, seeking whether there is 'something' to be seen, the contexture may split into a figure and its ground. Whatever figure you see it stands against everything else that constitutes the ground. Even for the same person, there may be multiple figure–ground constellations. Thus, the duck-rabbit (Fig 3.2b) exhibits itself as a duck or as a rabbit depending on how you look. The same ink traces lead to very different perceptual forms. The material ensemble in the form of an ink trace is a contexture, depending on our dispositions, separates into different figure–ground configurations. As such, the figure determines the ground as much as the ground determines the figure. As soon as we have one, the other is given simultaneously. Any consideration of movement requires a ground against which the movement becomes movement. It is in such a ground that all our conceptions are rooted – i.e. literally grounded or, as suggested here, *enracined*.

In the preceding section, I articulate how our ways of speaking and our being- and becoming-in-the-world constitute a rooting that provides us with a sense of deep understanding. The familiar soil that we walk (upon) is the firm foundation of our sense of being rooted (grounded). This fundamental knowing the way around the world constitutes a ground on which all of our instructed and learned under- standings are founded. At the most fundamental level, as a precondition for the experience of motion and rest, there is an experience of a ground against and in reference to which motion and rest come to stand out as figures against the ground. This ground retreats into the back so that the figure can become salient. It is from such a perspective that the earth (-ground) does not move.

We may distinguish between two ways in which to appropriate the reports, de- scriptions, and assertions (findings) of others. The first exists in illustrating the horizons of a ready 'world concept', as it has been formed before and in anticipa- tion. The second exists in the renewed constitution of the world concept from an already finished concept. Husserl emphasizes the fact that the earth initially ap- pears in our lives as merely another body among bodies, such as the Copernican conception of the world requires. Instead, the world is lived as the foundation (ground) of everything we know. It is only through subsequent events that the earth is constituted as an earth-body. The earth itself, in the original conceptual figure, neither moves nor rests. It is only in respect to the earth as ground that rest and movement become intelligible. To bring this statement into greater relief, consider this. Any letter or image presupposes a ground against which it can become figure. If there were to be no ground that withdraws so that the ink trace could stand out, no *thing* (i.e. nothing) would be seen. In Fig 3.2a, it is only when part of the con- texture withdraws, becomes context, that a figure (text) comes to show itself. It is through and by means of the ground that the visible figure of the text emerges from the invisible through the unseen to become the seen. The same is the case for mo- tion and rest, which can emerge only against a ground that in its very nature does not move. Returning to our case, therefore, once movement and rest are intelligi- ble, the earth, too, may move or rest. That is, even in the constitution of the move- ment or non-movement of the earth, the movement transcending earth as ground is required. Rest and motion lose their absolute nature when the earth-ground be- comes earth-body. Any dispute of this becomes possible only when the situation is considered from the modern perspective rather than from that of a world conceived in very different ways.

My own, originary animate body is lived internally as a constituting body with which I move and feel, and as a body in motion, against a ground that is at rest. The sense of movement and the sense of my animate body as a material body arise from the same life, as *something* in *movement* with respect to a ground from which it is separate. Any confirmation, any demonstration, and any understanding ulti- mately is anchored and rooted 'in my perceptual field and in the oriented presenta- tion of the segment of the world about my flesh as the central body among others, all of which are given intuitively with their own essential contents at rest or in mo-tion'.[9] My animate body in its relation to the surrounding world is the ultimate anchor ground, so that even when sitting on a moving train or in a car, I consider these at rest unless I look outside of the window, at which time I perceive myself as moving with respect to the earth-ground. For the earth to be moving, I have to consider it no longer as the ground with respect to which everything else moves, but as a body among other bodies. I have to take a relativistic perspective, that is, a perspective that includes the perspectives of others. The earth can move only in a social world, a world I share with others. I have to make a switch similar to that I make when I step onto the train. But this earth cannot be stepped on and off as in the example of the car or train, and, therefore, cannot be *sensed* in terms of rest and movement. Thus, 'as long as I do not have a representation of a new ground, as one such that the earth can have in its coherent and circular orbit the sense as a self-contained body in motion and at rest, and as long as I have not acquired a represen-tation of an exchange of grounds such that both grounds become bodies, just so long is the earth itself really the ground, but not a body. *The earth does not move –* I may say perhaps it is at rest'.[10] Husserl here provides the argument for why the earth does not move, and even when it eventually comes to move, a non-moving earth already is the essential sense upon which the understanding of movement and rest come to emerge and to be constituted (passively). Like Herbert Mead, Husserl notes that the understanding of space itself derives from early sense of moving about, where the about-ness of the about is itself a product of the movement: movement is the generative source of space, bodies, and time. Even the birds that fly relative to the earth are no different than humans who walk, because their flying is part of a totality of kinestheses that is related to an 'I can' of the organism. If we could think of having two earths, stepping from one to the other so that we might think reaching relativity of the grounds, we could still conceive the one and the other as separate only when we already had constituted our bodies on the basis of the true ground.

We cannot therefore abstract individual development from the historicity of humankind and the common sense governing the human relations into which we are thrown at birth, which surrounds us when we grow up, and in which we are permanently dwelling. The earth can no more loose its sense as the primordial ground – a sense that founds the sense anything can make – than my body can lose its unique sense as the primordial animate body. This is the same as saying that we always already are dwelling, even if we attempt to repress this fact with ideas about the construction of knowledge or identity. Husserl points out that he is not contradicting Galileo's *Eppur si muove* by saying that the earth does not move. The earth does move, but it is the original dwelling – which he considers being something like an originary ark – that makes possible the sense of movement in the first place and all rest as a modality of movement. This originary rest, however, is a mere modality of movement. It lies prior to any possibility of awareness of movement and rest. The situation is an analogy to the relation with others in dwell-ing, which is the ground for Self and Other to emerge. Like the earth that does not move, the social relations with others constitute the ground against which every possible figure makes sense.

The earth as ground is part of the totality that we live, live in, and live through; in fact, it is the ground against which any thing can take shape. That is, for example, even a simple letter on this page is a letter because it is set against a ground from which it is distinguished without that the ground itself enters consciousness. Yet it is only because the letter distinguishes itself and is distinguished from the ground from and against which it arises that we perceive it as letter. It is there and not there simultaneously. The earth provides the ground that enables all of our knowing, because it is with respect to it that our kinesthetic experience takes place and in reference to which our bodies are felt as such. It is the place that we inhabit and in which we are dwelling. But this earth is not lived as a collection of things that are or have been brought together. The 'together' of the things arises from whatever project we are involved in – the same desk and chair that have a particular function in our office work totality appear to us very differently than when they are used as support in the process of changing a light bulb. The familiar world of the child is of that kind: it provides the fundamental ground against which its sense takes place, where sense is possible as such only because of the ground, even if it is not itself apparent in consciousness. In this field, every object that enters anew always already is apperceived as a part of the thing totality. As a result, 'the apperception of the object as object as such is the first universal typification – precisely the typification of the object as object of experience, a perceptual object, and the typification of the units as configuration of objects'.[11] The totality of the earth ground, in its presence as object totality forms a unity that arises from and exists in the configuration as a whole – a happening or duration. It is within this whole that discrimination takes place. For Husserl, as much as for Mead, we first live the configuration of the world as a whole and then proceed to living its parts. A configuration always appears before its parts. We live the configuration with our animate body, which is something like a ground, that is, part of the constitutional origin. This is so because the consideration of parts of it as being at rest and being in motion is lived against a more fundamental, originary animate-body-as-ground that is at rest and whose self-movement is confronted with resistance that keeps or brings it back to rest.

The world of our dwelling provides us with a unity of self-evident facts that constitute the foundation of all evidence we can gather. The totality of fundamental evidence tends to be closed off as subsequent learning is layered over and on top of it, sometimes undoing it all the while retaining it in its very foundation. This is the case in the cultural-historical evolution of the formal (discovery) sciences, including mathematics. Thus, for example, William Harvey, an English Renaissance physician, overturned the then-common understandings of the function of the heart and provided an argument for the existence of the circular system of blood flow (see chapter 4). As others, he had started out with the common conceptions then in place, fundamentally an Aristotelian view of the human body. However, the revolution emerging from his keen observations and descriptions did not get rid of his prior understanding. Instead, his new understanding was enabled by his prior understanding, which provided a ground, the objects, and the tools for arriving at a new understanding that overturned what anteceded. The old forms of understanding were both overturned and retained, as sediments and ground, in the sense that they were essential for the new to emerge, on which the new is founded, and in which it has its roots. The interesting aspect of this is that learners today can re-live this and similar transitions. They can follow the path of understanding (*Nachverstehen*) as they produce again (*Nacherzeugen*), in a movement of active and passive constitution, the historical processes that have led to new cultural (see chapter 4). In this way, the emergence of any ideal form of more modern theories can be lived again and taken on in events termed *Nachverstehen* [understanding-again/after] and *Nacherzeugen* [producing-again/after]. That is, today we may re-live the genesis of a new understanding in ways that both overturn and retain what we understand before. The objectivity of the sciences – the fact that its experiments and empirical evidence can be produced at any time by anyone – arises from these phenomena of re-understanding and re-producing the cultural-historical genesis of knowledge.

Crucial in this process of cultural-historical genesis of knowledge is that any subsequent sense totality – e.g. atomic physics as it exists today – is not already the intention from the beginning. The evolution of the sciences is non-teleological; and it is this aspect that a truly *genetic* education retains. Every science emerges from a first appropriation, from first creative activities, which lead to further activities in a forever continuing appropriation. Everything attained before is retained in the constitution of the new. Tracing the evolution backwards, there have had to be more 'primitive' antecedent sense of how the world works enabling a first constitution based on what inherently was (self-) evident without that this self-evidence could be questioned any further. In this original step, the new could not have been anticipated because it was transcending, going beyond, and, therefore, was initially only darkly awakened. The truly new is unseen and therefore unforeseen – it is discovered. These are new in*sights* in the sense of the word, occurring quickly precisely because they could not have been anticipated incommensurable as they are with what has existed before. Unfortunately, the constitutional ground of our commonsense world is eclipsed, as 'the originally intuitive life, which creates its originally self-evident forms through activities on the basis of sense-experience, very quickly and to an increasing degree, falls victim to the *seduction of language*'.[12]

The original materials for the first foundation of sense, the original premises exist, prior to all science, in the world of common sense that is part of a prescientific but nevertheless cultural world. In the course of growing up, we come to find ourselves thrown into this world before actually capable of grasping it; and we talk a language that is not our own because it always already has come from the other. In this language is sedimented a fundamental, constitutive common sense that can be unearthed. Thus, for example, the Proto-Indo-European root *per-*, which appears in such common words as ex*per*iment and ex*per*ience, was used in the context of 'going through something', 'underdoing an (adverse) situation', 'peril', and 'trial'. When we reflect upon those situations where we use the words 'experiment' and 'experience', we do become aware that they in fact are associated with the original sense of the etymological root. It therefore is not necessary to reconstitute the whole of the sciences, to traverse the entire chain of foundations from the original and originary constitutions to the present day. Instead, in the tradition of the sciences, because sense is founded upon (preceding forms of) sense, the earlier forms enter the latter forms. A few exemplary situations suffice for the individual to re-live and re-constitute the nature of the process of sciences, from its foundations in the originary forms of self-evidently givens to the present day. On the other hand, if this going back were impossible, 'without the actually developed capacity for reactivating the original activities contained within its fundamental concepts, i.e., without the "what" and the "how" of [their] prescientific material'[13], the sciences would not constitute a tradition that has or makes any sense. Husserl adds that this was, in his day, unfortunately the situation in which the European sciences found themselves.

The aforesaid has consequences both for philosophy of science and for education. Thus a phenomenological philosophy cannot take but a genetic approach if it wants to respect the temporality and feeling of time that comes with the originary sense of going-through and undergoing. A genetic conception cannot be causal, where temporality is but a simple element. The lived taking of roots and the novelty of knowing are irreducible to each other. That is, the everyday (common) sense is the ground, the tool, and the object of a transformation into new forms of sense that in a way transcend and even reject the earlier forms. Yet the two forms are irreducible: the new (scientific) sense cannot be explained on the basis of prior sense; and yet the former is possible only because of the latter. The approach also has consequences for education. In the following section, I provide an argument for a genetic approach to education, which has the purpose of rooting any new understanding in the ways students live (witness and feel) their lives.

Fostering the Taking of Roots

Simone Weil once noted that the setting of roots possibly is the most important and most misunderstood need we human beings feel. In English, there is a rarely used word for having taken roots, being rooted: enracined. It has its origin in the French verb *enraciner*, to root, to implant; to this verb corresponds the noun *enracinement*, rooting, taking roots, deep-rootedness. 'L'enracinement' is the title of an essay written by the Weil, which, because of the lack of an equivalent word, was translated into English as 'The Need for Roots'. The taking of roots in common ground and common sense is an important aspect of knowing, whereby individuals remain grounded in and connected to the familiar worlds that surround them. In contrast, uprooting occurs in cases of brutal suppression of all local traditions, including the 'brutal' suppression of the forms of knowing available to everyday folk. This brutal suppression thus not only occurs in the case of indigenous students confronted with Western science but also in the case of all students rooted in their mundane ways of being in the world. It is associated with the forms of knowing imposed and assessed by others until the moment that another form is imposed for a time period unknown to the person – which is what students experience when a form of knowing correct today (a particular atomic model, a particular way of factoring polynomials) is considered false tomorrow. In education, especially when it is practiced superficially, the empty assurance that what we see is only appearance leads to uprooting and a sense of a loss of safety and feeling-at-home in / with nature that arises from, and with a sense of, dwelling. In fact, the various scientific revolutions have led to a general uprooting and loss of the security of home; but they also have come with a gain because the sciences have led to greater control over our condition (e.g. in the case of disease and illness).

Education – and perhaps science education more than any other discipline-specific school subject – has been concerned with changing the ways in which children and student understand the world. Teachers are encouraged to e*radica*te the misconceptions students are said to have or encourage in them in *radical* conceptual change, and students are to be encouraged to abandon their misconceptions in favor of other, more scientific understandings. Not surprisingly, students undergo science education as deeply uprooting, especially when they feel coerced into accepting explanations that do not immediately make sense and may even be counterintuitive. Even cultural approaches are cognizant of the fact that students' everyday language, which they bring from home and which characterizes a particular form of being-in-the-world, conflicts with the language that they are to acquire at school. Some scholars therefore speak of boundary crossing experiences and the building of bridges, whereas others see students constitute a third form of culture, being-in-a-third-space, where they cobble together ('synthesize') the cultures of the home and that of science for the purpose of form a third space where science is synthesized. But thinking education in terms of bridges, which comes with associations of gulfs and abysses separating two radically – i.e. literally, from their root up – separate realms, is not the same as thinking it in terms of taking roots and rooting where new forms of knowing are allowed to emerge from what already is. Gardeners know of this when they graft a branch from a more fragile fruit tree onto a root that makes it more resistant or controls its growth. The rooting and grafting metaphors allow new forms to grow on old roots rather than tearing them out and replacing them. Too often, however, youths – not only those indigenous ones that were removed from their families and familiar grounds to attend residential schools in Canada and Australia – continue to be torn from the worlds that they inhabit and build in dwelling, making them repeat statements that appear to reflect understanding the world in new, more scientific ways. The loss children live through is profound, and comparable to the loss of the world that indigenous children live through when confronted with Western science.

The point is not to eradicate children's original relation to the earth and the heavens but, while keeping it in transformed and transforming ways, to associate to it the new relations that correspond more closely to science. Teachers should allow children and students to learn that the new perspective on the earth and heavens, as significant and fascinating it may be, also constitutes a narrowing of the perspective that comes from the objectifying rationalist and rationalizing gaze. This narrowing comes with a loss of a sense of reality – such as when our marveling comments about the beauty of a sun*rise* or sun*set* are countered by a comment about the falsity of this conception and by an explanation based on the mere rotation of the earth. The teaching of astronomy does not have to undo and overcome the original and originary, non-distancing but identifying perception of the earth – which is home, ark, and ground of everything we know. It does not have to rob us of our world that speaks to us in its concrete reality.

In the face of such simple phenomena as the eclipse of the moon – frequently demonstrated by means of shadow play, which high school graduates may explain drawing on book learning, but which they seldom have experienced themselves – school knowledge constitutes a corruption. This is so because the bookish knowledge students acquire intervenes between the phenomenon and the person and, thereby, actually eclipses the moon for a second time so that the individual never comes to really see the moon. Because eclipses of the moon are infrequent, silent documentaries of the phenomenon might be played repeatedly. In an era when most students have access to computers, they could replay such video sequences over and over again in the attempt to make observations that they subsequently describe in their own language and in terms of their familiar world.

The genetic approach grounded in the everyday world that students inhabit allows them, by means of a small number of concrete examples, to re-live the original transformations that have led to a more or less radical change in the sciences (see chapter 4). A singular case, in which students delve in considerable depth, becomes a mirror of the whole of science, the whole world in a single raindrop. A lot if not everything characteristic of mathematics could be taught by and understood through considering the ancient proof of the fact that the series of primes is infinite. Such a consideration would lead to a more profound sense of what mathematics is about than the one that most college-entering students ever develop. The single consideration of what happens to a rock dropped from the top of a tower can bring to light the physicists' ways of thinking and experimenting generally; a similar case can be made if students were to truly engage – not just for verification processes – to seek an answer to Galileo's question what happens when a ball is rolled down an incline. In this particular case, we know that (a) if students really were to try investigating the phenomenon, they likely would learn to understand how the phenomenon can be lost in more ways than in the way it is actually seen and (b) if the teaching is too superficial, even college students in science methods courses tend to lose their ground, become uprooted, and 'get lost'. The study of a few phenomena in great depth may provide students with a good sense of how the world works and, in the process, they can get all the exposure to scientific processes and contents that might be of interest to a general education.

Re-living some of the fundamental transformations in human understanding could and does lead to uprooting – if done hastily. Because we live the movement through a conceptual revolution as uprooting, education simultaneously has to offer ways of finding a new ground. In this way, while losing ground in being uprooted, students simultaneously set their roots in a new ground that allows them to retain their taking roots. That is, students have to engage with a field of inquiry to such an extent that they develop a sense of being at home, at which time the phenomenon or concept to be learned reveals itself. Thus, all the while students are active, what they learn comes in and as a revelation. Elementary insights come almost on their own, accompanying the activity, in a form that that may be called *collateral learning*. In as far as it concerns general attitudes orientations, or dispositions, collateral learning may be more important than the few bits and pieces of content area knowledge that tend to be overemphasized in schools as much as in high-stakes testing. Truly fundamental and formative happenings have to be *moving*, in the intellectual and affective senses of the word.

Central to the foregoing description is the idea of living through something that happens to us, that we suffer, and that we do not control. This affects us cognitively and emotionally. In English, we tend to use the verb 'to experience' for marking that we witness and are affected by the happenings that we live through and that change us. Because the notion of experience is problematized in chapter 8, it suffices here to state that 'experience' is taken in the etymological sense of the Proto-Indo-European root *per-* articulated above, especially as denoted by the verbs to try, dare, and risk, put oneself in danger, carry over bring, fare, and to lead towards. Experiencing and experimenting, though they lead to new understandings, also come with perils, for example, with the danger of losing ground. A fundamental principle of the genetic approach to education is the concept of rooting and taking roots: or grounding. This concept points us to the effort to *ground* education in the current knowing of children and students rather than in the effort of making them abandon the rootedness in their familiar worlds. Genetic teaching does not seek a splitting of individuals, asked to adopt a new world while abandoning its denigrated origins. A genetic approach heeds the description of scientific revolution that emphasizes the non-teleological direction of evolution of the sciences and scientific knowledge: If scientists already knew before what they eventually will have found once they look back, that is, if there is not an aspect of surprise in what scientists come to know (discover), then there would be no need to engage in this endeavor. Thus, there is always something new – in terms of facts and theory – and there is therefore a phenomenon of emergence, where scientists (as well as everyone else) know only after the fact what it was they were doing and what they have truly pursued. And after the fact they can and generally do give a 'because' reason that links what they knew before to what they know now. The genetic approach focuses on this emergence of the new, and how this new comes to be integrated in and transforms what is already known.

Following the principles of the genetic approach means that children and students are re-living this sense of the open and undetermined future of knowledge that emerges from their efforts rather than searching for something predetermined already known to others. There is a passive genesis of new knowing, which, precisely because unknown only moments before its emergence, cannot be anticipated: what is emerging as the new way of knowing is unseen and therefore unforeseen. The living present is constitutive only 'because emerging in its radical novelty of a past immediately constituted, it grounds itself in it and does not appear to itself in the present other than over the ground of a passive continuity with the instant before'.[14] *Emergence* names the coming of a new order. It is associated with a new form of sense because an object or event in the old order (i.e. sense–giving contexture) comes to be part of a new one, thereby changing the figure–ground constellation. This immediately leads us to sociality, which is 'the situation in which the novel event is in both the old order and the new which its advent heralds. Sociality is the capacity for being several things at once'.[15] This *passive genesis* grounds the individual in its own past. On the other hand, the teleological aspect of education – where they merely come to reify pre-existing and pre-determined forms of abstract knowledge – leads to students' uprooting; it is instruction as conceived today that is responsible for students' experience of uprooting.

On Getting the Earth to Move

Readers should not be led to the quick conclusion that educators generally have used the genetic approach. Finding a way of teaching an idea through a genetic process is as difficult as the originary movement that has led to the initial idealization on the cultural-historical plane. We already see from the interview fragment featuring Mary that what we learn to say about the universe fundamentally is grounded in the original and originary ways in which we live the everyday world: The sun rises, moves across the sky, and sets. Our senses provide us with the foundational sense that is the ground in which may root any scientific sense that follows *even when the latter overturns the former*. It is precisely in making us distrust our senses that education leads to an uprooting. Although Mary has had lessons in geography and astronomy as part of her early school life, her ways of describing the universe generally and the phenomena within the solar system specifically derive from experiences that antedate her science lessons. Some science educators – including those from Mary's own Taiwanese culture – suggest offering curricula that bring about cognitive conflict and conceptual change in students such as Mary. The genetic approach, on the other hand, intends to provide experiences that lead to taking roots in the face of the uprooting that scientific revolutions constitute when re-lived on the part of the modern individual. That is, only when education offers a place where students can grow new roots in their existing sense of how the world works – because they are familiar with a phenomenon – can they also go through the movement of uprooting | taking roots that provides them with the safety of a new home while they lost their old.

Teachers may all too rapidly move to the formal discourses that are the specified contents of the official curriculum. This uproots many children and deprives them of their familiar world because the new discourse requires rejecting the old. The genetic description and explanation of development has to exhibit the continuity of something from something it is not, for example, from an animistic view to a scientific one. In the same way, the genetic approach to teaching has to emphasize the historical roots of ideas from their incommensurable predecessors, from the absence of objectivity to its opposite. But Galileo himself, celebrated to be an ingenious scientist, acknowledges that the Copernican system is not easy to comprehend. In a marginal note of his text he comments: '*The* Copernican *Systeme difficult to be understood but easier to be effected*'.[16] If he considered the Coperni-can system difficult to apprehend – e.g. on the part of his readers, many of whom, heretofore, have described the universe in Aristotelian / Ptolemaic terms – then we surely can expect similar difficulties to be experienced by those who, at the current time, describe the universe in similar terms. In his text, Galileo describes Coperni-cus' writing as 'obscure'. Teaching understanding does not mean to tell or prove to children something that they have to admit the new whether or not they understand and believe. Genetic teaching means that children can gain insights into why hu-manity could and can arrive at certain ideas – e.g. because nature offered and con-tinues to offer certain resources for seeing phenomena in this or that way. Thus, for example, Aristotle's insight that the earth must be a sphere, which he took from the fact that lunar eclipses always leave the same curved shadow on the moon, was also available to Copernicus and Galileo, two of the key personalities during the Renaissance that came to be associated with what is now known as the Copernican (scientific) revolution.

The genetic approach – where the adjective has to be heard as simultaneously being exemplary / exemplifying and dialogic (Socratic) – is conceived to allow children and students to work through some of the essential *groundbreaking* situa-tions in the sciences all the while allowing them to honor their non-scientific ways of being in the world. The genetic approach is not just historical. It distinguishes itself considerably from the historical approach in not presupposing the necessity of the scientific concepts that are arising during the genesis of ideas. The genetic approach allows children and students to move through some of the original consti-tutions of science that arose on the basis of, using the tools provided by, and focus-ing on the characteristic objects of a culture at a certain point in time. They do so in a dialogical way, in open conversations among each other and with the teacher. In astronomy, this might be some of the early Greek observations that led to the conception of the earth as a sphere, the first conceptualizations of the relationship between earth and moon, or the evolution of an argument for a heliocentric model, including its now as faulty recognized explanations given by Galileo based on the tides and tidal movement. Indeed, the dialogical approach likely would include discussions of when and why it makes sense to talk in the Aristotelian / Ptolemaic terms about sunrise, sunset, and the movement rather than about the rotations of the earth and when and why it does not make sense to do so. In the case of physi-ology, children and students could engage in tasks that allow them to make pre-cisely the kind of observations that led to the first constitution of the function of the heart and circulatory system (see chapter 4).

In the early days of astronomy keen observations of the heavens – sun, moon, stars, their movements and changes with movement – without any instrumentation, provided the primary materials for thinking about the earth. *Astronomy* derives from the Greek meaning bringing order to (Gr. *nemein*) celestial bodies (Gr. *as-tron*). The Pythagoreans had indeed thought of the earth as moving; only Aristotle, drawing on keen observation and reasoning, provides a proof for a stationary earth. In his works, Aristotle does not simply fantasize but grounds what he writes from his own and on the accounts of others' experiences. This occurs, for example, when he distinguishes between the different forms in which the moon appears in the sky. He appeals to the perceptual senses to provide evidence supporting the hypothesis of a spherical earth: 'How else would the eclipses of the moon have the sections of the circle?'; and, the moon, during 'an eclipse, always has a curved line, which distinguishes it'.[17] He distinguishes the shape of the shadow during lunar eclipses with the shape of the moon as seen in the course of a lunar month when it is straight, gibbous, and concave.

Already in Aristotle's days, the curvature of the earth – that it is round and of small and unimportant magnitude [Lat. *parua magnitudo*] – was derived from keen observations that can be made while traveling: 'If we move even a little to the south or north, a different horizon [Lat. *finiens orbis*, literally end of the world] shows itself, and in the stars overhead there is a considerable change, and the stars are seen differently when going a little to the north or south. Because some starts that are seen in Egypt and in Cyprus are not seen in northerly directions: and stars that in northerly locations can always be seen, there go down/set [*occidunt*]'.[18]

Copernicus later makes the same argument about the spherical nature of the earth, which has to be round because all masses press towards the center. The argument is based on the fact that certain stars are seen in the north but not seen in the south and the reverse. Just like Aristotle, Copernicus draws on specific observations, talking about starts that are permanently seen in the north whereas they are not even rising in the south. He draws on the same observation and description as Aristotle in his argument that the earth is a perfect sphere: '*From this it is obvious that the shape of the earth and the surrounding water has to be, as its shadow shows: it eclipses the Moon with absolutely circular circumferences (arcs)*'.[19] The astronomer then moves to introduce relative motion into his argument, whereby the movement of the object or the movement of the observer may produce an object's observed changes of place. This observation also is familiar to the moderns driving a car, or sitting in a train, where, when, for example, reading a book, our train appears to be leaving the station when in fact the train on the next track is moving while our train remains still: '*Now that it has been demonstrated that the earth has the form of a globe I have to also show whether its form follows motion and what place it has in the universe, without which it is impossible to discover the certain reason of what is to see in the heavens*'.[20]

It is this part of Copernicus' strategic move that may become a central aspect to teaching astronomy according to the genetic approach. Children may discuss and try out relative motion, when they move with respect to others or others move while they remain at rest: '*For every apparent change in place occurs by the movement either of the thing seen, or by the observer, or by the necessarily unequal change of both. For when things move equally in the same direction, no movement is perceptible relatively to things moved equally in the same direction, I mean between the thing seen and the observer*'.[21] In this quotation, we see how Copernicus introduces relative motion between the observer and the thing seen, a phenomenon that Galileo later will take on in his work on the subject (Fig 3.3) and the addition of velocities. In fact, Copernicus does not claim to have originated this

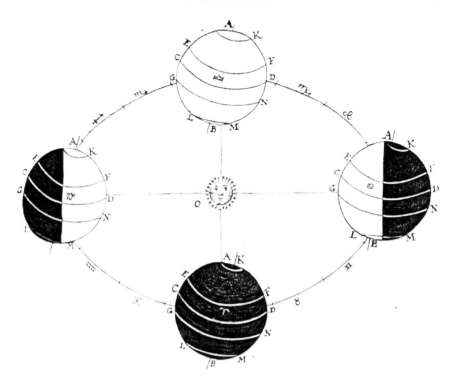

Fig 3.3 In his *Dialogue*, Galileo includes a diagram that is described, in his own words, as 'A plain scheme representing the *Copernican* hypothesis and its consequences'. He had in fact borrowed the diagram and further enhanced from the original text by Copernicus.

idea. In the foreword to his book, addressed to the reigning pope, he clearly attributes the idea of the moving earth to the Pythagoreans, who made the earth move. He then considers the movement of the earth based on what he himself has seen and thought.

It is precisely this shift from considering relative motion of object and observer that presupposes the phenomenon of movement, which itself is the observation of something in motion with respect to something at rest. This observation is even more originary and, therefore, the very condition for the subsequent change to a scientific description of relative motion. Cultural-historically, this shift only occurred in the sciences rather recently, during the Renaissance. It constitutes a tremendous shift in which the earth-ground becomes merely another object among objects. It means that the children and students have to uproot, give up the position in their familiar world and familiar language, and now look upon the earth, sun, moon, and planets from the outside. This outside may in fact be considered a new ground. But its possibility rests on the originary earth-ground, which is both abandoned and kept in the transition, sedimented in the very possibility of considering objects once we have roots in some ground. Without that ground nothing happens;

and without it, a total disorientation sets in. That is, if astronomical education does not provide for a having roots then students lose their old ground without gaining a new one on the basis of which to understand both their old and new ways of considering an object or phenomenon.

It should be clear at this point that children and students of science do not have to learn every topic that currently populates the science curriculum. Anything that they can learn will always by an infinitely small amount of what humanity knows. Therefore, anything whatsoever chosen for inclusion in the curriculum is more or less arbitrary. Instead, closely investigating a few topics – such as the historical transition from a geocentric to a heliocentric conception of the solar system – allows children to relive a scientific revolution, complete a conceptual movement again, and produce again, in active and passive synthesis, the crucial transition from an earlier to a later worldview (see chapter 4). Those few situations may then serve in exemplifying ways for other conceptual revolutions, reflecting the entire universe of science in one drop of rain (a small number in any case).

Uprooting | Rooting

Rooting appears to be a foundational principle for an education that heeds students' biographies and the ways these co-constitute the sense of what they encounter anew. Over the past decades, an increasing number of studies has shown that education uproots, where familiar ways of dwelling – e.g. feminine, indigenous, African American, working-class, and other everyday ways of knowing – are confronted with 'Western' science without providing students with relevant situations that allow them to find a new home where they can set new roots. Science here serves as an exemplary case – as Simone Weil shows, uprooting and alienation may occur in social sciences as well, such as when Polynesian students – e.g. in New Caledonia, part of the French overseas territories – are asked to recite phrases concerning 'our ancestors the Gauls'. That is, education leads to an uprooting without providing opportunities that simultaneously lead to a new form of being rooted together with a sense of safety that comes with the feeling of being at home with something. As transnational migrants know from their own lives, feeling at home again in foreign lands takes time, frequently a lot of time. This is reflected in the genetic approach, which emphasizes the slowness of the process by means of which students regain what they have lost. However, recent efforts in teaching science concepts still tend to go in the opposite direction, as exemplified in the various, worldwide attempts to teaching science and literacy learning among students generally and among indigenous students specifically. Rather than allowing indigenous students to evolve the familiarity necessary to grow roots and feel at home, recent curricular efforts attempt to *accelerate* learning. But there are no quick ways to rooting. The economy of the genetic approach does not come from constituting a fast lane on a unidirectional highway to specific content knowledge but rather from its emphasis of being rooted in understanding. Even the best teachers do not know what and when children will learn, for they are unable to anticipate the latters' personal contributions to classroom conversations only seconds hence. Teachers cannot anticipate what a learner will say in response to what they will find to have said once their current saying has ended. In fact, the fundamental problem with education is that it is thought from the outcomes, that is, the specific contents to be inculcated despite all the rhetoric about the personal construction of knowledge. This approach *cannot* be the answer because students, by the very fact that they do not know the concepts, cannot have these as goals toward which they could actively orient to learn them.

In this chapter, I offer the dialectic of uprooting | rooting as a way of understanding what happens when we are asked to abandon our familiar worlds in favor of scientific views – whether these are created in the natural sciences, social sciences, or humanities. I articulate the ways in which our familiar world is the unmoving ground in which we have grown roots. Education, in telling us that we have to distrust our senses, is uprooting. This conceptualization is consistent with the fact that so many students – often women, indigenous, working-class, and others with firm roots in everyday ways of understanding the world – drop and drop out of science, technology, engineering, and mathematics. Education can be different. The tremendous learning that was observed in my community research among female, indigenous, and learning '*dis*abled' students can be understood, here, in a new way: These students were not only working on familiar grounds, a creek in their community, but also had opportunities to grow roots in new grounds as they developed ways of investigating and describing their creek in ways consistent with Western science.[22] In the process of uprooting | rooting, these students grew new roots upon their old ones.

The earth moves; yet it does not move – the dialectic of uprooting (brought about by the moving earth) and rooting (brought about by the earth that does not move) is captured precisely in this incompossible statement. For the earth to be able to move, it has to be foundationally at rest. For humanity to evolve, there has to remain firm ground on which it rests and in which it dwells. Too often, however, students do not have the opportunity to become familiar with a topic or phenomenon to regrow roots in a soil that becomes a new home, in an extension of the roots from old to new ground, from an earth that does not move to one that moves. The genetic approach to teaching – which I ground here in the commensurable phenomenological philosophy – emphasizes this dialectic or uprooting and re-rooting that serve us as an anchoring ground for our ideas of a more appropriate approach to education. The genetic approach is based on the phenomenon of dwelling.

The genetic approach fundamentally is cultural and materialist. Children and older students come to engage in the very processes that allow the tradition (in the sense of handing on) of science, which occurs when they re-live the original creation and evolution of scientific sense, both rooted in and uprooting from an original earth-ground. The historical presence of science derives from the totality of human `history; and each new understanding act and understanding conception is rooted in the fundamentally pre-scientific world on both cultural-historical and ontogenetic levels. Individuals always learn in the present, which is a culturally and historically specific world. As a consequence, learning ends up being a form of cultivating the

always already cultivated. The figure of cultivation – already invoked in the ancient meaning of the verb 'to build' deriving from the Proto-Indo-European *bheu*
(chapter 2) – is related to the figure of uprooting | rooting, as every gardener or
farmer knows. Without the ability to set roots, nothing grows and cultivation becomes impossible; and what is uprooted (e.g. weeds) dies. For many plants that can
in fact be transplanted, disturbing the roots as little as possible – leaving the clump
surrounding the young plants undisturbed – allows these to push from the clump
into the surrounding soil and, thereby, become anchored in the new ground without
having the old clump removed.

The genetic approach, with its attention to extended depth rather than shallow
breadth, lends itself to cross-curricular integration. For example, Copernicus' *De
Revolutionibus* contains a lot of geometrical argumentation, which offers many
points of contact with and integration of mathematics. The conversational form of
Galileo's *Dialogues* and the argumentative manner of presenting alternative
worldviews contained in it provides opportunities of literary analysis generally and
of the genre forms specifically, including the argumentative methods currently en
vogue in (science) education. For the small number of students taking Latin classes, many original texts, which are written in that language, are easily available
online.

Notes

[1] '*The earth* does not move'. Edmund Husserl, 'Grundlegende Untersuchungen zum
phänomenologischen Ursprung der Räumlichkeit der Natur' in *Philosophical Essays in Memory of
Edmund Husserl* ed. by Marvin Farber (Cambridge: Harvard University Press, 1940), 313.

[2] George Herbert Mead, *Philosophy of the Act* (Chicago: University of Chicago Press, 1938), 147.

[3] Mead, *Act*, 434.

[4] Leonard Lawlor, 'Editor's Note', in *Husserl at the Limits of Phenomenology* by Maurice Merleau-
Ponty (Evanston: Northwestern University Press, 2002), xli.

[5] Simone Weil, *L'enracinement* (Paris: Gallimard, 1990), 62.

[6] '*Perspicuum est igitur, terram in media mundi sede locatam esse oportere, &* immobilem', Aristotle,
De cælo (Paris: Gabrielis Buon, 1560), 40r.

[7] On the Revolutions of the Celestial Spheres.

[8] Weil, *L'enracinement,* 62.

[9] Husserl, 'Räumlichkeit der Natur', 311.

[10] Husserl, 'Räumlichkeit der Natur', 313.

[11] Husserl, 'Räumlichkeit der Natur', 335.

[12] Edmund Husserl, *Husserliana Gesammelte Werke Band VI: Die Krisis der europäischen
Wissenschaften und die transzendentale Phänomenologie. Eine Einleitung in die phänomenologische
Philosophie* (The Hague: Martinus Nijhoff, 1976), 372.

[13] Husserl, *Krisis*, 376.

[14] Jacques Derrida, *Le problème de la genèse dans la philosophie de Husserl* (Paris: Presses Universi-
taires de France, 1990), 111–112.

[15] George Herbert Mead, *Philosophy of the Present* (Chicago: University of Chicago Press, 1932), 49.

[16] Galileus Galileo [Galileus Galileus Linceus], 'The system of the world in four dialogues', in *Mathematical Collections and Translations vol. 1* ed. by T. Salusbury (London: William Leybourne, 1661),
345.

[17] Aristotle, *De cælo* (Paris: Babrielis Buon, 1560), 41r.

[18] Aristotle, *De cælo*, 41v.

[19] Nicolas Copernicus, *De revolutionibus orbium cælestium* (Nuremberg: J. Petreius, 1543), 2r.

[20] Copernicus, *De revolutionibus*, 3r.

[21] Copernicus, *De revolutionibus,* 3r.

[22] See, for example, Wolff-Michael Roth and Angela Calabrese Barton, *Rethinking Scientific Literacy* (New York: Routledge, 2004).

4

Cultivating Culture

The constructivist metaphor for learning and development tends to come with the implicit idea of some underlying Self that constructs its world, meaning, identity, and knowing. This is so because 'to construct' is a transitive verb, which requires a subject and an object on which the former acts or which it produces as a result of acting on things. Construction also has a motive, the end product, an image of which constructors have in mind before they begin – a point made by both Karl Marx and the early Lev S. Vygotsky using the comparison between the bee and the human builder.[1] In opposition to such an epistemology – which inherently is incapable of describing how human culture has emerged in the first place – I develop in the preceding chapters the idea of dwelling as a condition to building and thinking. 'To build' etymologically derives from a root that also means 'to cultivate'. To cultivate means to grow; and to grow anything requires a ground for the roots to grab hold onto and from which to draw nutrients (unless we are dealing with the conditions of hydroculture where the medium is water requiring external support for the plant). In the preceding chapter, I suggest that education needs to make use of and build on the grounds of our everyday lives so that it does not become alienating and uprooting. Education thereby becomes a way of cultivating the very ground that is required for the new ways of knowing to take hold and grow. When an education is grounded in our commonsense ways of knowing that come with dwelling, new forms of knowing can take hold that overturn what we have known before without every completely eradicating these – as we see in the astronomers' ways of marveling at the beauty of a sun*rise* or sun*set*. In this chapter, I show how an education grounded in our familiar ways around the commonsense world allows us to re-live (a) the overturning of common sense that scientists earlier lived through and underwent and (b) the re-understanding that emerges from that overturning.

The literature shows that school students frequently are turned off by and away from science. It is the result of the uprooting that the adoption of science requires. Yet people of all walks of life frequently express an interest in particular forms of science by engaging with popularized representations of scientific concepts – such

© KONINKLIJKE BRILL NV, LEIDEN, 2018 | DOI 10.1163/9789004377134_004

as recent advances in genetic science, the discovery of the Higgs-Boson particle, or string theory – as reported in textual, audio-visual and other media. I know from my own teaching that interests arise in such a manner. Students often enrolled in my physics courses not because they wanted to be scientists but because they heard about the philosophical discussions we have had. One of those students – whom my fellow teachers talked about as a looser and whose marks had been low, especially in mathematics and science – was keen to take physics because he hoped it would provide him with the tools for understanding *A Brief History of Time* by Stephen Hawking. He had bought the book on his own, because of some interest that did not come from his previous school science. Not only did he end up with an A in physics (contrasting the many sixties in all his other subjects) but also, after some seeking of his way, completed Masters and PhD degrees and today is a professor in a biology department.

How do such persons – as well as children in school – learn something from the electronic media (e.g. a YouTube clip) that might involve the overturning of a long-held believe about the natural world? How does anyone of us move from an everyday, common sense to the new, scientific sense of the world when the scientific sense is not *directly* derivable from what we already know? How can this new scientific sense be unrelated to, but at the same time integrally grounded in this prior understanding? The problematic is framed in educational psychology as the *learning paradox*. It has not been solved in the constructivist literature, as the question of how a cognitive organism transcends itself by building new structures that move substantially beyond present tools, structures, and materials has not been satisfactorily answered. Moreover, the associated question of how, while being engaged informally with popularized media representations, we come to learn something that lies beyond and outside our current horizon of comprehension is not generally posed and even less frequently addressed. In the literature on the popular or public understanding of science, the process of change in individual understanding itself rarely (if ever) is made problematic. Thus, for example, there exist descriptions and explanations that emphasize the diffusion and integration of scientific information, which apparently makes it into everyday thinking. Other discourses theorize learning in the public sphere, as it may occur at open-house events, in terms of categories of consumption of scientific culture, scientific consumption behavior, and the accumulation of cultural capital; and some discourses use constructivist references to the constructive integration of diverse images and scientific language. But these descriptions and explanations are problematic, for we know from history of science studies that what is information in one paradigm is not information in another.

In this chapter, I further elaborate the preceding chapters and the fundamental idea of dwelling that constitutes the ground for building and thinking. Specifically, I develop the idea of *Nacherzeugung* and *Nachverstehen* to describe how engagement with broadly educational materials, non-initiates undergo processes in which they effectively 're-live' the accomplishment of scientific principles out of pre-scientific understanding is effectively re-lived. *Nacherzeugung* literally translates as producing (Ger. *erzeugen*) something again or after (Ger. *nach*); and in this re-production someone else who has done this before is followed. *Nachverstehen* denotes the process of coming to understand in the way someone else has come to understand. Like the English words 'after' or 'following', *nach* can mean both 'subsequently' and 'according to'. In the present context, these dictionary definitions refer to the process of transitioning from everyday, common sense to a scientific sense, and to do so following or according to popularized representations of scientific findings. Each time individuals come to know science personally they in fact personalize the history of (scientific) culture. The media contributes to culturing this culture, where culturing also means working the ground in which the scientific takes its roots. To illustrate these ideas, I analyze in the following a YouTube video and historical documentation associated with the first idealization or discovery of the modern scientific view of the operation of the heart and circulatory system. I do this to exemplify how everyday folk may come to learn and become interested in science as they relive a transition from prescientific to scientific understanding. I am not referring to the use of fiction to get students interested in such areas as biology or in issues such as human cloning, genetic screening, or evolution. Nor am I thinking about online science materials as tools that may be used to 'combat' what some note to be a widespread 'scientific illiteracy' – as urgent as that might be. Instead, these materials are means to generate and 'live again' a first idealization of scientific sense.

Cultivating (an Interest in) Science

For the purpose of making my case, I use an example from the medical field, in part because of the importance of the sixteenth- to seventeenth-century British physician William Harvey to the development of science specifically and because of the potential role of health as a context for developing student interest in education more generally. Anyone with pre-scientific views, wanting to be informed about how the heart and circulatory system works, has opportunities to find relevant resources online. In fact, many academics and teachers praise the presence of Internet materials for the possibilities they offer to student learning. For the following illustrative analysis, I randomly took one of the items that resulted from an online search for videos using the terms 'heart' and 'circulatory system', which turned out to be from a popular science series for children and youth: Bill Nye the Science Guy. Typical comments accompanying the video suggest that viewers of all ages appear to benefit from it – e.g. 'Lol this made my day. I've been studying for the exam tomorrow for over 4 hours a day for 3 days. This video made me understand it better, in a kinda fun way. :P' and 'lol I'm a college student, and I'm still learning from this guy'. The *Nacherzeugung* and *Nachverstehen* that this video may make possible differs, however, from Harvey's originary idealizations – and the circumstances he offers for their reproduction – in the sense that the common sense of the early seventeenth century was different from the common sense we have today. The following is the main part of the transcription of a recording from the Bill Nye series available on YouTube. It concerns the heart and circulatory system. The commentaries accompanying the recording give testimony to the fact that even college students may find it useful and learn something they had not known before. What is it in the recording that provides resources to the activities of people who, for one reason or another (e.g. studying, reviewing, trying to get some information) watch the show? In the section below, I provide some answers to this question.

0   ((*Bill Nye in a fighter jet doing a loop; Nye loses consciousness as the G-forces increase in the manoeuver; BN climbing a rope into a gym, with his heart rate shown to increase through the exertion; BN then moves forward, eventually appearing on a split screen, the other half of which is occupied by representation of the hear.*))

1   BN: * It's our larger than life heart model of science.

2   Your heart is a pump.

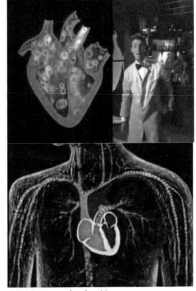

3   VOICE OVER: * It is the pump.

4   BN: It pushes blood all over your body.   ((BN portrait shot))

5   VOICE OVER: * It's the heart's job to keep the blood in motion.

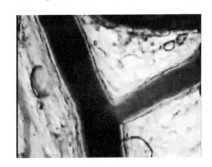

((*Return to illustration, turn 2*))

6   BN: ((*BN, portrait shot*)) Your blood carries fuel, energy from your food and oxygen. Plus your blood caries your body's waste away, too. (((*Il-*

lustration, turn 1, with movement of blood through upper body.)) Your heart sends blood in two directions every time it beats.

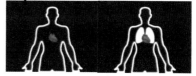

* The blue blood has very little oxygen * and your heart pumps it to your lungs. ((*Blue in "lungs."*))

7   where it gets recharged with oxygen. The read ((*red in "lungs"*)) oxygen rich oxygen gets pushed from the lungs back to your heart.

8   And from there it is sent to all the other parts of the body, what we call your system.   ((*split screen, as in turn 01*))

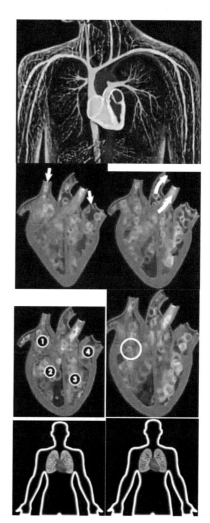

9   VOICE OVER: * The heart powers the circulatory system. It is the pump.

10 BN: * ((*Split screen, with* heart)) To send blood two ways at once … your heart has two sides. And each side has two parts, or chambers, so.

11   * So all together we got four chambers.

12   * Now to make that work, your heart has valves, like gates, between the top chambers and the bottom chambers. ((*Different valves highlighted with circle*))

13   Without the valves, this pump wouldn't work. It's a cycle, your heart pumps blood to your lungs back to your heart.

14   to your system and back to your heart ((*Underlying beat*)) and it does it all the time and it's only this big ((*shows fist*)) and you don't have to think about it.

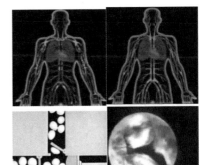

15   * Valves keep a liquid flowing in one direction. * ((*sequence of three valves in action, tricuspid, pulmonary, mitral, and aortic valves*))

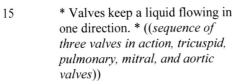

16 VOICE OVER: ((*Change to excerpt appearing as if from old documentary, voice reads text also seen*)) Warning, what you are about to see is a real human heart. This isn't going to be another rubber prop heart. Nope, this baby is real. A real working pumping human heart, surrounded by lots of blood and guts. If you are faint of heart or get queas- ((*shift in image*)) Parents do you [have] eyes over your hands yet?

17 VOICE OVER * ((*Documentary voice*)): Take a look. Your heart. ((*Dramatic music*)) ((*The documentary shifts to show an auscultation*))

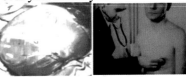

18 ((*Shift to a scene on the lawn. Teenager sleeping, awoken by noise, jogging on spot; an older female provides a description of what heart does.*))

Nacherzeugung and *Nachverstehen*

The video makes available a wide range of resources that offer the possibility of *Nacherzeugung* and *Nachverstehen*. Though any one particular viewing might be insufficient to produce a complete scientific understanding, the possibility to do so indeed is given with the resources provided. That is, familiarity with the ways in which the everyday world works, we come with sufficient capacities for the materials provided in the video to make sense and thus develop to the point that we can say understanding something that we have not understood before. Note the passive construction in the preceding phrase, according to which *the materials* make sense rather than some subject making sense of the materials. In this section, I provide an analysis of the video rendered by the preceding transcription. I focus on four issues. First, we may observe those aspects of the tape that allow the movement from commonsense to scientific sense. Second, I show how the videotape makes visible crucial aspects of the phenomenon such as to enable and foster *Nacherzeugung* and *Nachverstehen*. Third, there are obvious appeals to everyday, practical forms of common sense mobilized in facilitating the movement from commonsense to scientific sense. Finally, the video appeals to other modes that may serve analogical function in the movement of sense.

From Common Sense to Scientific Sense

There are at least two forms of familiarity to which videos appeal that are of the type transcribed concerning the motion of the heart. On the one hand, there is the fundamental mode of being in the world and knowing our way around the world, *dwelling*: persons exerting themselves, losing consciousness in an extreme flight manoeuver, standing in a doctor's office, or being auscultated. Second, these fundamental commonsense ways of dwelling become the basis of an extension into the scientific view of the heart and its motions in the way that these were conceived of by the English physician William Harvey (1578–1657) and, subsequently, his successors who have reproduced and handed on the paradigm. We may find that the present-day materials teaching about the motion of the heart and the circulatory system appeal to the same kind of sense experiences that the founders of the current medical view drew upon when initially presenting a new conception. In this case, it was Harvey, who still is celebrated in school biology textbooks as the founder of modern physiology and as a co-founder of modern science.

On the vertically subdivided screen in the video – one part continuing to show the busy exercise room – Bill Nye emerges on the right, as if from exertion; the left part of the screen features a cross-section of the heart, partly filled with a blue, partly with a red substance in which there are floating things. An appeal is made to relate the heart to a representation of exercise in the gymnasium behind Nye. This may evoke in the viewer memories of having exercised and of the sound of the beating heart, which is audible together with the noise from the gym. That is, the memory event begins with the imagery and sound of the recording before any interpretation could take place – if it does take place at all. The image of the heart (turn 2) is a representation or, in the discourse of the social studies of science, an *inscription*. It is no longer a naturalistic depiction, shown together with the lungs that René Descartes graphically represented (Fig 4.1) or that were verbally described by William Harvey. Instead, it is a cross-section that as such would not be available to natural observation. It is also a form of presentation that at the time of Harvey was not yet used or known. Contemporary illustrations typically show figures with incisions, layers of skin and muscle flayed to reveal hidden bones or organs – with minimal schematic simplification.

In the video, we observe a slight pumping action – a narrowing and widening of the lower part of the animated representation of the heart (turns 2, 10–12). This is evident when the two extreme configurations of the heart (turn 10) are plotted unto each other (Fig 4.2). The periodic expansion and contraction is of the kind that Harvey's description in *De motu* appeals to as visual experience: 'the heart is erected and rises upward to a point … it is everywhere contracted, but more toward the sides, thus, using less magnitude, it appears longer and more collected'.[2] That is, the animated illustration makes an appeal to the same form of visibility that emerged in Harvey's careful, *in vivo* studies of the hearts of different animals, especially in situations where the heart movements were sufficiently slow to make precisely *these* observations that could become the decisive evidence for the asso-

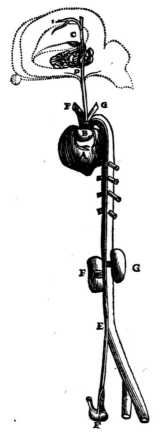

ciated idealization. The observation is based on and rooted in the everyday sense of the world, against the resting earth as a ground. The motion, in contrast to rest, itself is perceived and perceivable only against a nonthematic ground.

Harvey had begun his investigation not with the intent to overturn the standard explanation that was reigning at the time. Rather, his goal was to see the motions and characteristics of the heart [*usu cordis*] via his own inspection rather than by what he could read in other people's books. An important dimension of the video is that it makes these motions visible for its (generally non-scientific) audience. Harvey found this a 'truly difficult' exercise to the point that he felt God alone could understand the meaning of the heart's movements. He initially could not tell systole and diastole apart, and dilations and constructions were 'like a flash of lightening [*quasi trajectore fulgure*]'. The systole appeared to him at one time here, the diastole there, then reversed, varied and confused. As a result, he could not reach a decision about what to conclude on his own and what to believe based on the writings of others. It is in the course of his investigation of cold blooded animals and his observation of the hearts in dying creatures that he came to identify those moments in the heart's motion that are so unproblematically depicted in the Bill Nye video. That is, this 'larger-than-life' (turn 1) model *facilitates* making the crucial observations that Harvey's original transition to a scientific idealization required.

Fig 4.1 Depiction of the heart and part of the blood vessels from *Tractatus de homine* by René Descartes, where the body is described as a machine.

Harvey's text makes reference to three significant observations to be made: (a) the heart rises to the apex (where it strikes the chest such that it can be felt); (b) the heart contracts, particularly on the sides, which makes it appear narrower and longer (Fig 4.2); and (c) the heart feels harder when it moves then when at rest. He adds that in coldblooded animals the heart is lighter in color during the motion phase than during the resting phase. The translator of a 1928 publication of Harvey's work comments on these observations in a footnote to the English text: 'This is the first of that remarkable series of extraordinarily acute observations on the motion of the heart and blood so simply and clearly reported by Harvey in this book'.[3] These observations can be made in different parts of the excerpt (turns 2, 7, 9) but especially when the cross-section of the heart is shown as it pumps the blood to the pulmonary system and into the body (turns 10–12; Fig 4.2).

Fig 4.2 Comparison of the two extreme positions in the depiction of the heart (turn 10). Solid lines show the largest outline, whereas the dotted lines feature the other extreme. When animated, the heart can be seen pumping.

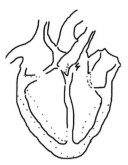

Central to the perspective Harvey developed was the fourness of the chambers of the heart and their relative sizes. This fourness is also made explicit in the Bill Nye video, already apparent in turn 2, but especially from the image and text in turns 10 through 12. What Harvey first articulated as the different roles of the two sides of the heart – one in the circuit to the lung and back, the other in the circuit to the periphery of the body and back – is indicated in the video in the different coloring, blue for the left, and red for the right (from viewer).

Visibilization

The motion of the heart is only very indirectly accessible to everyday experience and, therefore, is not subject to the same kind of clear and incontrovertible evidence that provides us with our everyday, common sense of the world. The blood circuit is also not available to observation as such. It may therefore not surprise that these features – the heart as an integral element of a blood circuit – do not generally appear in children's drawings or that even teachers have misconceptions about this system. In his days, the blood *circuit* was not available to Harvey. At the time the body was thought of more as a collection of different organs – much in the way today's children represent the corporeal elements. In fact, the translator of the 1928 edition of the book on the motion of the heart notes that Harvey, in his philosophical orientation while doing his work, still is fundamentally Aristotelian. A change from the Aristotelian to the Galilean description and explanation of motion requires the same kind of changes that occurred culturally and historically when Galileo introduced his new way of conceiving moving phenomena. One way of describing this issue, therefore, is in terms of a transition Harvey was making from an Aristotelian view to what subsequently came to be recognized as the first modern description of the motions of the heart and blood and a first modern explanation of its circulatory function.[4] That is, on the grounds of an Aristotelian worldview, as embodied in the work of the second century Greek physician Galen, arises a new and very different worldview. In and through new representations (e.g. turn 9, turns 13–14), together with the intimated movement of the blood, and our everyday encounter with liquids flowing and under pressure, we are afforded first (or confirm subsequent) idealizations of the circulatory system. That is, although not visible as such, the presence of a circulatory *system* is enabled through the use of inscriptions, which in turn draw on having lived in the technologized world as resource.

Appeal to an Everyday, Practical Sense

Our lifeworlds are the intuitively concrete worlds that are antecedent to the scientific world. Philosophers and social scientists of very different ilk – with respect to natural and social objects – have shown that action and praxis involving things always precedes the intellectual comprehension. We know what an instruction means to say after we have succeeded in doing what the instruction describes. In action and praxis, things (objects and tools) always are comprehended in the sense of being included, and the acting subject is comprehended in the world as a whole. That is, as far as it concerns the constitution of sense, intellectual comprehension always is grounded in, and relates to, our being comprehended in the physical and social world. Any scientific object, any scientific discourse, is based on our mundane, everyday common sense – however much the former might seem to contradict the latter (see chapter 3). This comprehension is extended metaphorically to the aspects and functions of the body that are not immediately accessible by the senses.

Following the part that heavily draws on representations of the heart and circulatory system (turns 2–17), the video appeals especially to everyday experiences in a scene shot on a lawn involving a narrator and a 'subject'. The narrator, a young woman, talks about the normal heart rate and compares to it the rates while sleeping (lower, with diminished need for oxygen), when surprised or scared (when the heart rate speeds up), and while doing intense physical exercise (the body needs more oxygen). In the background, a young man sleeps (Fig 4.3a), is suddenly awakened by the loud sound of crash cymbals (Fig 4.3b), and then jogs (Fig 4.3c). The video finally shifts back to the documentary, where a doctor auscultates a baby and an old man, while explaining that the heart beats about two hundred billion times over an average lifetime. Harvey, too, appeals to the everyday experiences of the pulse and its change with various activities: 'It is not supposed to be that the uses of the pulse and the respiration are the same, because, under the influences of the same causes, such as running, anger, the warm bath, or any other heating thing (as Galen, the ancient Greek physician says) they become more frequent and forcible together … but in young persons the pulse is quick, whilst respiration is slow. So it is also in alarm, amidst care, and with the anxiety of mind; sometimes, too, in fevers, the pulse is rapid, but the respiration is slower than usual'.[5] In this paragraph, Harvey appeals to the everyday experience in the same way just as the video from the Bill Nye series does. This highlights the specific observations that can be made in such situations: after exercising – exemplified by Nye, who is moving into and through the gym or in the teen's jogging – is associated with the sound of an accelerated heartbeat. These, then, become part of the (what shall become the scientific) argument that respiration and blood flow are two separate systems.

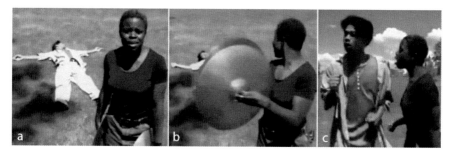

Fig 4.3 Scenes from the Bill Nye video. a. The young gentleman is sleeping. b. He is woken up by the sound of crash cymbals. c. He begins to run. The narrative concerns the different heart rates associated with different forms of activity.

Prior to Harvey, a particular, communal sense certainly did exist about the heart and blood in the human being. Shakespeare, for example, writes of 'a voice is-su[ing] from so empty a heart', and then confirms that the saying is true because 'The empty vessel makes the greatest sound'.[6] The sense in each case is based on what in the lives of the people generally and scientists specifically existed as self-evidently true (apodictic); and how the ways the heart appeared in life had been available through other apodictic forms that come in and with dwelling. Harvey's discoveries arose from and over against this common sense. But because Harvey himself grew up in this culture, in and through his scientific practice, a new sense started to work against, and overcame, his existing common sense. If we were able to plot his thinking, there would be something like a duration in which the old and new existed simultaneously. In this duration, the new appeared. The old sense, however, did not completely disappear: It continues to exist in the general culture, as shown in the (science education) literature concerning the ways in which people from all walks of life conceive of (talk about) the heart and the circulatory system. Here, it takes on a particularly figurative valence. At the same time, aspects of this sense, such as the heart being a vessel, provide resources to others to make the same trajectory as part of the *Nacherzeugung / Nachverstehen* movement. Because sense is grounded in sense – new sense unpredictably emerges from previously existing sense – at least some aspects of the old sense have entered the new sense but in a new form. At the point of emergence, two very different orders coincide.

In catastrophe theory, such points are classified as *crises* or *catastrophes*. Catastrophe theory provides a way of describing and classifying morphogenesis, that is, the genesis and emergence of new forms.[7] Here, the new form is a way of describing aspects of the human body. At first, there was the Aristotelian way of talking about the heart, blood vessels, and blood (Fig 4.4, left of 'crisis'). Later, a new way of talking about these issues emerges in the sciences (Fig 4.4, right of 'crisis'). But this is not the only way of talking, for the old ways continue to exist (lower branch, Fig 4.4). This classification also allows us to understand the moment of emergence, the crisis, which is experienced today when young people with Aristotelian ways of talking eventually come to talk about these matters in the customary ways of the sciences.

Fig 4.4 Catastrophe theory provides descriptions of the emergence of new forms, such as new metaphors. In and through the work of William Harvey, new metaphors emerged for talking about the heart, blood vessels, and blood. The old metaphors did not disappear. Even today, they constitute the earliest forms of talking so that at some point in our lives, we undergo the same kind of revolution that Harvey underwent (*Nacherzeugung*) and we grasp the phenomena in the way he came to grasp them (*Nachverstehen*).

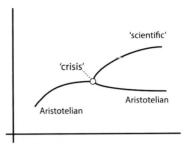

The Nye video, finally, is characterized by a *functional* discourse the emergence of which was one of the historical changes that the idealizations first articulated by Harvey helped bringing about. Harvey generally did not write using a discourse of functions – such a language would only develop during the later part of the seventeenth century. In his text, the word *ūsus* [use] and its inflections is much more frequent than the word *fūnctiō* [function]. But his descriptions, by means of *Nacherzeugung / Nachverstehen*, continue to make it into general culture and into other sciences: they not only lent themselves to such further developments but also became the sources for metaphorical and analogical extensions into other fields, such as economics, where the idea – one might even say the 'culture' – of continuous circulation took hold. It was only after Harvey that the idea of *circulation* within a system became a fundamental analytical tool useful for talking about other phenomena in other fields. Then, a century later, the term *function* took on the dominant role over structure in the associated descriptive approaches to organisms.

Appeal to Other Perceptive Modes

Besides the visual mode, the video also provides material for the auditory sense. Throughout the video, there are periods when the audience can more or less clearly hear the beat of a heart (e.g. during the opening part, when Nye shows up on the split screen next to the heart, turn 2) in the background. In one instance, the video shifts to a clip from an old documentary, where a doctor auscultates a male patient. Underlying the narrating voice and the music, one clearly hears a heart beat. The voice articulates the text in a highly rhythmic manner:

Day and night, in steady rhythm, there operates within

```
 /   -   /   -  / -  /    -  / - /   - /
```
the human body a MARvelous machine: The heart.
```
 -  /  -  / - /  -  /   -  /  -  /   -  /
```

In this representation, each slash corresponds to a stressed, each dash to an unstressed syllable. It clearly makes visible what may also be as a 'da-dam' pattern, which also is typical of the heartbeat including the occasional irregularity. Thus, for extended parts of the recording, the soundtrack provides the sound of a pounding heart, which gives – what in music is called – a basso continuo to the narrator's

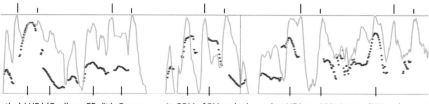

thebLUE blOodhas vERy little Oxygen   it COMesfrOMyourbody   andyourHEArt   pUMpsit toyour lUNgswhereitgets

Fig 4.5 The longer and shorter vertical lines above the volume (continuous, green) and pitch (dotted, blue) transcription indicate the strong and weak beats of the heart. Syllables in capital letters mark the stresses.

voice (Fig 4.5). The effect is amplified by the voice, which, in its stresses, parallels the basso. The video continues with above-mentioned situation with the young man sleeping and exercising (Fig 4.3). The beating heart can be felt and the pulse is easily accessible when the fingers are placed at different parts of the body: we learn early in life how to feel the pulse on the side of the neck or near at the base of the thumb. It is a common phenomenon that offers opportunities for an idealization of the heart as part of a circulatory system. Harvey uses the analogy of a horse that drinks, whereby the movements of the throat can be heard and felt. A similar case exists in the heart, where with each portion of blood transduced in the veins and arteries, 'a pulse is made, and can be heard in the chest'.[8] Harvey was one of the first to note and record the observation of the sounding heart. Today, such as in the video, no special mention is necessary that the pounding we can hear while exercising is associated with the heart. We hear the pounding as the pounding of a heart.

The underlying soundtrack is not the only way in which rhythmicity is exploited as a means to appeal to everyday experience. The narrators' voices, too, are very rhythmic. For example, in one instant the narrator says: 'When you are sleeping, your body doesn't need as much oxygen, so your heartbeat is lower'. On the soundtrack, underlying the soundtrack, there is a dull beat at a frequency of 1.00 Hz (60 beats/min), which is about the normal heart rate for most persons. Then the narrative concerns a scare, accompanied by the depiction of the current narrator beats cymbals (typical for creating an effect of excitement). The underlying beat accelerates to 2.66 Hz (160 beats/min). The narration goes like this: 'And when you are scared, your heartbeat speeds up. It's like your body is sending a message to your heart saying "pump more blood". Scientists call this the fight or flight response'. Being scared and running are precisely the same lived-through phenomena that Harvey has called upon in his description of situations that increase the normal hear rate.

Nacherzeugung, Nachverstehen, and the Cultivation of Culture

Central to the phenomenological conception of learning is the passive dimension of the first discovery or re-discovery of what is later accepted as a scientific fact. If there is something very new that has just emerged then it could not have been seen and thus foreseen. If it is not foreseen, then something new has unpredictably emerged. In popular language, we name such events 'insights': something suddenly has come into sight. Such emergence is an integral part of our everyday lives, where situations unfold unpredictably and without being under our (complete) control. After the fact, the new is tied into the old such that it appears *as if* the old had been the causal origin of the new – when it in fact was only the ground and condition.[9] That which emerges and sublates what we currently know – i.e. both overcomes and preserves it – is of necessity unseen and therefore unforeseen. We do not control it, but instead has 'come upon' us. Whatever 'it' is, *it* makes sense. That new sense that arises in the process of *Nachverstehen* initially 'dawns upon' rather than being painstakingly 'constructed' *by* us – there is a level of *passivity* in the reconstitution of sense: 'the passivity of that which is initially darkly awakened and emerges with increasing clarity belongs [to] the possible activity of a re-remembering in which the past experiencing is lived through quasi anew and actively'.[10]

Moving from the prescientific ('unscientific') to the scientific is problematic because the learner does not have a preconception of the new ground or a presumption of the change from the prescientific to the scientific ground. The prescientific therefore cannot be an object in itself to be discarded because it is constitutive of the ground and horizon of sense that comes with dwelling, just as the immobile earth is the substrate for all subsequent determinations of movement (see chapter 3). Our dwelling and its associated common sense are the foundation of what we can live and on the basis of which any science develops.

Science is a human achievement that 'historically and for every learner presupposes the existing generally pre-given, intuitive *Lebensumwelt* or everyday environment or world'.[11] The mundane lifeworld that we inhabit on a daily basis from our births therefore constitutes the foundation of every science. Our everyday experiences and immediate perceptions almost certainly constitute the reason why researchers in education and psychology continue to find Aristotelian 'conceptions' of (i.e. ways of talking about) motion among children and their adult teachers. It also presents a tremendous, almost insurmountable resistance force to any change of ways of talking, e.g. to a Galilean or Newtonian language about how the world works. But in a process of *Nachverstehen*, every learner can be said to attain something similar to the discovery that led to the first articulation of the science: from everyday sense, as the ground and resource for the new sense, to the new ground for the evidence that ascertains the scientific as such. Because of *Nacherzeugung* and *Nachverstehen*, the lifeworld itself changes: human culture, modes of being, and common sense (in which mutual grasp is grounded) shift, as it were, beneath the very feet with which we are standing.

Constructivist learning theories suggests that every learner constructs his or her own understanding. This does not explain the objective nature of what is known, particularly in scientific knowledge. Nor does it explain why the simple, empirical, yet systematic investigations (experiments) that the anatomist Harvey initially developed can be conducted, anywhere in the world and at any time, yielding precise-

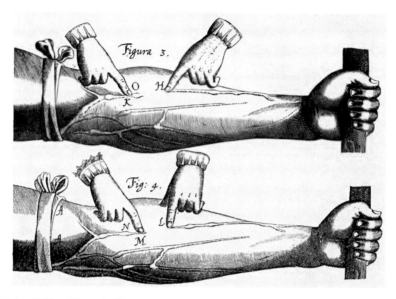

Fig 4.6 William Harvey's illustration for how to see the presence of valves and direction of blood stream.

ly the same observations. The illustrations included in Harvey's book *De motu cordis* indicate how to conduct such an experiment. This is an experiment that proves that the blood is moving in the veins from the periphery toward the heart. Harvey offers the means for the re-production of his knowledge and for achieving their own understanding (*Verstehen*) after (*nach*) his own. When the actions described are performed (e.g. tying up the arm as for phlebotomy to collect a blood sample), then specific observations can be made. Thus, if a finger is held as in the second drawing (Fig 4.6), then the observer will see what Harvey has seen and described: no influx of blood from above. Together, his text and the associated images constitute a sort of recipe or instruction for reactivating one of the origins of modern anatomy and the scientific revolution concerning the circulation of the blood and the function of the heart. It is a recipe, for all one has to do is what is depicted: press on an artery and move toward the heart, and one can see on the forearm the equivalent of what Harvey depicted. In so doing, we re-produce what Harvey has done and, in its wake, we can see what he has seen, and grasp the same idea that had *come to him* while doing what he captured in his instruction (Fig 4.6).

In the context of medical science, such a reconstitution is as valid today as it was five hundred years ago. The historically first achievement of a scientific discovery forces the radical revision or overturning of some aspect of pre-predicative grasp of the lifeworld. This aspect of the lifeworld then can be said to gradually become a ground that provides for the validity of the scientific achievement. Those willing to engage in re-understanding can do so by ways and means that others have taken before them and that can be taken again, for this very reason, by anyone else to arrive at the apodictic evidence that led to the first realization and its re-production. Husserl therefore suggests that *Nacherzeugung* and *Nachverstehen* are the reasons for the objectivity of science, a concept based on the fact that some observation is independent of the individual subject, location, and time of the *Nacherzeugung*. If it is independent of contingencies, then the observation is objective. In this way, students and laypersons can reproduce a scientific sense by taking the same route taken during the first idealization, undertaking a contemporary performance that makes present again the originary activity of idealization and the consciousness for the self-evident identity of the ideal formation.

In this chapter, I use Husserl's phenomenological perspective on the question of the overturning of prescientific sense through that very prescientific common sense and sensuous observation and evidence. The prescientific sense comes to be sedimented in, and to form the basis of, scientific sense even as the former is overturned. The essence of the proposal runs like this: In every constitution of (scientific) sense that occurs as someone engages with online materials such as a YouTube video on the human body, something of the original constitution and sense of the animate body is reenacted and relived. However, because culture has changed, the constitution as a starting point is no longer exactly the same: as that which is apodictically self-evident, everyday common sense itself has changed.

Such a phenomenological approach is fruitful, as Husserl articulates a key problem that few philosophers, educators, and educational researchers pose, let alone consider and attempt to resolve. How does the way in which live (witness, feel) the world everyday – the world that is the world of our concrete, real experience, which in fact gives sense to the word 'world' – often lead to ways of talking that make no or little sense, which is in manifest in the contradictions with the commonsense ways in which everyday phenomena appear? Even more fundamentally, how can our mundane, everyday sense be used as a resource for achieving a form of (scientific) sense that ultimately transcends the quotidian? Why try to lead laypersons to abandon their common sense that has served them well in all or most situations that they find themselves? As many philosophers suggest, in our prescientific life, we participate in the Heraclitean flux of changing, sensual-objective givens. Although things change, we are certain to see, touch, and hear them, that is, grasp these things in their properties as objectively real things that are in this and not in another way. This (sense) certainty of things, and the associated apodictic certainty that we associate with the everyday world, also gives us a sense of objectivity and reality. Our normal, everyday, mundane, and practical lives are characterized by this sense-certainty, to which the Nye video fundamentally appeals. We share this sense with others, because of the common ways in which we live our pathic lives. This sharing of sense also is the ground of em*pathy* and sym*pathy*. It therefore becomes the basis upon which the pedagogical function of the video rests. This everyday, common sense constitutes the ground and horizon for everything else we do and learn. It circumscribes the source of sense on which other, newly acquired sense is built in a continuous expansion and transformation.

Any quick look at the literature will reveal that people of all ages are said to hold incomplete and scientifically incorrect concepts and accounts of the human body. These concepts are *essentially* rather than *incidentally* inexact; therefore, they are nonscientific. This is so because scientific terms, including *force* or *pressure* (e.g. exerted and produced by the heart), denote phenomena that cannot be seen and often are counterintuitive. Indeed, such phenomena are not initially there but arise from dwelling and by means of complex processes that build on the felt resistances coming from pushing and being pushed against things in the proximity of the material world. There is then an 'identification of the individual organism with the object', and resistance, 'which finds its expression in the kinaesthetic experience of effort', appears in the object 'in so far as *the effort is located in the object*'.[12] Scientific phenomena, such as force, therefore cannot serve as *apodictic* evidence and, thus, already constitute (part of) a transformation to scientific sense. The closed circle of the blood cannot directly be perceived and, in Harvey's work, arose from *inferences* rather than from observation (e.g. compressing veins, generalizing from decelerated function of the dying heart to the normal function of the healthy organ).

In the online video, viewers come to be presented with the image of a two-color circuit. It is a finished result from observations and inferences not thematized in the video. In Harvey's *De motu cordis*, on the other hand, we can clearly observe the descriptions that serve as the basis of the physician's inferences. Some of these descriptions were provided by others and, therefore, also were part of the Aristotelian description that was integral to Galen's doctrine about the heart and blood. One of the ideas that Harvey created in and with *De motu cordis* was that of a continuous circuit as part of which the heart has a special role: that of pushing the blood into the arteries right to the peripheral vessels. The parts and their names already existed. As discussed above, it was the *function* and the *functional whole* that changed with the work of Harvey. There is empirical evidence that everyday folk today have to move through the same sort of process to achieve a first idealization. Thus, experts and novices with respect to complex biological systems, including the human respiratory system, exhibit little differences when it comes to their talk about structures, but there are significant differences between their ways of talking about functions and causal relations. Similar developments are born out when people are asked to categorize, where shifts have been observed between categorization according to domain towards causal relations across domains.

In the Bill Nye video, the heart is presented as a pump. The idea of the pump is repeated in the images of a mechanical pump pushing particles from one pipe into another with the aid of gates functioning as valves (Fig 4.7). Harvey himself did not explicitly see the heart as a pump operating in a closed system to keep the blood flowing. It was Descartes who articulated in 1668 – i.e. twenty years after Harvey's *De motu* was published – the idea of the human heart as a pump, the blood vessels as a circulatory conduit system, and the human body as a machine. The video clip appeals to this commonsense being in the world, in which learners of all ages encounter the function of liquids and gasses being pumped and under pressure in a range of technical contexts (e.g. swimming pools, hospitals, bicycle repair). That is, just as Descartes analogically transferred the ways in which machines are seen and seen to work to the human body, the Nye video appeals to a transferring of our everyday sense of machines to that of the human body. That

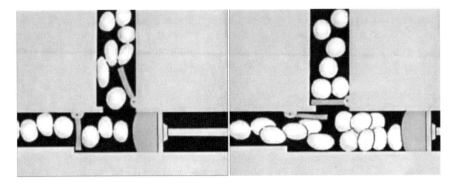

Fig 4.7 The idea of the heart as a pump in a machine is reproduced in the analogy with a pump pushing material (in the form of white bubbles) from one pipe into another pipe with the aid of gates that open only in one direction. It was Descartes who introduced the analogy of the human body and a machine, an analogy that is prevalent in many discourses today, including those of alternative approaches to health.

same mechanism is at work in the ad for a brand of cooking oil popular in the health food world. Its motto is 'oil the machine' – which also is the name of the homepage – and the ads tend to feature endurance athletes. 'Like any machine', the ad goes, '[ultrarunners] require oil to run their best'.[13] The everyday familiarity with machines is the ground for the argument that the human body requires an oil to work well. In the course of human cultural history, however, the ways in which machines are encountered changes. Thus, what was part of the everyday ways of being in the world at the time of Harvey was different than those ways into which we are born today where pumps, plumbing and other machine systems are part of the everyday world that constitutes common sense. They therefore constitute the background against which we every new encounter makes or does not make sense. These provide resources for grasping the heart and circulatory system as systems, powered and sustained by the systemic operation of machine parts that together form a coherent and interdependent whole.

It may sometimes be thought that scientific breakthrough itself cannot be shown in film. In this chapter I suggest that viewers of visual online materials can relive an (aspect of an) originary scientific breakthrough such as the originary constitution concerning the motion of the heart and circulatory system by engaging with visual, online media and a lifeworld replete with technical examples of the principles at stake. This approach throws into relief the talk about information available, because the sense-giving act that provides the person with a scientific sense also constitutes a change in perception, the horizon of sense, and, therefore, in what the nature of information is. That is, there is a revolutionary process at work, in which prescientific forms of apodictic evidence are both overcome and kept in the new forms of evidence that constitute the new, technologized scientific sense.

University-based educators and teachers often deplore the apparent resistance of students to conceptual change and the cultural continuity of existing conceptions. The phenomenological perspective developed here provides an alternative to this literature. It extends this literature in that it has an answer to the apparent persistence of non- or prescientific discourses. First, all science is grounded in our everyday sense that comes from knowing our way around the world; and the most fundamental of these ways have not essentially changed in the course of history: We continue to see the sun rise in the morning and to see it set in the evening; and we continue to feel the cold come into the door rather than heat being lost to the outside. Second, the initial sense does not disappear with the adoption of a scientific discourse. Rather, the original worldview comes to be sublated in and with the new, that is, it comes to be both overturned and kept alive, sedimented in our understanding as the foundation upon which science is built. This is captured in the catastrophe theoretic framing, where the old, in some version, continues to exist next to the new scientific. As already suggested above, despite the Galilean revolution (see chapter 3), physicists and astronomers continue to marvel at and enjoy a beautiful sun*rise* or sun*set*, even though at work they would label as naïve or unscientific any person who seriously supposed the sun to be moving (around the earth). The real marvel that we observe daily in the world around us is that people do learn science *and* continue to talk about the everyday world in pre-scientific terms. Once seen in this perspective, it is evident that we do not need to eradicate prior (mis-) conceptions but rather design education in a way that allows people of all walks of life to hang onto their familiar ways of getting around the world, including language, all the while accessing new phenomena and developing new forms of (scientific) language that are useful in special purpose contexts (science classrooms, science careers).

Notes

1 See Karl Marx, and Friedrich Engels, *Werke Band 23: Das Kapital* (Berlin: Dietz, 1983), 19. Vygotsky quotes and builds on this passage in Lev S. Vygotsky, 'Consciousness as a Problem for the Psychology of Behavior', in *The Collected Works of L. S. Vygotsky vol. 3: Problems of the Theory and History of Psychology* (New York, 1997), 63.

2 Guilielmi Harvei Angli, *Exercitatio anatomica de motu cordis et sanguinis in animalibus* (Frankfurt: Guilielmi Fitzeri, 1628), 22.

3 William Harvey, *On the Motion of the Heart and Blood in Animals* (Springfield: Charles C. Thomas, 1928), II.29.

4 Harvey, *On the Motion*, II.44.

5 Harvei, *Exercitatio*, 15.

6 William Shakespeare, in *Henry V*, Act IV, Scene 4.

7 See Wolff-Michael Roth, '*Neoformation*: A Dialectical Approach to Developmental Change', *Mind, Culture and Activity*, vol. 24 (2017), 368–380.

8 Harvei, *Exercitatio*, 30.

9 See, for example, George Herbert Mead, *Philosophy of the Present* (London: The Open Court, 1932).

10 Edmund Husserl, *Husserliana Gesammelte Work Band VI: Die Krisis der europäischen Wissenschaften und die transzendentale Phänomenologie. Eine Einleitung in die phänomenologische Philosophie* (The Hague: Martinus Nijhoff, 1976), 370.

11 Husserl, 1976, *Krisis*, 123.

12 George Herbert Mead, *Philosophy of the Act* (Chicago: University of Chicago Press, 1938), 427.

13 http://oilthemachine.com/

5

Emergence of the Image

In chapter 3 I quote George Herbert Mead writing about the idea that permanent space and motion are consequences of percipient and prehensive events that are at the origin of consentient sets and perspectives.[1] If space and motion are consequences of percipient and prehensive events, the objects that populate our life-worlds should be even more so the consequences of such events. More importantly, whereas these percipient and prehensive events occur in the animate body of the individual who grasps a thing, 'the attitude must have been assumed before either the thing or the organism can appear as an object'.[2] Both organism and thing emerge as figures against the ground of dwelling. The required attitude that Mead writes about, however, is the result of the intimate relation an individual has with others. The thing that stands out over and against the Self (as much as the self) is possible only because of the social relations that precede the thing and the self. The social relation is the model for the self–thing relation. In Mead's philosophy, social relation also is the birthplace of the self–other distinction. On this point, he does not differ from Karl Marx and Friedrich Engels, who note that the relationship of humans to nature determines the relations among each other, and the relation among each other determines their relation to nature.[3] Thus, unlike the various versions of embodiment and enactivist theories, which are grounded in the individual and therefore have to construct the social from what they already know, the intellectual traditions on which I build here emphasize the primacy of the social – including the emergence and existence of natural things. The relations that are at issue here are those of dwelling. Before there can be building and thinking, which require objects and (associated) ideas as phenomena standing out in consciousness, there is dwelling, which also includes the community of dwelling with others. We thus have come to the same double constitution of mind that the Russian philosopher of psychology Felix T. Mikhailov arrives at: (a) *'the relation that gives birth to man is his relation to nature'* and (b) *'a relation generative of man is nothing other than the affective, sense-giving relation of our animal forebears, in the first instance, toward one another'*.[4]

A classical problem in the cognitive science is the 'grounding problem', that is the question how mind and its abstract knowledge are connected to the material world. In some theoretical approaches – including constructivist, enactivist, and embodiment theories – relations already are postulated between the human body and knowledge. Many scholars have noted the requirement to critique the (constructivist) idea of the homunculus in all of us, who, as the reflective subject, constructs knowledge and applies schemas (concepts) to the world it perceives. What is required instead is an understanding of human knowledgeability that is arising from the confrontation of persons with the world in a pre-intentional present – pre-intentional because what we will have learned lies by definition outside our previous knowledgeability and therefore cannot be intended. Studies associating themselves with the constructivist, embodiment, or enactivist approaches emphasize 'sensorimotor' activities. However, the emphasis on the 'motor' aspects of human behavior misses precisely what is most important about movement: kinesthesia. Thus, to 'arrive at veritable understandings of kinesthesia and the fundamental concepts generated in and through movement, embodiers need to wean themselves away from sensory-motor talk'.[5] Instead, what we need is an approach that creates descriptions of and works from the basis of our *sensory-kinetic* being in the world. Researchers need to think in terms of movement itself instead of (mental) schemas and other transcendental (abstract and abstracted) forms that then (somehow) need to be *embodied* (put back into a body) and *enacted*. Movement, on the other hand, and the associate feeling of movement, kinesthesia, essentially implies the animate body and, on evolutionary grounds, is a *condition* of life and cognition. Thus, it makes little sense to talk about movement in the absence of animate bodies that move and feel. *Living* consciousness, and therefore living cognition (knowing and learning), essentially derives from kinesthesia, our sensible bodies felt in various ways while we move rather than from purely motor aspects or motor aspects associated with sensations. Instead of a 'motorology', we need to pay attention to the 'living and lived-through dynamics as it unfolds and of that living and lived-through dynamics as a kinetic melody'.[6] It is therefore not so much the physical body that needs to be theorized to understand cognition – knowing, learning, education – but the animate body with its movements and kinesthesia. This would then allow us to distinguish physical robots that learn bottom up from interacting with their physical and social environment, but do not undergo life as animate beings do (e.g. who suffer their pathic lives, are affected, and feel sympathy and empathy for others).

The constructivist metaphor describes learning in terms of the intentional construction of knowledge. Numerous studies show, however, that the source of thinking, knowing, and learning is *pre-reflective*, which gives an essentially pathic (passive-active) dimension to learning. Empirical work provides evidence that learners cannot aim at the knowledge to be constructed precisely because they cannot *see* it beforehand. This new knowledge will be apparent to them only at the end of or following some task: thus, that which will have been learned was unseen before and therefore unforeseen. In fact, the words *know*ledge (as *cog*nition) and *nais*sance (birth) have the same origin. Both derive from the homonymic Proto-Indo-

European syllable *ĝen-, ĝenə-, ĝnē-, ĝnō-*. One of the two homonyms has the signi-fication of 'to bear', 'to *gen*erate', and made it into Latin as *nātu*; and, from there via the French, it developed into the modern words *naissance, naissant, née, nas-cence*, and *nascent*. In another line of linguistic evolution, the same aspect of the root develops into the birth-related words *genesis* and *generate*. The second part of the homonym has the signification of 'to know', 'to recognize'. In fact, both verbs – 'to *know*' and 'to re*cognize*' – and the nouns and adjectives built on these, direct-ly derive from the root. The verbs 'can' (and its equivalent verbs in numerous Germanic languages) and 'gnostic' (relating to knowledge) have the same origin. That is, there is an historical association of the words knowledge, on the one hand, and naissance (birth), on the other hand. Knowledge is birth: it comes forth from the pregnance of movement. The difference between knowledge and naissance is undecidable. Knowledge is born in movement, because knowledge, unlike what Jean Piaget and all sorts of constructivists think, is not somehow abstracted from movement but is born in an excess of movement, pregnant with the new. Move-ment always means change; and in humans, the movements of the body – whether we move through space, move a member, or move in speaking – always are related with changes in the accompanying thinking. It makes no sense to think (theorize) the animate body separately from mind. In English, the term *reconnaissance*, a term born from the same root, refers to an advance into a terrain to discover its nature prior to making the real advance: it is a movement ahead of itself. In recon-naissance, as in Melissa's movements described below, knowledge is born in a process of transcendence, when aspects of movement come to stand out in aware-ness and against everything else. Just as in any birth, that which is born, here knowledge, does not anticipate itself: coming among its own, knowledge will not have foreseen itself. In the next section, a case study is provided of how the new and unforeseen arises in and from movement.

Other recent work on cognition and learning, such as the work on the situated, embodied, and enacted nature of cognition also places an emphasis on the body. In this book as a whole and in the present chapter specifically, no recourse is sought to embodiment, enaction, or schemas, which are central features in recent dis-courses that seek to integrate cognition and the physical body. Rather, I develop a phenomenological account that is fundamentally grounded in movement, the asso-ciated feeling thereof (kinesthesia), and the sensation that arises from tact and the contact of the animate body with the surrounding world at its sensory periphery. That is, although the proposed conceptualization of learning is grounded in bodily movement, it distinguishes itself from those other frameworks because it explains those aspects of knowing that the embodiment and enactivist approaches presup-pose.

In the here-presented approach to education and learning, dwelling and living in the world begin with and *precede* intentional orientation towards ready-made ob-jects. Objects are taken as Mead presents them: the end result of movement and social interaction with others. The structure of this chapter follows this temporal relation of and between (a) events we live through and undergo and (b) any related knowledgeability that emerges. Thus, I begin with the empirical description and then proceed to an unfolding, deepening analysis of what we can see and learn from the episode presented.

An Empirical Case

The empirical materials that follow were collected in the course of a specially designed unit on three-dimensional geometry for second-grade students. The study results show that through this curriculum the children came to work at developmental levels with respect to three-dimensional geometrical objects beyond the levels that the variously existing theoretical models attribute to that age.[7] The unit, which stretched over a fifteen-day, seventy-minutes-per-day period, includes tasks in the course of which children explore and talk about three-dimensional objects in small group- and whole-class configurations. For example, in the first lesson, the children were asked to sort mystery objects one object at a time, and, in so doing, build a category system. In the lesson from which the data presented here derive, the students were asked to gather in groups of three and to build plasticine models of a mystery object hidden in a shoebox and accessible only to touch by entering a hand through a narrow hole in one of the walls covered by a curtain. One of the cameras used followed the group including Sylvia, Jane, and Melissa. The following description centers on Melissa.

The video shows Melissa, after having her hand in the shoebox for twelve seconds, laughs, as if some idea had come to hear; and she then begins to work her mass of plasticine. The latter slowly takes what we recognize to be cubiform shape. About two and one half minutes later, Melissa says to Jane, 'You know what is, I think it is a cube'. Jane exhibits a questioning facial expression and Sylvia, while having her hand inside the shoebox, responds while shaking her head: 'It's not a cube'. About fifteen seconds later, Melissa turns towards Jane and, saying 'I checked the sides like this', moves her cubiform model (a) exposing one face, holding the thumb and index finger of the left hand in a caliper configuration to it and then (b) continuing to rotate the cube to expose the next side, again holding the caliper configuration to it (Fig 5.1).

Another ninety seconds later, Melissa holds up the plasticine model that she has continued to fashion towards the research assistant shooting the video and says, 'I think it is a cube'. The research assistant videotaping the group asks, 'Why do you think it is a cube?' As before, Melissa brings the right hand into a caliper configuration holding it across one face of the cube (Fig 5.2a), then turning the cube to expose a second face orthogonal to the first one she holds the same, unchanged caliper configuration to it (Fig 5.2b). She turns the cube again, exposing a face orthogonal to the second one (Fig 5.2c), and finishes exposing the first face while holding the caliper configuration against it (Fig 5.2d).

Following this second articulation of the object, having gone through another episode of entering and presumably exploring the mystery object (we do not know what the movements actually are), Melissa goes through the same kind of again another two minutes later. She turns the cube while holding the fixed caliper con-

Fig 5.1 Melissa moves the cube to expose one face orthogonal to the first, in each case holding the thumb and middle finger of the right hand in a caliper configuration.

Fig 5.2 'Because it is the same ... because it is the same ... shape'.

figuration to the different sides of the cube. The research assistant asks, 'What does it have to have to be a cube?' Melissa responds, while moving the cube and holding a caliper configuration to the different face pairs, 'It has to have the same ... sides' (Fig 5.3). Following exchanges with her peers, who assert that they do not think that it is a cube and describe to/instruct Melissa what and how to do feel that the mystery object has the shape of a (flat) rectangular prism. For example, Sylvia repeatedly configures her two hands in a praying position, which we can see as descriptions of and instructions for sensing the flatness of the mystery object. However, Melissa appears in a position not unlike the infant, whose 'actual transfer of sense from the visual body of another to its own tactile-kinesthetic body is unexplicated'.[8] Our account therefore will have to provide an explication of the conditions under which Sylvia's descriptions can make any sense to Melissa.

The research assistant recording the happening subsequently asks Melissa, 'Why do you think it is the same?' Melissa's hand moves through a variety of configurations as if she were moving about the different faces of a cube and says, 'I feel all around it, and it is the same' (Fig 5.4).

Eventually the teacher arrives at the table (nearly ten minutes into the task). At that time, Melissa goes through the same movements, turning the cube in and with her left hand to expose different faces, and holding a caliper configuration across pairs of sides, saying that it has to be the same. The teacher, however, having grouped Sylvia's and Jane's models separate from the one Melissa has shaped, suggests that the three need to come to agree on *one* solution to the task: there is only *one* mystery object, and there can therefore be only *one* type of model. After repeatedly rearticulating her assertion about the cubiform nature of the mystery object, Jane eventually takes Melissa's model in her left hand, moves and touches it while having her right hand in the shoebox. Jane asserts that that the mystery

Fig 5.3   'It has to have the same … sides." Melissa applies the caliper configuration to a face and then turns the cube to apply the same configuration a face orthogonal to the former.

Fig 5.4   'I feel all around it and it is the same'.

object is not a cube, and, as Sylvia before, invites Melissa to do a comparison using her model.

Melissa takes Jane's model in her left hand and enters her right hand into the shoebox (Fig 5.5a). We can see the left hand moving: rotating / touching the model with one of the large square faces pointing upward. Jane, with an open palm, touches the exposed face and suggests, 'Feel this part' (Fig 5.5e). Jane suggests turning the model on the other side. We again observe movements, which hold and turn over the model, followed by a touching movement (Fig 5.5i). As a result of the next movement, the model comes to stand on one of its narrow faces (Fig 5.5j), followed by a series of movements that rotate and feel the object (Fig 5.5j to 5.5n). Melissa then directs her gaze – which up to this point was oriented toward Jane's model in front of her – into the air, puckers her lips, and begins to grin in an apparent expression of surprise. Continuing the movement, she returns the model to Jane and then immediately begins to reshape her cubical model, which eventually takes on a rectangular prismic form.

From the instant when Melissa first put her hand into the shoebox to the second idealization of the nature of the mystery object, exactly fifteen minutes have passed, during which Melissa has reached into the box eight times for a total of a little over three minutes. In this episode, a new form essentially arises twice – first the 'cube' then rectangular solid – from, and is wedded to, the movements of the left arm, hand, and fingers, which, presumably, parallel the movements of the right

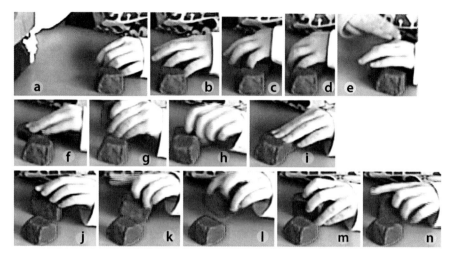

Fig 5.5 Melissa moves the object and feels it while her right hand is inside the shoebox: On one of the flat sides, she feels and turns the object four times. Turning it over, she feels the other flat side. Putting it on the narrow sides, she feels and turns Sylvia's model six times.

hand and fingers. The shape that emerges has its origin in proprioception, the kinesthetic doing and feeling, and the associated sensory affectations deriving from the meeting with the material object.

Recon/Naissance: **From First Movements to Symbolic Gestures**

In the preceding case study, the rectangular prismic form emerged in, through, and indissociably from the movements of the hands, inside and outside the box. It is indissociable from the movements, because any denotation of the form by means of one or the other sign (e.g. word, model, symbolic gesture) is *rooted (grounded) in* what she has lived and undergone before. The associated movements, when mobilized again outside the box to show what she has done (Fig 5.4) and why it is a cube (Fig 5.1 to Fig 5.3), reproduce a kinesthesis. But such a movement does not require cogitation and awareness. Rather, just as we walk without having to think how and where to place our feet, the memory of the movement is sedimented in the capacity and habit to move. This allows reproducing the movement at any one point in time and, thereby, leads to the same kinesthesis and sense: alone, in the absence of the object, to the sensations in the presence of the object. In fact, the naissance of form (i.e. idea, knowledge) occurs twice in the episode: first, when the cubical form emerges from the movements in the initial encounter and, second, when the rectangular prism form emerges during the eighth comparative exploration of the mystery object together with Jane's model. As the following analyses show, this is not 'embodied experience'; it is the sense of a body in movement. The sense pertains to what the body senses, including its own movements. Everything we see in Melissa is movement, from the first demonstration of how she knows that the mystery object is a cube to the exposition of how she had previously investigated the mystery object, and to the repeated exploration of the mystery object in the right hand and the comparison objects in the left hand (Fig 5.5). In moving one's own body, there is a *sense of effort*, of which the source is the subject itself because of the distinction between the subject of the free effort and the term that immediately resists with its own inertia. The effort may not be apparent when we pick up a cup of coffee, or move a hand and arm in our everyday familiar ways – but it becomes immediately apparent, for example, if we attempt to do something unfamiliar or something that we recognize to be beyond our current capabilities (e.g. trying to keep up with another cyclist who just passed us). Here, I develop a phenomenological account of learning and transformation, which takes into account the empirically demonstrated fact that without bodily movement no change in knowledgeability is observed. *Know*ledgeability is born (*née*) in movement.

In classical epistemologies and associated constructivist research projects, including those of Piaget, objects are taken to be given as such. That is, children and other learners, such as those I followed in this project, are assumed to be interacting instantaneously with objects as wholes (e.g. 'cube' or 'rectangular prism'). However, in the lesson fragment, Melissa could not have interacted with the 'mystery object' as *one* thing – putting her finger or hand somewhere does not give her the thing as a whole, for example, as a cube or a rectangular prism. At the instant when she begins, this object is distant: it will be the end result of the series of movements that constitute the exploration (Fig 5.4). Even a face of such a geometrical object would be the result of her groping *about* rather than of an instantaneous apperception. If anything, there is the feeling of something that becomes a facet, and the thing is the totality of a series of connected facets, one unfolding into another in the course of movement. What she feels has integral and irreducible kinesthetic and sensory dimensions. The video shows how Melissa, with a facial expression of concentrated and focused activity, apparently moves about in the box. Then, suddenly, she breaks out in a smile. She withdraws her hand and, eventually, tells Jane with accompanying hand movements why the mystery object has to be a cube (Fig 5.1). The same is observable in the symbolic constitution of the object through the hand movements in the presence of the cubiform model. Finally, the new form emerges from unfolding movements that follow each other rather than are given in an instant. At the heart of coming to know an object, there is therefore a sequential series of movements that come to be coordinated and thereby make the object as such. Readers who are not convinced may return to the depiction consisting of blotches (Fig 3.2, p. 45). Before finding what I embedded as figure, readers' eyes are required to wander until that time when the eyes do so in a very specific way at which point the figure of a killer whale (orca) appears. It is quite apparent that the external form will have guided the reader's eyes to move in a way that makes the form appear. The form appears because they eyes have moved about following a particular form, which then is perceived as the image of the killer whale. The form has taught the eyes to move such that a killer whale is seen. As a result, the killer whale is given to the person rather than being the result of a construction.

The upshot of these considerations is that what will be known exists in and arises from the series of movements. Thus, for example, the rectangular prism – recognized as such on the part of Melissa immediately preceding the instant when her body configuration manifests surprise – emerges from a sequence in which first one of the large faces, then its opposite, then the sequence of narrow faces come to be in contact with the fingers. Each of the faces itself is the result of a series of hand movements. The specific form of the entity as a whole arises from and is constituted by knowing what happens when the object is turned and followed along, turned and followed along, turned and followed along. That is, when Melissa explains *why* the mystery object is a cube, she expresses it in a sequence of connected movements (e.g. Fig 5.3 and Fig 5.4) rather than in the geometer's abstract properties (e.g. 'six equal squared faces' or, what a mathematician calls, 'an object with O_h, *432, or achiral octahedral symmetry'); but without such sensing, none of the formal, abstract properties would make sense.

The foregoing actually is reminiscent of the celebrated but in education little attended-to analysis of the experience of a cube, only recently confirmed by neuroscientists to be correct. Accordingly, we never feel or see a cube as such, that is, a cube as geometry theorizes it. Instead, the cube is given under a given horizon and in the form of a particular perspective (e.g., a hand holding a caliper configuration to a side [Fig 5.1 to Fig 5.4], or the fingers or palm pressing down on the exposed face of a rectangular prism [Fig 5.5e, f, & i].)

When Melissa first puts her right hand in the shoebox, she does not and cannot know what the form of the mystery object is. In moving about, the hand eventually comes into contact with a mass different from and detached from the shoebox. But this mass does not and cannot appear as a complete form. To have any hope of finding out what kind of form the mass in the shoebox has, Melissa's hand needs to move over, about, and around it. The object as such cannot emerge other than as a sequence of feelings associated with the movements she makes. There are therefore two forms of sense that arise: the one deriving from the auto-affection of the animate body (i.e. kinesthesia) and the sensory one deriving from the contact with the material world. Historically only the latter has been associated with knowledge, made thematic as epistemic movements. Whatever the *form* that eventually emerges, it is the result of a *series* of movements – which may be of the object turned about itself or of the hand moving about a stationary object. Before Melissa senses the mystery object for a first time, her hands cannot 'enact' the symbolizing movements that we subsequently see (e.g. Fig 5.2 and Fig 5.4). The required sensation of movement, kinesthesia, comes from the first execution of the movement – i.e. reconnaissance – to be subsequently recognized in its reproduction, rather than having its origin in the brain. We may think of this as a series of innervations, and this series of movements constitutes something like a *kinetic* melody. Once triggered, the movement as a whole unfolds without requiring any further outside control. This is why the movement can be executed again on the basis of what the organs 'know' themselves, and even the knowledge that the present movement is the same as a preceding one is based on the kinesthetic sense. The movement is not represented in the brain; and it does not originate in the brain – though the brain certainly is part of the happening as a whole. Thus, for example, I do not need to represent in mind my hand and fingers that do the typing of this text. Even though the hands and fingers may be innervated by something that happens in the brain, the brain itself is dependent on what it receives from those organs. These organs rather than the brain are in *immediate* contact with the world. That is, conscious will does not determine the movement of an organ: Consciousness intervenes to get the movement going and recognizes subsequently, in the effect of the movement, whether the intended and the actual movements have been the same.

As a consequence of the movements, some whole comes to establish itself, an idea, which goes beyond (i.e. *transcends*) the actual kinesthesis and sense – like the sensations of the blind men in the well-known story from the Indian subcontinent who touch an elephant. The fact that Melissa does not anticipate sensing either the cubiform or the rectangular prismic form can be seen from the facial expressions, which, in each case, express the arrival of something unforeseen. The intentional orientation towards the mystery object as an object of a specific type – in Melissa's case, a cube – cannot but exist *after* its initial constitution. It is the result of a series of movements and the associated kinesthetic and tactile sensations. And all signs speak for a pathic and passive rather than a construction: the first as the second idea *come to* Melissa rather than being the result of a construction – in the same way in which (novel) insights arise in problem solving. In that process of an idea that emerges to become itself – a process we may term *ideation* – a new quality to the subsequent movements related to the mystery object comes about. The new can come about because what we intend or can anticipate never limits itself to what we already know. Movement is pregnant with new things although it is not aware thereof. This leads to the fact that 'that which is seen, to the contrary, is of such a nature that one has to discern in it that which is really seen, given in itself, "in person", and that which is but "emptily aimed at [*visé à vide*]"'.[9] At the instant Melissa aims at the mystery object, only one of its facets is self-evidently given at a time – a surface, line, edge, corner – but the others are not really being given and thus can be aimed at only in an unspecific manner.

When Melissa moves her hand through a series of positions, symbolically indicating what she has done (Fig 5.4), the feel is reproduced but the sensation is absent. On the other hand, the symbolic movements in the presence of the cubiform model not only reproduces kinesthetic sensations but also the sensory ones that come from and go with contact. The very existence of mind arises from the dehiscence between anticipated sensation and actual sensation, in other words, in the coincidence (appearance) of the past and (in) the present.[10] There is therefore an abstraction in the sense that the material object no longer is needed but the movement still underlies the symbolic form produced in and through the gesture. We therefore do not need to speak of the 'enactment of a schema' or the 'embodiment of the cube and rectangular prism' because the movement itself constitutes the original and originary memory of the associated forms. If schemas existed then high-performance athletes could articulate, by the very nature of schemas as something transcendental, the difference between their movements and those of another athlete coming in second could be made explicit. But athletes or scientists studying them cannot articulate in just what the difference exists between the first and the second: it is always only after the fact that tenuous explanations for the observed difference in performance are given. Athletes, however, can reproduce the movements and, in so doing, exhibit masterful performance. Thus, arising out of the contact with the world, the movement has become independent of it, constituting its own memory, and, thus, begins to exist abstracted from the situation. Melissa can show what she has done later in a whole-class session, away from the particular object and in a different part of the classroom. She might even return home after school and go through the same movements again to show what she has done on that day in the mathematics classroom.

There is a problem when we theorize thinking and learning through the processes that a constructivist metaphor proposes. Thinking learning through assimilation and accommodation actually destroys the internal structure of the object for the acting and feeling subject. Thus, a cube *never* is perceived in terms of its geometrical qualities, *six* equal square faces, eight vertices, twelve edges, ninety degree angles, and so on. Indeed, 'the cube with six equal faces is only the limit idea by means of which I express the carnal presence of the cube, which is there, under my eyes, in my hands, in its evidentiary presence'.[11] I never perceive the cube or its projections but always the concrete properties of the thing. More importantly, Maurice Merleau-Ponty suggests that when we hold the cube in our hands, turn and feel it, *we do not construct the idea* of the geometrical object that then explains why we feel the different. Instead, the cube is there before our eyes and hands and discloses itself through these perspectives. A perspective is the relation of the individual to an object as much as the relationship of the object to the individual; and this perspective on the object inherently is social because modeled on the caring social relation that we entertain with others.[12] I do not have to objectify and look at what I go through from the outside to discover the cube behind, so to speak, the one-sided appearances in which it is given to me at the moment to reveal its real, objective form: the object and the different perspectives arise at the same time. Essential to Melissa's pathic constitution of the rectangular solid, to how she knows and knows about these objects, is knowing-what-happens-if the object is turned or if she moves around it. As we can see in the data (Figs. 5.2 to 5.4), when the cube is turned, the same, unchanged caliper configuration also describes the subsequent face that is at a ninety-degree angle with the previous one. We do not need to think of the cube in abstract and abstracted terms but simply in terms of a continuity of movements – here of the left hand rotating the cube around axes that are ninety-degree angles with respect to each other – and the continuity of observation (sensation), here, the constancy of the extensional aspects of the exposed faces. The movement of or around the object is associated with correlated feelings, and these are what knowing the object bottoms out to be. The sense of the body therefore constitutes the body of the sense (here the object).

The constructivist metaphor suggests that learning arises from the interpretation of objects and events – I know this to be the case, as it became evident when I discussed these issues with some of the internationally most well-known mathematics educators who fly the banner of constructivism. They did not accept that when we move, there is a sense of movement that arises from the movement itself without interpretation. In their view, everything was mental. Yet intentional movements are associated with particular kinesthetic sensations that allow moving in this manner again and, in so doing, recognizing that movement. In the effort, such as the one I bodily produce to get these words onto the computer screen, an effort that I perceive and reproduce at the instant, there is no excitation, no foreign stimulant – yet the organs are put into play. That is, 'the contraction effectuated without any cause other than that proper force that feels or perceives itself immediately in its exercise, and without that any sign can represent it in imagination or to a sense foreign to its own'.[13] The French philosopher Pierre Maine de Biran thereby describes the origin of symbolic movements (gestures): they arise from the first kinestheses in spontaneous movements of the body often arising from work or exploration of the material world. Once it also has symbolic character, the (gestural) movement can be associated with other symbolic forms useful in the same setting. When a hand adapts itself to a form, such as Melissa's hand in the black box that follows the surface of the mystery object, the double sensation arising from kinestheses and sensations may be a first-time-ever constitution. Recognition arises from this, when sensation and kinestheses of subsequent explorations of the mystery object come to be cognized as having occurred before. There is an initially spontaneous movement, giving rise to kinesthesis and sensation, before there can be a capacity to make the movement present again symbolically, that is, in its absence. The preceding statement captures what Karl Marx and Friedrich Engels write about consciousness more generally: it is life that constitutes consciousness rather than the reverse. Consciousness cannot ever be anything else but conscious being: consciousness is and arises from the dehiscence of being (past) and its presence in the present. It is only after the fingers of Melissa's hand *have moved* (notice the past tense) that the insight can emerge that the object was something other than the previously claimed cube.

Initially, therefore, there cannot be for Melissa an object independent from the movements of her hand and fingers; in fact, the movements of the hand (fingers) are tied to the material (form), which provokes particular kinetic forms as the fingers follow the surface and contours. That is, whatever form emerges – the first instant of which Melissa announces in her smile followed by the verbal articulation of 'I think it's a cube' – is the result of the material form giving shape to the movement trajectory of the hand. The trajectory constitutes a particular kinetic form, a movement sequence or kinetic melody, which will come to be characteristic of the ideal geometrical form that will be associated with the movement. The actually cognized form is the result of a sequence of movements, characterized by characteristic feeling. Even if the form comes to be denoted as a 'cube' or, subsequently, as 'rectangular prism', having arisen from the movement, it is essentially grounded in this movement. Movement means kinesthesis, a sense of the effort, and sensation that comes from the contact with the world. This is why 'the geometer … by ascending to the first element of objective knowledge, does not yet seize this element, completely abstract as it is, then in its sensible form'.[14] As experimental research shows, it is through tact and in the contact it implies that we come to know the world rather than through vision alone. Thus, touch truly is the geometrical sense: any idea, any schema, or any ideal notion of geometry arises from, and therefore is grounded in and wedded to movement. There is no 'grounding problem' because geometry – as subjective knowledge or objective science – does not exist without movement. What researchers refer to as ungrounded or abstract does not deserve inclusion in the category of *knowledge*. Maine de Biran and Mead agree that only tact and contact can be the basis of originary synthetic observations. That is, even if a person were to encounter a synthetic description first, it could make sense only when there are antecedent (tactual) *sens*ations; even if a teacher provided some descriptions and instructions for exploring some unknown object, the *sense* of these *always* would follow the actual kinestheses that come from moving about/around the object.

In the episode, we twice observe the arrival of a new sense, announced as such by the learner herself. Her movements and the object encountered are pregnant in the sense that something new can come forth. Pregnance means transcendence, so that in contact with the world, new things emerge. In this situation, we witness the coming of a specific thing – *this* rather than *another*. Thus, in *empirical pregnance*, our knowing-how concerning, and knowing-about, a thing is of a kind 'of which we can have an idea only through our carnal participation in its sense, only by espousing by our body its manner of "signifying"'.[15] As a consequence, the emergence of a figure from an indefinite ground thus situates us outside those philosophies that begin any analysis in terms of a pre-existing subject that encounters an object. That is, this emergence of a figure situates us completely outside of constructivist metaphor in all its various forms (e.g. radical and social). This requires us, therefore, to move towards a post-constructivist account of learning such as the one proposed here.

When Melissa begins moving her right hand over the mystery object she does not require a representation. In fact, in the same way that military patrols move about a field in an act of *reconnaissance*, Melissa is on a reconnaissance mission where the mystery object is going to give itself because Melissa, not knowing it, cannot intend constructing it. She cannot have a *re*presentation of the object until some future moment when, in the absence of the object, she can make it present again. This is what she does in her explanations to Jane and the research assistant (Fig 5.1 to Fig 5.4). If anything, such movements *generate* representation – as we know especially from recent work on mirror neurons. These neurons, which are active when the neuron associated with movement is active, are required for recognizing the same movement in the behavior of another. Thus, movements can be repeated without representation; and, when these movements were associated with touching some object, they lead to the recognition of form and all the affective experiences associated with their first occurrence. This may be the reason why Sylvia's gesture of the hands held as if praying do not resonate with Melissa. It is only after kinesthetic and sensory experiences such as in Fig 5.5e, Fig 5.5f, and Fig 5.5i that the shape of the gesture and the shape of the mystery object come to be sensed and make sense. This possibility gives rise to repetition of purely symbolic forms. Thus, in Fig 5.4, the movements – which initially had ergotic (work) and epistemic function and which are associated with kinesthesia and sensations – now also have a symbolic function. They do not require representation but, following a trigger, unfold as a whole, like a kinetic melody without separate, symbolic mental representation. (I once described the experience of having forgotten a phone number but, upon putting my hand to the keys, dialed the correct number: the phone number was present in the hand movements but not represented in my mind.[16]) To develop anything such as knowledge that transcends the movements of the body, the latter have to exist in repeatable form and prior to any schemas that are said to underlie them. To have a schematic representation of a movement, the movement has to exist as such and prior to the fact that it can be present again.

In the episode, we see something new appear from the movements of Melissa's hand. This is possible because an experience is open towards its end and, therefore, multiplicious, even though it may initially appear unitary: there is always another way in which something can appear, always a new form of sensing and feeling, always a new way of understanding something (here mathematically). It is this multiplicious nature of things that constitutes *pregnance*. In abstract ideas, such as the one denoted by 'the cube', the multiplicity of sensations is lived in a unity. So the movements, such as the ones Melissa has engaged in the shoebox are *fecund*, giving rise to new ways of feeling and, ultimately, to new ideations resulting in new forms of ideas. Psychologists forget this productivity and fecundity that comes with and from pregnancy, a power of the bursting forth of the new. The notion of pregnancy as productivity not only of new orders but also of new perceptions is completely outside of constructivist perspectives. There is an original and originary constitution – an *Urstiftung* in the sense of Husserl – rather than simple accretion to something already there, any existing or accommodated schemas. From the perspective of the learner, there is transcendence rather than immediate recognition of an a priori concept. But there is more to such an emergence of ideas from movements and ideations, including the *inherent* intersubjective (objective) nature of knowing and its historically developing form.

Ideation Implies Intersubjectivity and History

In and through the formation of an idea, time itself is born (and therefore history and biography). This is so because the new is seen as different from the past – which Melissa specially marked by recognition and surprise in the first and second emergence of form. That is, there is a delay between the first contact of what comes to be cognized as one object and the related idea of the thing; there is a second temporal dimension in the emergence of becoming aware (see chapter 6). Melissa marks, in her facial expressions, the appearance of something (cube, rectangular solid). There is a tension-laden transition from whatever was to the newly emerging idea. The transition does not occur all of a sudden but has a microstructure. Thus, recognition and surprise, as we see marked in and by Melissa's face, both require a past appearance to be present again together with the new. That is, in the first emergence of an idea, which arises from and describes something that has preceded it – movement – also emerges time. This is captured in the idea that time is the emergence (of the new) and the absenting (of movement), as a coming-going to presence. Time arises when a past event comes to presence when it actually has disappeared. For Heidegger, Being [*Sein*] has disappeared when we grasp it as some being [*Seiendes*]; and time precisely is that gap between Being and beings. In Melissa's case, the movements have ended when she grasps the ensemble of feelings as a cube or rectangular solid. That is, ideation implies temporality and, therefore, historicity. But because historicity requires the making present of a past presence – i.e. representation and repetition – ideation also implies intersubjectivity. That is, even if one of the three children were to arrive at a radically new idea about geometry, it would immediately be reproducible, because of its very nature, by the same and other students; and, therefore, it would be *intersubjective* and historical. This contradicts the constructivist notion of knowledge as something singular and subjective.

The most primitive forms of thought and mind arise with the sensation of a wanted action or effort in the direction of a distant object – which, as seen above, may be just another facet of the mystery thing in hand; Melissa turns this thing to be able to feel out another one of its sides. This wanted effort, together with the double sensation of resistance in the body attributed to the object, lies at the basis of all cognition. In the constructivist approach, however, scholars claim that the learning and developing child *constructs* for it*self* the world – through assimilation to existing schemas preceded or by the accommodation of existing schemas. Apart from the fact that this does not take into account the changes of both (interpretive) horizon and object, the constructivist approach does not explain how the *tools* and the *subject* of the construction come to be constructed in the first place. The tools and subjects themselves *emerge* as the result of contact, kinestheses, and sensations. In ideation, the birth of the idea that we observe in the episode from the mathematics lesson, the object, subject, and tool all emerge, unpredictably, at one and the same instant. The object does not exist distinct and independent from the subject and its movement. The object essentially is given in, as, and through movement. The perception of external things and the perception of things that happen within the body thus vary together, they are but two aspects of the same act, a position that both Merleau-Ponty and Mead have taken. Moreover, the separation of the external from the internal is possible only because of the antecedent social relation that serves as its model. Ideation, the appearance of the object as over and against the Self is social through and through. The object exists generally or it does not exist at all – a point that the German philosopher Ludwig Feuerbach already made[17] prior to the independent discovery on the part of Mead.

The proposed framework also allows us to rethink the origin of time, which Piaget suggested, thereby revising Kant's notion of time as an a priori, to be the result of a construction. However, the above-noted analysis of the fundamental nature of everyday human consciousness suggests a different relation between *Being* [*Sein*] and *time*. How the two are connected to learning has not been explored

beyond Piaget in the educational literature but is an integral consequence of an
epistemology that gives primacy to movement, which movement creates as much
as occurs in space and time. It can therefore be felt as having a particular form of
qualitative dynamic. In the emergence of an object (idea) into consciousness, there
is an essential temporal aspect. The new object, as we see above, is not given once
and for all. It arises from kinesthetic and sensory movements. Then all of a sudden
the realization of the form, a realization that itself marks a difference from what
was there before, a cube, to what is there now, a rectangular prism. Ideation is a
process that itself constitutes time, as the new comes to stand against what was:
what is present is different from a past presence, and this difference itself constitutes time. There is a decalage (but not of the Piagetian kind) between movement
and idea or between Being and beings (things). The process of ideation itself, the
realization of a difference, *constitutes time and temporality*. But for the past to be
present requires the capacity of *making it present again*: re-presenting it. The past
is past only in reference to the present in which it is present. With ideation, therefore, comes the historicity of the idea. But, if the past can be made presented again,
represented, then it can be made present again not only by the same subject but
also by other subjects. The standing out and being present to consciousness implies
its iterability in general and, therefore, community and intersubjectivity. That is,
rather than having to be constructed and, in essence, being unachievable – as this is
assumed in the constructivist account – intersubjectivity is given with the very possibility of making something present again. Intersubjectivity thus also means (in-
ter-) objectivity and historicity: geometry, as science, can be performed over and
over again, simultaneously and across time, without changing. The same experiments and the same proofs lead to the same results whoever conducts them whenever.

Besides temporality, there is another problem in constructivist approaches to
knowing: how can two or more individuals know the same world in the same way?
The problem arises because knowing is theorized in terms of individual consciousness and constructions rather than in terms of an inherently shared passibility of the
incarnate, animate body. In other words, intersubjectivity as a problem is an arti-
fact of theory in the constructivist, enactivist, and embodiment approaches. This is
not the case in those theoretical takes that are based on the primacy of the social in
the emergence of consciousness from movement. It is precisely because we move,
because we *are* animate bodies in movement endowed with passibility, that we
share in common sense. The biological bodies that make us have senses in common: in and through our sensual bodies, life affects itself, and, in so doing, shows
itself to itself in the body of sense.

In the initial encounter of a worldly object, the movement of turning, turning
around, and sensing the object – both cube in demonstration and mystery object in
box – there is a first sensation not yet idea but no longer just raw in nature. In the
first contact between hand and mystery object, the movement of ideation has begun, a movement that reaches from the invisible to the seen. It has been said that
'this original layer above *nature* shows that *learning* is *In der Welt Sein*, and not at
all that *In der Welt Sein* is *learning*, in the American sense or in the cognitive

sense'.[18] Because the logical predicate (e.g. 'is *In der Welt Sein*') constitutes what we assert about the logical subject (e.g. *learning*), *In der Welt Sein* is what we can assert about *learning* rather than the other way around. We cannot assert about *In der Welt Sein* that it is learning. When Melissa learns – as marked in the surprise visible in her face and the subsequent actions that turn the cubiform model into a rectangular prismic one – then we can assert about it that it is a form of *In der Welt Sein*, being-there in and with an animate body in movement. Learning is indissociable from the animate body and, therefore, the knowing-how and knowing-that associated with it. In other words, a material body does not imply learning but learning implies an animate, sensual body that inherently is material as well.

Multiplicity, Bifurcations, *Pregnance*

In the literature we can find intimations that students are to be exposed to discrepant events and counter intuitive demonstrations. However, the present observations suggest that we cannot automatically assume that a situation is contradictory from the perspective of the learner. Through the eyes of Melissa, the cubical model was the appropriate one fitting her sense of touch and thus her sense, and there was no evidence for her to assume otherwise. Whenever she tested the mystery object during the preceding seven times, it was consistent with the experience of the cube in the way she demonstrated having tested (Fig 5.4) and articulated the features (Fig 5.1 to Fig 5.3) that made the mystery object resemble the model she had shaped from the plasticine, that is, a cubiform entity. If there was a contradiction, it existed between the models Jane and Sylvia had constructed and her own. But the evidence that *she* had collected spoke against the contentions of the others. Initially, therefore, there was no contradiction between Melissa's kinesthesia and sensations related to the mystery object and cube. It is only when she does the comparison (Fig 5.5) that all of a sudden the differentiation emerges from kinestheses and sensations and, in this, a contradiction between an earlier claim and the one in the process of emerging.

Initially, the movements of the right hand/fingers lead to the production of the cubiform plasticine object. What has given itself to the right hand and fingers came to be associated to the figure known as cube. Initially, and in response to her peers' assertions that the mystery object was not a cube, Melissa shows how she moved around the object with the caliper configuration (Fig 5.1), which, because it remained the same, was evidence for her that there was a cube. Later, when asked by the research assistant, Melissa twice does indeed provide both a gestural (symbolic) and verbal description consistent with formal geometrical properties of a cube. In fact, there appears to be a contradiction between the movements in the first three articulations of the mystery object as a cube (Fig 5.1 to Fig 5.3) and the gestural description of what Melissa says to have done (Fig 5.4). The subsequent movements of fingers and hands (Fig 5.5) give rise to a certain form of tactile sense, which is recognized to be the same as the one in the other hand, and which, in the instant of the recognition, is marked as surprise. Something unexpected has occurred: where one form of sense may have been the anticipated one, something else is born: the commonality in the kinesthesis and tactility of both hands. The movements and sensations in the right hand and fingers emerge as corresponding to the corresponding movements of the other side. Here, cognition of the object in the right hand is tied to recognition: cognition is irremediably associated with cognition, which also goes beyond what was previously known to be there.

In the present situation, a problem occurs only after a new kind of sense emerges. Melissa initially feels what she articulates to be a cube. Thus, she is modeling and holding the plasticine cube in her hands and follows its outline with her hands, a contradiction between the initial kinesthesia and sensation and the one that subsequently is related to the movement does not appear. The two forms of kinesthesis and sensation, the one inside the box and the one outside the box, appear to be the same. It is through cumulative encounters with the object that an infant comes to know that kinetic deformations in perceptions arise from the kinetics of its animate body. The process is actually a little more complicated, as there are situations where we are deceived, such as when, as noted above, we sit in a train at the station believing it to move when in fact it is the train next to it that is pulling out; and the reverse may also occur. It is only through analysis or further perceptual clues that we may be able to distinguish between the two situations.

A contradiction, however, does not initially arise for Melissa when Sylvia and Jane say that the mystery object is not a cube, when Sylvia uses symbolic gestures to describe the mystery object, or when Sylvia and Jane show their own models (descriptions of the mystery object). We can understand the episode when we think about the kinesthesia and holistic sense that comes to be differentiated in ongoing and subsequent transactions, sometimes requiring particular exchanges with others. Thus, initiated by the demonstration that Jane provided and the encouragement on the part of Sylvia, Melissa uses another model to conduct a direct comparison with the mystery object. It is in this unfolding that the differentiation occurs, which then allows distinguishing between cubical and rectangular prism forms. In fact, the feeling in her hand initially means likeness between the mystery object and the model, which itself is different from the initially postulated and modeled cube.

Such differentiation is a general movement observed in development, such as in that pertaining to concept words. Thus, for example, students often use 'heat' to denote not only the phenomenon that scientists associate with the word (i.e. energy) but also the ones referred to as temperature and entropy (Eng. hot → heat; Ger. warm → Wärme; Fr. chaud → chaleur). As those interested in food know, with continued exposure the senses of smell and taste become increasingly differentiated and knowledgeable about differences between foods to the point of being able to indicate during the blind tasting of chocolate, wine, or olive oil such specifics a the geographic origin, varietal, or soil type.[19] Differentiation allows a reconfiguration of sense. Such a reconfiguration of sense also is well known to those producing transcriptions of classroom videotapes. Even seasoned transcribers find that what they originally heard was said changes when someone else offers a different possible hearing, or sounds that are heard but not recognized as words all of a sudden turn into clearly recognizable words.

Movement and the Birth of Form

In this chapter, I articulate a theoretical reorientation from the material body to the movements of an animate body endowed with passibility. An empirical example shows that rather than simply being embodied and associated with abstract movement schemas somehow enacted, our knowing-how and knowing-that emerge from movements of the animate body. In such an account, therefore, the distinction between knowing and knowing one's way around the world (i.e. moving in a knowledgeable way) has been erased. It is only in this way that the body of sense (of words, language) is the reverse side of the sense(s) of the body. It is not that abstract knowledge has to be grounded, that there is a 'grounding problem', but rather, anything that can lay the claim to being epistemic, arises in and from the movements of the body. This is so whether we perceive them (e.g. as the movements of hands or the body as a whole) or not (e.g. our eye movements required for seeing anything at all). Adjectives such as embodied and enacted are artifacts of epistemologies that begin with and privilege the mind over the body rather than constituting epistemologies that are sound on evolutionary and cultural-historical grounds. If such adjectives and concepts as 'enacted schemas' and 'embodied concepts' are to have any sense, the very origin of these schemas and concepts needs to be demonstrated. On biological grounds, (human) schemas and concepts are evolutionary latecomers. Their origin has to be explained without drawing on a priori and innate knowledge – a form of reasoning that uses what is to be explained (i.e. the philosopher's *explanandum*) to explain that which explains (i.e. the philosopher's *explanans*). The post-constructivist approach proposed here simultaneously is a pre-constructivist epistemology. It establishes the possibility for any so-called embodied or enacted schema (if they exist at all). Before a process of construction can set in, the origin of the tools of the construction need to be explained. On philosophical and evolutionary grounds, which reconstruct the beginning of life in motility and sensation, self- movement and self-affection are the origins of any higher conscious form of life. Because movement and kinetic melodies constitute their own memory, no (mental) schemas are necessary. In fact, the mental schemas are the result when movement comes to be spontaneous rather than being instinctive and, therefore, transcend themselves so that any schema can emerge. Willed acts come about when spontaneous movements come to unfold after some conscious mental act consistently triggers their release and unfolding.

The geometrical object – such as the (ideal) cube – is a limit idea arising from continuous refinement of actual objects encountered in practical experience (movements), a refinement that can only in the unachievable limit become consistent with geometrical properties. Practical activity is sedimented in and underlies any geometrical knowledge. In the present study, we observe a differentiation that is required before the refinements of the cube can occur: the differentiation of cubical from other, similar forms. This differentiation itself comes to be sedimented to constitute the fundamental sense, the ultimate ground of any geometrical concept of three-dimensional forms.

In the episode, we observe hand movements both over a model object (Fig 5.1 to Fig 5.3) and on their own (Fig 5.4) used to explain why the mystery object should be a cube. There also is observable a conceptualization, a mode of transcendence. Thus, Melissa shows what she has done, repeats the movements that have earlier arisen while following and sensing the mystery object (Fig 5.4). These movements, however, differ from the ones she previously used to 'prove' why the mystery object has cubical form: the caliper configuration held to the model is the same for the different faces. We do not know whether Melissa's hands have moved like this ever before. In any event, to be *intentionally* enacted, the body needs to know that these movements are among or one of its powers. That is, it has moved in this manner at least once before. The same movements can be executed in the absence of the original form associated with them; and they can be *re*cognized only when they have been cognized before. Thus, it is in this way that there is a transfer from the movements that the hand has made *following* the mystery object to gesturing the movements as part of the argument that it has cubicle form. It also lies at the origin of the recognition that occurs when some other material of the same form is followed.

To conclude, the original movements in the shoebox are the originary and original signs of diverse elementary perceptions related to them; these movements cannot be separated from the primary qualities that come from the resistance of the movement to itself (associated with kinesthesia) and the resistance deriving from the outside object. The movements, therefore, can actually serve to recall, bring back, the ideas associated with them; and this recall, in turn, is the fundamental memory in which words and language are grounded. Whatever we know about the world always and already is grounded in and arises from the movements of the animate body. Or, to be more exact, from the kinesthesia and sensations associated with these movements arises anything we can be knowledgeable of. When we say that something 'makes sense' or 'is meaningful' then we address precisely this association of sound-words with original movements, kinestheses and sensations, in, tied to, and toward the social and material world.

Notes

1 George Herbert Mead, *Philosophy of the Act* (Chicago: University of Chicago Press, 1938), 147.

2 Mead, *Act*, 146.

3 Karl Marx and Friedrich Engels, *Werke Band 3* (Berlin: Dietz, 1978), 31.

4 Felix T. Mikhailov, 'The "Other Within" for the Psychologist', *Journal of Russian and East European Psychology*, vol. 39 no. 1 (2001), 25 and 26.

5 Maxine Sheets-Johnstone, 'Body and Movement: Basic Dynamic Principles', in *Handbook of Phenomenology and Cognitive Science* ed. by Shawn Gallagher and Daniel Schmicking (Dordrecht: Springer, 2010), 221.

6 Sheets-Johnstone, 'Body and Movement', 230.

7 Cf. Wolff-Michael Roth and Jennifer Thom, 'Bodily Experience and Mathematical Conceptions: From Classical Views to a Phenomenological Reconceptualization', *Educational Studies in Mathematics*, vol. 70 (2009), 175–189; and Wolff-Michael Roth and Jennifer Thom, 'The Emergence of 3d Geometry from Children's (Teacher-guided) Classification Tasks', *Journal of the Learning Sciences*, vol. 18 (2009), 45–99.

[8] Sheets-Johnstone, 'Body and Movement', 230.

[9] Michel Henry, *Incarnation: Une philosophie de la chair* (Paris: Éditions du Seuil, 2000), 53.

[10] Contact is so important in Mead's philosophy that the term appears more than 570 times in *Philosophy of the Act*.

[11] Maurice Merleau-Ponty, *Phénoménologie de la perception* (Paris: Gallimard, 1945), 236–237.

[12] Mead, *Act*, 116–117.

[13] Pierre Maine de Biran, *Œuvres inédites tome 2* (Paris: Dezobry and Magdeleine, 1859), 211.

[14] Pierre Maine de Biran, *Œuvres inédites tome 1* (Paris: Dezobry and Magdeleine, 1859), 102.

[15] Maurice Merleau-Ponty, *Le visible et l'invisible* (Paris: Gallimard, 1964), 258.

[16] Wolff-Michael Roth, *First-Person Methods: Toward an Empirical Phenomenology of Experience* (Rotterdam: Sense Publishers, 2012), 97–101.

[17] Ludwig Feuerbach, *Sämtliche Werke zweiter Band* (Leipzig: Otto Wigand, 1846), 308.

[18] Merleau-Ponty, *Le visible,* 262.

[19] Roth, *First Person Methods*, 75–87.

6

Becoming Aware

In the preceding chapter, we observe how objects (perceptions) and ideas (conceptions) emerge from acting in the world. In the specific instance we notice what appears to be a *sudden* appearance and recognition of the form that a hidden mystery object takes when it feels different (like a rectangular solid) from what it felt before (like a cube). But the objects that enter our lives do not have to be mysterious, at once being of familiar *kind* and not having existed in parts of our familiar world up until an instant of insight. In the course of my life, I have had repeated 'sudden' discoveries, each of which left such an impression that I remember it to the present day. The phenomenon occurred to me (note the passive tense!) for the very first time while taking the daily bus ride to the city where I attended secondary school. For years I had taken the trip when one day, 'all of a sudden', I saw the city's renowned Marienberg Fortress from a point and under an angle where I had never seen it before. I was surprised over seeing something that I had never seen before and began to wonder about how it was possible that I had taken this trip for so many years but had never seen what I just had seen for a first time. Given the circumstances, there can be no doubt about the fact that I could have seen the view before so that this 'fact' existed retroactively. Some twenty-five years later, already in my late forties, I started attending closer to the phenomenon and to its implications for epistemology and for educational practice. I had realized that precisely because I did not know about those views ('facts'), I could not intentionally orient toward them. In one case, it was a giant feed silo next to a road that I had been cycling along for seven consecutive days for the purpose of simulating learning events; in another case, it was a little church on the way to work, which I had taken for eleven years before actually becoming aware of for the first time.[1] For extended periods I was unaware of the existence of these things until, after having become aware, they were present in my awareness. In each case, the world in which I *dwelled* was enlarged, contained more things that I was able to act on, talk about, and make use of. It was only while writing this book that I found that George Herbert Mead already conceived of the emergence of things, which he articulated in the context of science but that also are valid in our everyday lives: 'Things emerge, and emerge in the mechanical order of things, which could not be predicted from what has happened before'.[2] That is, these new things became objects that I could use in *building* and *thinking*. For years I thought about the phenomenon as something that occurs suddenly, in a flash. It was only more recently that I began to attend to the *phenomenalization* of the seen from the unseen and therefore unforeseen. It turns out that the appearance of a new thing is not sudden, as if occurring in a flash. Instead, it is an event* with its own temporality, which, admittedly, tends to be rather fast so that we do not attend to it as such. In this chapter, I describe *becoming aware* as something that happens. Given the right circumstances, when something in the course of happening unfolds slowly enough, the phenomenon can be studied in its different phases.

Between the 1960s and 1980s, there was a lively debate about the appropriate epistemology to be taken when studying student learning. Behaviorism, Jean Piaget's stage theory, information processing approaches, neo-Piagetian theories combining stage theory with information processing, and conceptual change all were part of a panoply of theoretical frameworks available to the learning scientist. Since then, however, constructivism, in its various forms, has risen to become a master theory (narrative) of how we learn. Yet there are a many different forms of learning that cannot be explained using a constructivist metaphor – especially the different forms of learning that have to do with the human capacity to be affected and suffer, that is, with passibility.[3] With respect to learning, the inherent unavailability of the future and the openness of a happening (here sometimes denoted as event*) that becomes a definite event only after the fact, make it impossible for students to construct knowledge in the manner that this verb implies. The verb *to construct* is a poor theoretical choice because the verb is *transitive,* requiring a definite subject and object. It is a poor choice because we inherently cannot know what we will have learned, that is, the future knowledge that is the ex post facto object of the learning, which is revealed to us only as a consequence and end product of the finalized (learning) event. Indeed, numerous philosophers and psychologists – including George Herbert Mead, Maurice Merleau-Ponty, and Lev S. Vygotsky – have pointed out that we do not know the contents of our own physical and discursive acts (i.e. *what* exactly we are doing or saying) until after the fact. That is, we neither 'construct' our physical actions and phrases nor construct the 'meanings' thereof to implement them afterward. Instead, these are emergent phenomena, unseen and unforeseen until after they have arrived.

The unsuitability of the verb 'to construct' and the associated epistemology is familiar to pragmatic philosophers of language. Thus, for example, Richard Rorty uses the case of the 'craftsman [who] typically knows what job he needs to do before picking or inventing tools with which to do it'. He makes the contrast with 'someone like Galileo, Yeats, or Hegel (a "poet" in my wide sense of the term – the sense of "one who makes things new") [who] *is typically unable to make clear exactly what it is that he wants to do before developing the language in which he succeeds in doing it*. His new vocabulary makes possible, for the first time, a formulation of its own purpose'.[4] Even the great poets are *typically unable* to make clear their aim until they have achieved it in the poem. That is, in the process of making something new, the poets not only are unaware of what they will have produced in the upcoming future but also are incapable of describing and explaining precisely what they are doing, which, in retrospect, will have been something new. Painters, too, do step back from their paintings, a move that enables them to see revealed, a posteriori, what their preceding brush strokes have yielded. The content of the quotation thus also questions the possibility to be 'metacognitive' when you are creating something new, that is, when you are learning.

These considerations suggest that *becoming aware* has the character of a happening (which is known *as* event only after the fact) and of *aspect dawning*. The use of the expression stating 'something is dawning on us' suggests that whatever eventually appears first exists only in vague and unclear form before it becomes clear upon entering full light. After the new has entered the clearing, those who have become aware of and perceive something new (i.e. have learned it) describe what they have been doing using the new language and linguistic expressions and, thereby, produce an *a posteriori account*. From the history of science it is well known that a posteriori accounts are teleological and constitute a form of Whig history, which makes it appear as if the actors had aimed from the beginning at making what they only after the fact knew as having done and produced. I know this to be the case because I was a member of a scientific research team that attempted to refine the description of a particular phenomenon that was explained by a theory for which its creator had received a Nobel Prize.[5] The data ultimately showed a very different pattern. This different pattern was dawning upon us only slowly. It eventually turned out that other research, too, had shown the same pattern. Our research report was written in this new light. We were in the same situation as David Suzuki, a famous Canadian geneticist turned journalist and environmentalist, who wrote: 'the report was a way of "making sense" of our discovery, of putting our results into a context and communicating it so colleagues could understand and repeat (if necessary) what we did. But it conveyed nothing of the excitement, hard work, frustration, disappointment and exhilaration of the search – or the original reason we started the search for paralytic mutants'.[6] The result is that a posteriori accounts do not have predictive qualities and, therefore, like Monday morning quarterbacking, have no *theoretical* value: they do not *explain* a thing. In this chapter I describe and (begin to) theorize precisely that movement from being unaware to being aware while the poets and learners do not yet know what they will have come to know when they are done. This movement I denote by the term *becoming aware*. Becoming aware inherently is a process of learning, because afterwards we are aware of something that we had known (been aware of) before. Becoming aware is a quintessential learning process that we need to know about because it involves parts that currently dominant epistemologies do not or cannot explain.

Aspect Dawning

The *dawning of an aspect* refers to the arriving of a new thing in conscious aware-ness – which is not and *cannot* be the result of an interpretation. A clear example in the literature on learning events in the sciences (i.e. 'discoveries') exists in the ac-count of how the DNA structure came to be *found*. James D. Watson had created cardboard shapes of the four chemical bases that crystallographic analyses had shown to be present in the DNA molecule they studied and for which the research-ers wanted to find the structure. Watson describes what happened that morning as having begun to shift the cardboard shapes into different possible pairings without already having in mind the way in which the pairings would look like. At one point, it suddenly was dawning upon him: the adenine-thymine pair, which was bonded by means of two hydrogen atoms, had a shape identical to that of the gua-nine-cytosine pair. Everything seemed natural, and no fudging was required to make for the identity of the two resulting compound shapes. In his account, Wat-son describes shifting the different material shapes of his model bases in and out of various configurations. He had to do so because he did not know what he would ultimately know: two pairs, with members placed in particular ways, were identical in shape. This knowing is not only of the perceptual kind but also one of conceptu-al nature. Moreover, not knowing what the DNA molecule and its rungs will be looking like once 'discovered', he could not have a plan to intentionally look for it. He tried this and that – a form of event often referred to as 'trial and error'. Quite accurately, he therefore describes that he was *becoming aware* that the adenine-thymine and guanine-cytosine pairs were identical. This awareness was both of perceptual and conceptual nature. For him to become aware, there had to be some-thing that he could become aware of: the configuration of the two pairs. These physical pairs *preceded* his awareness. Watson did not direct his awareness but rather, the identity of the shapes of the two pairs *offered itself to him* rather than him looking for them. He was moving cardboard shape looking what this moving gives. It was when he had become aware of the configuration that he knew it was what he was looking for – something like a reconfiguration of the colloquialism, 'I know it when I see it'. Prior to that he did not know and, therefore, could not inten-tionally construct the shapes. The ultimate configurations were unseen, and there-fore unforeseen, until he saw them and knew that this was what he had been look-ing for without knowing that he was doing so. This is why we might see in his description a case of trial and error. But trial and error implies that we do not know and that we come to know something when it works, when it turns out not to have been done in error.

Watson writes that he *suddenly* became aware – he had an epiphany. That is, he was describing an instance of insight, when something unknown up to a point came *in sight*. He uses the adverb 'suddenly', which has the sense of 'all at once' and 'without preparation or warning'. Such a framing, however, obliterates part of the description, which also notes the *coming* of awareness and the *becoming* aware. There is a happening at work, a movement, at the end of which we are consciously

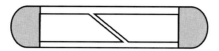

Fig 6.1 After 116 tests using the glow lamp, Birgit becomes aware of the gap between the electrodes. Three lessons later she becomes aware that one has to hold the glow lamp at the metal ends to make it work.

aware. Watson does not write that he *constructed* awareness. As Rorty above points out, he *could not* construct it because he was becoming aware of the equally shaped pairs almost despite himself *following* his moving about of the shapes. 'To construct' means that he had anticipated in some way what the outcome of his actions would be and he would have acted accordingly. The problem with the constructivist metaphor is apparent in chapter 5, where I describe the pregnance of movement, that is, its generative nature and the emergence of the unseen and thus unforeseen. Because we cannot construct awareness – we would have to be aware of our future awareness to do so – the phenomenon also contributes to evolving a post-constructivist account of learning.

We do not have to seek recourse to the discovery accounts of famous scientists – though there are recommendations on cultural-historical grounds to take the toughest and extreme cases for studying psychological phenomena. Instead, if we pay close attention then we can find evidence of the coming of awareness in the everyday classroom. We have already seen one example in chapter 5, where Melissa apparently explores and constitutes an aspect of the space surrounding her with the right hand (i.e. in the shoebox) while turning and touching her peer's model with the left hand. Then, her facial expression changes quite rapidly, exhibiting astonishment; she puckers her lips, then picks up her clay model and shapes it into a rectangular prism. Now, after eight tactile explorations of the mystery object totaling more than three minutes, the mystery object had given itself as a cube. It was during the eighth exploration that a new form was revealing itself to her hand. Here, too, we can say after the fact that she was becoming aware at that instant: the mystery object was taking the shape of a rectangular prism even though it had felt like a cube during, and as a consequence of, the seven preceding explorations. In another instance, I had studied a group of tenth-grade students in a course on static electricity. In one of the two groups recorded, the students had great pains to consistently reproduce an effect that the teacher had demonstrated. The teacher had rubbed some material, including an overhead transparency, and then held to it a little glow lamp (Fig 6.1). It lit up, which the teacher suggested was due to the static electricity. After having conducted 116 tests, following another series of inconsistent results, Birgit, one of the four students in the group, stared at the glow lamp and then said something like, 'Oh, it is broken. It cannot work!' It is at that time that she had *become aware* of the fact that there were two electrodes, which Birgit (incorrectly) described as a broken lamp. Because she did not know that a glow lamp has two electrodes rather than one continuous filament like a classical light bulb, she could not intentionally look for it. There was then a movement from not being aware to being aware; and this part of the learning event – after all, she did come to know something that she did not know before – requires a new, post-constructivist form of description. The movement itself requires an appropriate theory that is consistent with the nature of an event* as emergent. Emergent means that there are aspects that we cannot predict what comes based on what we currently know. Moreover, the phenomenon is not one that is typical of the individual. Instead, 'in so far as the individual takes the attitude of the generalized other toward the object there emerges an object that is universal'.[7] The object, the gap between the two electrodes, immediately is a universal thing, which can be seen in the fact that Birgit pointed it out to the teacher (as a material thing) and used it to explain the failure to achieve the successful investigation. The object immediately, that is, with its appearance, is social – rather than individual to be shared and negotiated with others, as constructivists want to have it.

My studies – those pertaining to physicists invited as experts to provide readings of graphs from first-year university biology courses – show that we must not presuppose the givenness of what is on a page. Thus, one physicist, when stymied, was told by the research assistant that she had to look at the value of the curves but she answered, 'I can't help but see [the] slopes [of the curves]'. It is not that she *interprets* slopes: she *cannot help* but *see* slopes. Mathematically, instead of seeing the values of birthrates as a function of population size, she saw the slope as a function of the curve. In another study of mine what was to be seen as a graphical sign for a biological phenomenon arose in and from the verbal exchanges of two physicists who experienced the *dawning of an aspect*. In that case, approximately parallel lines came to be seen as indicating levels in a third dimension similar to the elevation lines on a geographical map. Finally, *what* there was to be seen in two representations in an experimental biology laboratory – an image of the microscopic slide contents and a graph – was not given but emerged in the course of the verbal exchanges over and about the two; and the pattern in which the generated data related emerged as a form of a quickly occurring but not sudden gestalt switch within the research team. Without a thing, without an aspect, there was nothing to be interpreted; the latter process could start only when a new (perceptual or conceptual) aspect had dawned. Describing the movement from the absence of a sign or thing to the presence of a *new* and unknown sign or thing precisely is the object of this chapter.

An Empirical Investigation

In chapter 2, I refer to Karl Marx and Friedrich Engels, who, drawing on the creative possibilities of their German language, write that consciousness is conscious Being. That is, Being does not have to be consciously aware of any structure in practical activity and, on evolutionary grounds, is not inherently so. This is why Martin Heidegger places dwelling and Being (*Sein*) before building and thinking (beings), which, thus, are the consequences – and thus possible because – of dwelling. We may experience the primacy of Being when we are 'in the flow' or during meditation, when we are not conscious of Being and do not make it present make present (again), that is, re-present. The issue also can be observed among children while growing up. Thus, even though children come to speak a language in grammatically correct ways, they become aware of the grammatical rules and grammar only after already speaking their first language sufficiently well. It is only then that they begin differentiating subject, verb, object, and so on. Speaking is a mode of dwelling, but awareness of the parts of speech can come only when children already know to speak correctly. Like the poets referred to above, children can describe what they are doing with the words of their language when they already have learned this language, including that language with which they describe the grammatical rules. In this section, I provide an empirical account of the movement from being unaware to being aware (of something).

Every single example of the phenomenon (becoming aware) already sketched in this preceding section would lend itself to deep analysis for the purpose of exhibiting the invariant features. However, none of the related studies produced enough data and sufficiently thick descriptions suitable to accomplish my purpose. Thus, the particular situation analyzed and described here is part of a growing database in which I document – in the form of descriptive notes, analyses, photographs, and other inscriptions – learning phenomena, especially learning phenomena of types that are not generally described in the learning sciences literature. For many years I have kept entries in my lab (research) notebook on particular learning phenomena (a) in which I had 'suddenly' realized something, that is, have had a 'sudden' insight or (b) when I tried remembering something but could not precisely because I did not know the thing to be remembered. The following is but one of those many instances I recorded, some of the very same nature under similar circumstances. Although in*sight* frequently goes with perception, becoming aware pertains especially to conceptual issues.

On July 23, 2013, I have gone on a bicycle ride around the peninsula on which I live riding northwards along the highway (Fig 6.2) when I am *becoming aware* of my lips forming the word 'temple' just as I am passing something that I now remember as a green 'sign'. The 'temple' is still ringing in the ears just after and although it has gone. I am aware of having articulated the word 'temple' just after having completed it. A fleeting thought concerns the question whether an arrow (←) has actually been there as well, but I am already past the two signs that are visible in Fig 6.2b and cannot not verify its presence. After the fact – when I will have passed by here a few days later, at which point I also take the photographs – the arrow clearly is there; and now that it is described, readers will see the arrow in the photographs (Fig 6.2). But in this case study, we have to place ourselves at a point in time when the subject (this author) is not yet aware of the existence of a street sign pointing the way to get to the temple. On that day, after just having passed what I *now* know to be a sign, I am becoming aware simultaneously of having formed the words 'Indian temple' and have come to grasp it *as* 'Indian temple'. However, just before that realization and *while* the 'Indian temple' is on my lips, I am not aware of it – until the ending '-ple' has been coming off them. At that instant, too, there is a fleeting image of greenness – gone but still resonating with/in me; I am associating it *after the fact* with the ground on which the 'Indian temple'

Fig 6.2 View of the highway during a bicycle trip while approaching an intersection. a. Farther away. b. About 100 m closer.

has appeared. Having passed what I now know to be the street sign, I can no longer verify it. At that time I am *becoming aware of* three facts, each pushing its way into my consciousness where they become what they are: (a) I have not known of the existence of a sign pointing to an Indian temple; (b) I have not known that close to where I live – an area predominantly populated by white working and middle class (94%) and indigenous populations – there is an Indian temple; and (c) I begin pondering where the temple might be because I have never seen it or known of it; and I begin pondering whether it might be something like a meeting hall rather than a building that stands out because of its architecture.

The type of occurrence just described is not singular. In the course of that summer, I was tuned into this phenomenon and recorded many such events. For example, on that same day, I also recorded becoming aware of something that dawned into my consciousness in the form of a brown patch, which when I was already past, I will have seen as a dog. Something was dawning, and there was a movement from an indefinite brown blotch to a definite dog. On another day, riding my bicycle along the same familiar route, I undergo precisely the same type of event with another road sign that I have never seen before during the sixteen years of passing there (Fig 6.3). Every time that I have passed the spot since then, I have been wondering about the fact that for such a long time I had not seen the road sign and had not been aware of its existence – though now it stands out so prominently *every* time I am passing. Before that first time, I could not precipitate its presence in my consciousness. Here I focus on the movement by means of which the unseen comes to be seen and thus comes to be present in and to consciousness. It may in-

Fig 6.3 I was passing this stretch of the road for sixteen years before I became aware of the road sign.

deed be a movement from the invisible, and comes to be the present but unseen after it has entered the visible and therefore is seen.

From these cases, described in greater detail for the 'Indian temple', we may learn five important lessons. First, we note that at least when we know and are aware of the road panel ('Indian temple'), it is quite prominent – at least when we are close up (Fig 6.2b). Despite this ex post facto prominence, and despite having cycled past this place for years, I was becoming aware of it only on that particular day. Although we tend not to pay attention to such phenomena as part of our everyday lives – these experiences do not come to stand out in our awareness as interesting phenomena at all – these are actually quite common. Both looking and the thing *precede* the awareness. Now that I know of the roadside panel, I can easily attend to its future appearance on the next bicycle trip that I take on this highway and I can talk about it and my initial encounter with it. That is, once I have become aware of the phenomenon I can make it present again (e.g. by re-imagining it), anticipate it, and do other things with it. But until the instance when becoming aware begins, and right to the presence of it in awareness, to construct is not an appropriate verb for describing my relation to it.

Second, we note that there are temporal delays during the movement of becoming aware. The awareness of something green and the awareness of having formed with my mouth and lips what will have been the words 'Indian temple' were aftereffects. That greenness initially was only indeterminate in my awareness in the same way as (a) a word is indeterminate when it only makes its way up to the tip of the tongue without actually emerging from our mouths and into our minds or (b) we almost come to visualize something without quite arriving there (called *presque vue* in psychology). There was something like an indeterminate greenness inscribed with white at the beginning of the movement of becoming aware without that I could know that such a movement was in its course. That is, even the description 'becoming aware' is possible only after the fact, when I know that I was becoming aware of the thing that now exists in my awareness. Up until this point, it is an *event-in-the-making* or *event**, where the nature of the 'event' is available only after the fact. That is, the expressions event-in-the-making and event* both are incorrect in a strong sense, for, while some happening is in its course, the whatness of the 'event' is unknown. We know what is happening only when the happening has come to the conclusion and when we know any outcome or products. At that point we can grasp what has gone on before as a specific type of event and thus name it (e.g. *that* dinner in Paris). It is only with hindsight that I will have been able to say that 'something drew my attention'. In fact, this last expression shows that we live the phenomenon as one in which *something else* is acting (active tense of 'drew'), and, being subject to this action, my attention *is drawn* (passive tense). In the final stages of becoming aware, the preceding indeterminateness still is resonating, a sense of an emerging greenness, the sense of having moved the lips prior to comprehending what was happening as my (unintended) reading of a text. These movements still linger, though they are definitely in the past. This is what Edmund Husserl refers to as *retention* – that aspect of the (specious) present that has the character of pastness.

By the time I grasp *what* there has been, a road sign that points to an Indian temple, I have already passed it. Perceiving and grasping also have ended once they yielded the perceived and grasped (note the past tense). The awareness of green was associated with something still resonating in *retention*, that is, after it already has gone from the retina. At best, there is a dim sensation that remains, not the awareness of some/thing or the awareness of a green color. Similarly, awareness of the *what* of the sounds coming off my lips has followed their actual movements. (Most people reading with their mouths forming the words are unaware of doing so.) More importantly, the grasp of the contents of 'Indian temple' has occurred even later than the awareness of the text. This relation between forming a word and comprehending it were becoming evident to me three weeks earlier, when I just had become aware of having passed a roadside sign. My becoming aware was correlated with the sounds /'ask ju:/ ('ask you'), /a 'skju/ ('a skew'), and /ə'skju:/ ('askew'). It is in the movement through the different pronunciations that I was becoming aware of having passed what I subsequently knew to have been a realtor sign carrying the name 'Paul Askew'. Once I had fully grasped, the thought emerges into my mind that the name lends itself to making jokes and that the person might have been teased or ridiculed for it. There is a clear movement, though while it is occurring, there is not and cannot be a sense of where it is going. Only while writing these lines, four years after the original event, do I learn about the fact that G. H. Mead has written about the phenomena in terms of a *specious present* that becomes extended so that a formerly unrecognized individual thing 'has been drawn out of the shadows, and, in this novel temporal perspective … becomes one more figure in the world'.[8] In none of these processes does something like *construction* occur – 'receiving' or 'being subject to something other than ourselves' are two better ways for describing and naming what we actually live through.

Third, once I have become aware of the white-on-green-background inscription 'Indian temple', once it has become present in/to my consciousness, I can make it *present* again (*re-*). That is, whereas the same roadside sign had been in all likelihood on my retina before, I could not make it present again as the object of my intentional activity. *Being aware* (consciousness) is associated with the faculty of making something present again. The object that stands out over and against me is tied to the possibility to make it present in its absence – to represent it. But, as the empirical data show, there is a delay between presence and awareness of presence, the latter always only following the former. Philosophers make this difference thematic in various ways. For Heidegger, the difference appears in the above-noted distinction of Being [*Sein*] and beings [*Seiendes*], the latter including the things (signs, words) that allow the former to be made present again, to be represented, and therefore to be present in conscious awareness. For Mead, objects have a distant character, which comes with the 'promise or threat of possible contact experience' and where 'the final contact is the experimental evidence of the reality of the promise which the object at a distant carried'.[9] Objects – i.e. things that stand out – have this character of the distant thing even when they are close enough to be touched.

Fourth, *becoming aware* is a movement in the course of which awareness becomes what it is: awareness of something. But the awareness of something as something is only the endpoint of the movement. It is only its result. The movement tends to be so fast that under most normal circumstances we are not aware of it. We therefore refer to it as *insight*: something is coming (suddenly) into sight. Precisely because agency is shifted here, the verb to construct once again turns out to be inappropriate. Having become aware of *becoming aware* especially during bicycle trips, I come to think that in this particular kind of event attentional processes are slowed down to the point that they may become objects to be studied systematically. Thoughts come to me during bicycle training when and while I am not at all seeking to think about research. This, too, is a common aspect of innovation and a topic of study by neuroscientists, psychologists, and phenomenological philosophers alike. What I describe here is the *coming* of a thought, the *becoming aware* of an idea. We could construct this thought only if we already knew it in advance – like the craftsperson who knows from experience approximately what the end result has to look like – and, therefore, could represent it. But thoughts are more like the result of dialogical processes and, therefore are as unpredictable as the outcomes of all dialogical processes.

The fifth important issue for theorizing learning pertains to the mode of *becoming aware*. Because I neither knew nor was aware of the road signs, or knew that there was a temple, I could not construct them. I can engage in any construction only if there is already something there. Again, there is a vast difference between constructivists, who literally turn everything on its (their own) head. They do not heed the suggestion of Marx and Engels that I repeatedly refer to above: not consciousness determines life, but life determines consciousness. It is the physical sign

'Indian temple' that provokes consciousness into becoming aware rather than consciousness that 'constructs' the 'Indian temple'. Moreover, I could not even consciously start off becoming aware, because the movement arrives at an object – I
become aware of *some/thing* – and this object inherently is available only after the
epiphanic event. Instead, I *find* myself comprehending after the fact rather than
having intentionally produced comprehension. I could not make the sign the intent
of learning precisely because I did not know (of) it. Rather, becoming aware generally and becoming aware of *becoming aware* specifically is associated with a
particular (*passive*) sensitivity, (willing) *receptivity*, and attention.

A Post-Constructivist Perspective on the Coming of Awareness

In this chapter, I direct attention to a phenomenon that under normal everyday
condition tends to be so fast that we do not heed it, fail to notice it, and, therefore,
that we are not becoming aware of it: the movement from unawareness to awareness, from not-knowing to knowing. The phenomenon is not just one of the perceptual kind; in fact, it is conceptual through and through, because in everyday life
we do perfectly fine perceptually without conceptual awareness (e.g. we are unaware of our surroundings while walking through a city and talking to a friend or
colleague). That is, although it may appear on quick reading that this chapter is
about perception, it is, on a deep level, concerned with awareness and therefore
cognition and mind.

   In the classical constructivist approach, we learn by interpreting the world. This
presupposes the existence of whatever is interpreted. Radical constructivists maintain that we never have access to the world but perpetually are caught in the con-
finement of our subjective minds so that even intersubjectivity is the result of a
subjective construction. The present study shows that the constructivist presupposition is unfounded. In this study, as in the third person studies of students and scientists referred to above, there is no evidence of some thing being in consciousness
that the learner interprets. Instead, it is only at the end of the movement from unawareness to being aware that something – a new object, a new sign, or a new idea –
comes to stand out. That standing out over against the subject (a) is modeled on the
emergence of the Self and the Other from social relations and (b) comes with a
representative capacity (it is representable and there is something who makes it
present by means of something other).

   My investigation shows that a distinction is to be made between a continuous
seeing (understanding) of some aspect and the dawning (becoming conscious) of
an aspect that has not existed for us before. I describe the movement denoted by
becoming aware, that is, how we are becoming aware of something before it can
become the object of our conscious and deliberate (constructive) activity. It is not
that we see and understand something *as* something, that is, that we *interpret* it as
something. Instead, we are confronted with the (perceptual, conceptual) thing that
appears in our consciousness: we are patients rather than agents of this process.
Even if we are asked to have to look differently at a situation, we sometimes can-

not help but continue seeing it in the way we have done up to now – which is the case because we do not understand a thing according to an interpretation. Many may initially see one thing in images of the duck–rabbit (Fig 3.2b, p. 45) type, and, when asked whether they see another thing as well, may respond 'I can't but help seeing …'. The nature of the thing *as* an object is tied to multiplicity of perspectives so that seeing something as something always includes the perspectives of the generalized other. In chapter 5 I refer to Ludwig Feuerbach, who realized that something really exists only when the Other and I can agree on this existence, that is, when it exists for me as it exists for others. In a strong sense, therefore, we are confronted with what *is given to* our perception and understanding simultaneously.

Individuals are positioned differently. The same (material, social) object may not be same for every individual – a phenomenon we are familiar with as soon as we move about in the world and in the different ways in which we are positioned with respect to the same thing. A material thing – commodity, word, or gift – has exchange value for one individual while simultaneously having use value for the recipient. This is tied to the different ways in which the individual Self is constituted – buyer and seller, speaker and listener, or giver and recipient. Again, as noted above, the relation between individual and material thing reflects the relation between people, and the relation between people reflects the relation between people and things. Mead, too, suggests that the existence of the object comes with the multiplicity of perspectives. There are many phenomena in the psychology of perception with which many readers will be familiar, including the dual images of (a) a vase / two faces, (b) an old / young woman, (c) a duck/rabbit, (d) the double Maltese cross, or (e) the double (Necker) cube. Such instances tend to be taken as the result of constructions, where a person is said to interpret some material substrate in one or another way. But saying that people *construct* what they see is not at all what happens (e.g. you do not construct the killer whale in Fig 3.2a [p. 45], but *it gives itself* after some gazing at the ensemble of black and white blotches). From a physiological perspective, the killer whale is seen when the eyes have followed a specific path given by the outline of what is seen (has become figure) and the saccades away from and back to it.[10] As noted above, we generally cannot help but perceive something in a particular way (a graph, a mystery object), and sometimes only with extended effort arrive at perceiving the thing in a different way. Similar phenomena are reported when studies suggest that students look at graphs and are said to iconically confuse them with other images (e.g. maxima and minima of a sine curve and the turns of a race track). The way in which we come to see and understand, or rather, in which we are becoming aware, does not tend to be studied at all; and yet, when we do study it, it turns out to be not well described by means of the constructivist metaphor.

Readers are familiar with the phenomena at issue here, though precisely when *becoming aware* has not arrived at its conclusion: the tip-of-the-tongue, *presque vu*, and I-forgot-what-I-wanted-to-say phenomena. In the tip-of-the-tongue phenomenon, something we are trying to remember or say has not quite made it to our awareness. We know we wanted to add to an ongoing conversation but forgot what we wanted to say. This would also be the case if I had not quite come to grasp that there had been something green, or if the 'Indian temple' had not quite made it into my awareness. We are aware that something was in the process of becoming aware, sufficiently into awareness to the point that we have experienced the early stages without actually becoming aware of the thing as such. In the I-forgot-what-I-wanted-to-say phenomenon, something that we were apparently aware of has disappeared and never made it into awareness so that we can no longer say what we wanted to communicate. But the disappearance is not complete, for there is a trace that allows us to be aware that something had been close to or already in awareness without there being a sufficient trace to know *what* it actually was. When we say that something 'was dawning on me', then we actually refer to a temporal nature of an appearance that was known as something only after it had fully appeared.

The empirical evidence points to the fact that initially there is nothing in perceptual experience that could be interpreted: in the way Birgit was unaware of the gap in the electrodes, I was unaware of the roadside sign. The upshot of this investigation is that I cannot construct something as something if there is no *thing* to begin with. If construction were to be an appropriate description (metaphor), then I would have to presuppose the (material) presence of the thing (e.g. the materially inscribed trace of 'Indian temple') in the way carpenters have plans for the houses they construct. As this chapter shows, the written is not present in/to consciousness. There is a movement by means of which we are becoming aware. After having become aware I can then begin to ponder where there might be an Indian temple, as suggested by the roadside sign. That is, whereas construction might be the appropriate metaphor for describing/theorizing what happened after I had become aware, and in the context of what I already knew (had been aware) concerning the geography of my municipality, that which is consistent with our understanding of learning, the arrival of something we had not known before, is precisely what escapes such a description. Therefore, *construction* is not the appropriate metaphor for describing and theorizing learning. Passive receptivity as condition and *becoming aware* – a unit including unawareness and awareness as two of its manifestations – constitutes a more accurate way of describing the arrival of the new, and, therefore, of learning. Mastery in learning, whether we consider a school student or a researcher, exists in the capability of *letting* the unseen surge into the visible *by surprise*. Because this occurs unpredictably, learners need to learn how to attend to these otherwise fleeting aspects of our lives.

In this chapter I provide a description and analysis of b*ecoming aware.* The movement includes being unaware, latent awareness, and full awareness. Each of these three dimensions is but part of the whole movement that cannot be further reduced. Because of this, *becoming aware* is an appropriate unit/category – in the sense of the unit analysis that is to replace analysis by means of elements – of *learning* because it embodies change. Unawareness, latent awareness, and awareness are but manifestations of the whole unit. It is a true unit of learning because it is a (holistic) category of *change* (rather than the difference between two things). The phenomenon of *becoming aware* shows that there is more to learning than construction. There is an essentially passive dimension of learning that lies in the blind spot of constructivism with its exclusive focus on agency at the expense of passibility. Precisely because we are unaware of some thing that we will eventually be aware of, we cannot make it the object of our intention. In our world, it initially is part of the invisible that will have been an unseen only after it has entered the visible when it is seen. Even if we know that there is something that wants to become aware – sufficiently so that we are aware of the process without knowing what it is that wants to become aware – we still cannot do much about it, especially we cannot construct the thing or awareness thereof. Watson was looking for the structure of DNA without knowing what it was. He thus was not in the position of the person looking for the proverbial needle in the haystack. Instead, he is better thought of as someone going through the haystack looking for something that he does not know what it is or, at best, that he knows he might know when he sees it. Readers will have been many times in situations, where they were close to remembering something without ever getting there despite all their efforts to make this something present again.

If learning were a simple matter of construction, then how the way in which we perceive something could be changed once we are told that matters are different than how these initially appeared to be. However, as described in chapter 5, even if told repeatedly by peers and teacher alike, Melissa continued to perceive a cube when tactually exploring the mystery object. In the way the physics professor referred to above 'could not help but see slopes', Melissa could not but feel a cube. In that instance, something occurred that we might take as a lesson in (natural) pedagogy: another girl (Jane) actually comes up with a form of instruction that allows Melissa to move through a process of becoming aware that the mystery object felt differently. Whereas Melissa first touches the mystery object and then molds the clay or shows with the clay model why the mystery object is a cube during the first seven explorations, Jane demonstrates how the mystery object and its model can be felt simultaneously. When Melissa does the same using Jane's plasticine model, we observe her undergoing a movement of becoming aware, which, once awareness has arrived, manifests itself in her face as surprise. A reshaping of her model follows. In this case, two movements occur simultaneously: an unperceiving of the mystery object as a cube and the simultaneous emergence of a rectangular prism. *Becoming aware* involves both processes: some thing or some aspect of the ground disappears while simultaneously a figure appears. The figure itself, as object, comes with the property of representability. This is also why the object is instructable: Jane and Sylvia can endeavor to teach Melissa what to do so that she can become aware of the rectangular prismic form. In Jane's instruction, we see what kind of pedagogies might work for teachers to assist their students more generally. For example, teachers might then think about strategies that have the potential of assisting the physicist Anne to change from seeing slopes to seeing the values of the curves. Pointing and tracing gestures may play an important role. There is a wide-open field of investigative possibilities concerning instruction that fosters *becoming aware*.

The first-person study employed here provides us with a means to describe learning phenomena not accessible in other ways and, importantly, to draw conclu-

sions with epistemological implications: the limits and limitations of a constructivist metaphor for learning. *Becoming aware* may be the quintessential learning phenomenon – we come to be aware and know something that we had not been aware
of and known before. Because of its essentially passive dimension, this learning
phenomenon is not and cannot be described by means of a constructivist metaphor.
The same method also underlies the next chapter dealing with the learning that
arises in the encounter of illness.

Notes

[1] Wolff-Michael Roth, *First-Person Methods: Toward an Empirical Phenomenology of Experience*
(Rotterdam: Sense Publishers, 2012), 31–34.

[2] George Herbert Mead, *Philosophy of the Act* (Chicago: University of Chicago Press, 1938), 88.

[3] Wolff-Michael Roth, *Passibility: At the Limits of the Constructivist Metaphor* (Dordrecht: Springer,
2011).

[4] Richard Rorty, *Contingency, Irony, and Solidarity* (Cambridge: Cambridge University Press, 1989),
12–13.

[5] Wolff-Michael Roth, 'Learning in the Discovery Sciences: The History of a "Radical" Conceptual
Change or The Scientific Revolution that Was Not', *Journal of the Learning Sciences*, vol. 23 (2014),
177–215.

[6] David Suzuki, *Inventing the Future: Reflections on Science, Technology, and Nature* (Toronto:
Stoddart, 1989), 192.

[7] Mead, *Act*, 275.

[8] Mead, *Act*, 94.

[9] Mead, *Act*, 76.

[10] I describe this phenomenon extensively in Roth, *First-Person Methods*, 15–41 (chapter 2).

7

The Invisible Body

In attempting to understand learning, research of all kinds and in many disciplines – education, learning sciences, psychology – focuses on the mind, mental processes, and conceptions. The constructivist metaphor is used in many other scholarly fields as well. The metaphor is principally concerned with the mind, which is seen as the locus of the world as we know it – based on the argument that there is no information transfer from outside to the inside, a point that Ernst von Glasersfeld took up from the Austrian physicist and philosopher Heinz von Foerster. Whereas cognitive approaches see their efforts thwarted when attempting to show the relevance of the metaphysical mind in a world that is material through and through, the idea that there is something essential about the fact that mind exists in and is associated with the body escapes all of the aforementioned approaches. Although Jean Piaget already emphasized the role of 'concrete' actions, the body really came to be the central theoretical entity in more recent embodiment and enactivist theories. But these theories do not show how we get from a material body to something like thought and mind. In each theory, the mind is already presupposed – e.g. in the form of schemas – to explain how the body provides the ground to thought. For example Piaget postulated that mathematical operations 'are less discovered in objects than deduced or abstracted with the subject's own operational structures'.[1] How the operational structures get into the mind is not explained. All such theories also have a problem with the way they theorize the social: it has to be constructed after or as part of the individual's own constructions. In contrast, there are approaches where mind is thought of as an emergent feature of dwelling (Being) that always already involves others. The Self and the other, the Self and the object, and the Self and awareness all emerge together in what may be denoted a cataclysmic event – of the type that in morphogenetic terms is a fundamental crisis or catastrophe. All of these are manifestations of a continuously evolving and changing, once-occurrent life that seems to have become invisible among stable things and structures. *Life, aliveness*, and *living* are precisely what escape the 'life' sciences because they focus on structures, things, and processes.

Perhaps the most important and untheorized aspect is that we all have not just one but multiple bodies. Before working through this issue and what it implies, I describe when these bodies became apparent to me for a first and rather striking manner.

In the two preceding chapters, I note that the perception of an object always implies the perspectives of the generalized other. In life, we do not tend to be aware of this fact but live within our own perspectives – though in situations of conflicting views, we are confronted with those of others. This stance toward the world through the individual perspective tends to dominate when we engage in some physical activity like cycling. We *feel* tired or feel that our legs are tired, and everything seems to be more difficult than at other times. We do not tend to think in such instances that when something stands out then we also can communicate it to others. Our own perspective and description always already implies the perspectives of others. As a result, what stands out – the object, word, other, or Self – is social.

One day on the bicycle, while looking down at my legs, I was struck: what I saw was not at all what I could feel. I did feel 'tired legs', but what I could see were legs that continued to pedal as if this was the most normal thing to do. There is nothing like fatigue that could be seen. My perspective on my own legs was that of a doctor confronted with a patient who talks about some ailment, which the doctor cannot perceive and, at best, is an ailment that manifests itself in this or that symptom. What I would provide to the physician is a verbal account of something in the world that he has no access to: it is abstracted and abstract. But for me, what I describe also exists in another modality. At the time, while I was riding the bicycle, I had the simultaneous experience of seeing the legs as another would see it and at the same time I was feeling the fatigue. The phrase, 'my legs are tired' *made sense* because of the *sense* in my legs. At that point in my ruminations, I began to think about the description Maurice Merleau-Ponty provides of a hand touching another hand, one doing the tactile exploration the other one feeling that something is happening to it, both touching and being touched.[2] This feeling of something can be communicated and felt by my listener, to whose hand I do the same – in the manner that Jane teaches Melissa to touch the mystery object in the way she also touched the plasticine model outside of the shoebox. In communication, we – Jane and Melissa or my physician and I – use language. But language never is our own so that the fatigue as it appears in my phrases is not mine.

What I describe thus far was only the beginning of my considerations. How is it possible, I asked myself, that I identify something *as* 'fatigue'. Fatigue is only the classification and explanation of something else of which I then *became aware*. Anything that stands out in my consciousness – as seen in chapter 6 – always already is something that stands because of the social relations underpinning consciousness in general. But, I was thinking at the time, what stands out for me in consciousness can only be a manifestation of something more profound. In what stands out as fatigue, my animate body (muscles) manifests the resistance of the body against its own effort. What normally appears effortless and has disappeared from consciousness now is lived as effortful. There is thus an invisible body that

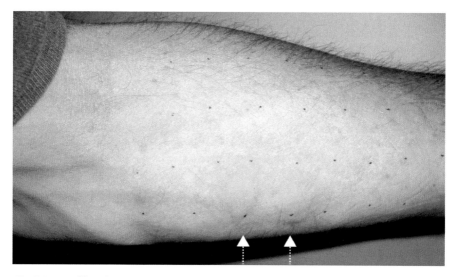

Fig 7.1   Manifestations of the living, animate body in the allergy test. The arrows mark those two of thirty-two testing points (plus two controls), each corresponding to a different substance, where irritations appeared and thus mark particular allergies.

manifests itself in some way – here by means of something that we have come to know and label as fatigue. This invisible body is life itself. It is invisible and only manifests itself in and by means of self-affections that are similar to symptoms – here symptoms of a *living* body the life of which is invisible, as if hidden in a black box. Rather than the two bodies that Merleau-Ponty is writing about – the touching and the touched – there are three bodies and three ways of appearance.[3]

First, there is the living, animate body – *der Leib* in German and *la chair* in French philosophy. In and as *living* phenomenon, it is inaccessible. This invisible, animate body knows itself better than we could describe in whatsoever explicit description – a fact that exhibits itself in the gap between plans – our own or those others provide – and our situated actions. However, although inaccessible, this living body, which knows itself rather than *about* itself, nevertheless is the seat of the most fundamental aspects of knowing – e.g. the movements of our vocal tracts producing the sounds of language, saccadic movements of the eyes that underlie the phenomenalization of stimuli into real objects seen, or the knowing ways in which athletes act appropriately at the right instant without having to spend a single thought. It is here that we are touched – someone else cannot ever know what I feel as *my* pain – and that affect is situated. All those different tests that I was submitted to when doctors tried to find out the origin of my chronic fatigue, all those recordings that resulted (e.g. the one determining allergies, Fig 7.1), were actually missing the living, animate body that only *manifested* itself in various ways, in the symptoms of my mysterious illness. That is, we can only live but never access through discourse this 'real biological [i.e. living] phenomenon' as some believe it to be possible; talk and argumentation alone will never get us to live this phenomenon. Talking and writing *about* undergoing extreme passivity *is not* this passivity itself, is not the real feeling and sense thereof. We may *talk about* pathos – suffering – but will not truly understand, not be able to have em*pathy*, without having undergone in flesh and blood such pathos ourselves.

Second, there is the transcendental body, the one we are aware of subjectively, such as when we feel something in a muscle that we identify *as* 'pain'. This no longer is the invisible, animate body but the one that stands out, the one that has transcended the originary body that knows itself. Standing out means standing out in consciousness. The original body is accessible only subjectively; but the transcendental body, because it stands out against a background and has become a thing, inherently is social. My pain, though experientially real, is always my pain and nobody else can feel it. At the same time, standing out makes it namable, and both the name and the standing out is possible because our relation with others. For the infant, the discomfort of whatever kind does not stand out; and we can only ever guess what it might be based on what we have done just prior to the infant stopping to cry.

Third, there is the constituted body, that is, my body as body among bodies as it is accessible to others, doctors, scientists, nurses, and the like. This is the objective and objectified body.

The second and third appearances of the body also have been referred to as the constituting (sensorimotor) and constituted (objective) body. These two bodies are closely related. This is so because, as philosophers of very different ilk (e.g. Edmund Husserl and George Herbert Mead) have pointed out, I could not know another person to be angry or melancholic unless I had not already adopted the other's viewpoint on my own behavior. To be able to see a behavior as melancholic, I have to see together at once what stands out for me within and what others can see me doing from without. This is the condition for me to see and understand the bodily manifestations of another as melancholic. Unless they have gone through the relevant form of suffering themselves, common 'healers' – surgeons, physicians, priests, psychologists, psychiatrists, and the likes – only know the suffering symbolically, abstractly, but never concretely, never in the real form that it affects persons and their living, animate bodies. *Em*pathy is impossible when we have not undergone the same pathic experience. Already Spinoza realized that the pleasure arising from seeing our enemy suffering from some harm is associated with some feeling of pain on our part.[4]

The second and third bodies are known, transcendent, and thus not the bodies of passion (pain). It is only in the first body that pain and other passions are lived; it is only through the third body (external world) that I can share descriptions with others that then can be used to make, in the second body, a relation is established between my animate and my constituted body as an objectified entity. Together, these three bodies are required for *sympathy* and *empathy*. The first, invisible body is that of suffering. It is the ground for anything that can be articulated about my body, on the part of others (e.g. doctors) or on the part of the Self (e.g. when I describe what I feel).

Educators think about and make connections between learning, the body, and relevance. Thus, 'hands-on', 'experiential learning', and associated expressions have become rallying cries for many, even though schools by and large still teach in traditional ways that favor rote learning. Objects in the natural world are easily shared, because all participants in a learning situation have equal access to it – e.g. a hands-on experiment or science demonstration – these externalities do not really 'touch' us but are accessed via representations (e.g. words, images, graphs, and numbers). There are phenomenological reasons why the objectified world, though coming into being through our kinestheses, comes to be lived as separate from us. This separation – or, as materialist philosophers tend to prefer to say, this alienation – underlies the very split between knowing as it arises from being-in the world and knowing-about the world. The body plays a role in conceptual understanding that educators have not yet theorized: incarnation and the animate (living) body. In continental philosophy, there is a tradition of theorizing the material and the suffered body as distinct. This requires different concepts, which exist in the pairings Körper / Leib (Ger.) and corps / chair (Fr.) that are sometimes in the literature rendered as body / flesh but here are referred to as body / animate body.

The first body is of interest to education because it is here that we are really (rather than symbolically) affected. Health issues are of particular import to learning, because what we live (undergo) in our animate bodies and as incarnate beings – e.g. the source of pain, suffering – is inaccessible to another person in contrast to objects and phenomena (objectified forms) in the environment. At the same time, precisely because health *affects* us, it *touches us* physically and emotionally – it is a pathic phenomenon before it can be a mental phenomenon. Undergoing any surgery but undergoing a liver or heart transplant specifically fundamentally changes the ways in which we understand and relate to the environment.

There is confusion about what '"embodied" knowing' means because in the literature there tend to be only two bodies that are made thematic in the distinction of knower and known. Both of these bodies are related to forms of knowing that already are symbolic (philosophers use the technical term *transcendent*) and the relationship of these bodies need to be understood for arriving at an appropriate epistemology – one required to make the kind of link between environment, health, and knowledge that the post-constructivist epistemology elaborated here is all about. To understand the role of pathic phenomena in our lives, and, therefore, the role of the pathic in *all* of our knowledge, we need to understand the triple nature of our bodies. In this chapter, I achieve two related aspects. First, I propose a different epistemology grounded in the human capacity to suffer and be affected (i.e. possibility). Our suffering is not a human, individual or social construction, but real, felt, and predating any conception that we may have of pain. Second, precisely because being affected and suffering are fundamental to knowing, I propose it as a starting point and ground for thinking about and doing education. I start the reflection with an account of a long-standing illness that neither standard nor alternative medicines got into their grips. This illness taught me a lot about knowing and learning; and it was an integral part of my own changing epistemology that led me from the radical and social constructivist of my early career to the post-constructivist position articulated here.

A Mysterious Illness …

In this section, I articulate the different attempts to locate an illness. The failure to get a hold of it lies in part because the search is inappropriate, for it seeks to deal with the *manifestations* of a living thinking body, which is invisible even to our own consciousness that is but an instance of collective consciousness. This invisibility is the core of Spinoza's *Ethics*, where both the material body and thought are but two manifestations of a single and unitary *substance*; and it is central to a philosophy of the animate body (flesh).[5] As soon as I articulate something, it is but a manifestation of something else. And this something else remains invisible – including to myself. It retreats whenever we think we have grasped a hold of something and, in so doing, bring something from the realm of the invisible into the visible, revealing the now-seen as the previously unseen.

… in Flesh and Blood

One day in the summer of 2002 – having just arrived in my office to get ready for teaching a graduate class that afternoon – 'I' was all of a sudden struck by an extreme sensation of fatigue. In fact, there was neither an 'I' who felt nor a 'me' that was affected: there was but an intense sensation. It was so intense that it became impossible to decide what to do next. I did not know what had hit me, and the feeling was like the proverbial 'hitting of the brick wall'. There was just abandonment. I woke up some time later on the floor right at the place where I remembered to have stood last. A similar incidence occurred a few days later at home, where 'I' could not even decide to take the few steps to the couch only three meters from me to rest or sleep but dropped right where I stood, in the middle of the kitchen and on the tiled floor. The experience of passivity was radical in a double sense: (a) what was happening to me was not the result of intent but pure passion and (b) 'I' did not even have a choice of wanting to do something or not. Over the next few weeks, I found in and through my animate body–me that the fatigue was paired with the difficulty to recover from exercise. A day with a bicycle tour (short compared to what I had been doing before) was followed by a day when the legs felt tired and a subsequent day when I could hardly ride at all, requiring a resting day before I could start with light exercise. Using the stairs from the lower to the upper level of the house became difficult and almost impossible.

... in the Standard Medical System – Take 1

My family physician, worried that I might not get sufficient sleep, prescribed sleeping pills. Although I tend to be skeptical about medication, I was willing to try but abandoned when I experienced the stated side effects – including frightening nightmares and extreme sweating – after the first couple of times that I took the pills. He was also concerned that a chronic sinusitis was keeping me from breathing well and prescribed a steroid drug, which again only dealt with the symptoms rather than the causes. He said that someone eating as healthy as I do *could not be* ill and that I was in better shape than ninety-five percent or more of men my age. I had been tested, among others, for anemia, which would have expressed itself in fatigue. However, my father-in-law, a family physician in France, suggested that the problem might not at all be with regular anemia but with storage iron (ferritin) levels. The tests that I requested here in Canada revealed just that. My physician recommended supplementation. A follow-up test three months later revealed little change – my levels still were subnormal. He recommended doubling the dose: A follow-up test two months later showed that I was just below the threshold. He recommended tripling the normal dose of supplementation. Another three months later, the levels had crept just into the normal range. During this time, no other options were pursued as the physician wanted to eliminate 'one possible cause at a time'. The 'fatigue', however, stayed with me.

The physician then suggested testing whether I suffered from allergies. The allergist conducted a standard test for about thirty-two different substances; the test was positive for dust and mites (Fig 7.1). He recommended special bed sheets and other (expensive) things that I could buy from the store associated with his office. The doctor was relatively uninterested in the fact that I had been proactive by removing all wall-to-wall carpets and runners suspecting that I was allergic to dust, which was born out by the fact that a chronic sinusitis had diminished. I had already experienced the relationships between the environment and personal health. For example, over a forty-year span, my chronic sinusitis problems increased and became more intense when I lived in humid climates (e.g. Mississippi or Ontario in the summer). Symptomatically, when the conditions are very dry, such as in desert climates or on an airplane, there is no obstruction of the nasal passages whatsoever. I also had undergone a change when, in the early 1980s, I removed all carpets from a house I owned and replaced them with ceramic tiles and wood floors. There was a drastic decrease in the seriousness of the problems.

The rheumatologist conducted a number of tests and ordered X-rays. On the day I saw him to receive the results, I had particularly strong pains in my joints, especially the upper arm / shoulder (glenohumeral) and knee joints (femur / tibia, femur / patella). The rheumatologist, however, said that I there was nothing wrong with me. My living body-me was invisible to him. Even I did not recognize myself – the real me that was the source of what stood out for me and what I described as pain – in the X-rays that he had asked to be taken of my joints. He was not looking at *me* but at a representation, a manifestation of something from which the passion had been stripped. Not having access to my passion – singularized in and through my animate body – he could only rely on what the X-ray photographs showed: nothing, because what there really was had not externalized itself to make it onto his photographic plates.

I underwent repeated neurological testing, by the same and by different neurologists. Having participated in scientific research that measured the propagation of (heat) waves through human oral tissue, I found the tests interesting as the different graphs shows lag times in the pulses traveling through left and right leg. The neurologists in my city ultimately decided that there is a high likelihood of a neurodegenerative disease, a form of multiple sclerosis, with a small (5%) likelihood that I could be suffering from amyotrophic lateral sclerosis (ALS or 'Lou Gehrig's disease'). This is a degenerative motor neuron disease with a mean life expectancy of about three years – though a very small number of people, like the physicist Stephen Hawking, might be living more than fifty years after being diagnosed with the disease and given two years to live. In my case, only further testing would disconfirm or confirm this hypothesis.

The effect of the ALS diagnosis tremendously *affected* us (my partner and me), emotionally and cognitively. Three long months of waiting for admission to the premier specialist in my province followed. My wife and I considered various options and needs, like a ramp to permit wheelchair access to our home. Finally, during the examination, the prime neurologist of our province said that he understood why previous doctors were thinking that I might have ALS but that I did not have this illness based on what he knew from his long professional life.

While discussing these latest results with my family physician, he said that we had now exhausted all avenues and that – because the symptoms persisted – I should perhaps try alternative medicines (health providers).

... in Alternative Medicine

Stimulated and encouraged by the physician's advice, I began to search the Internet on alternative medical approaches but ultimately relied on recommendations for whom to consult with. The first doctor was a former graduate of my own university (BSc) who had specialized in traditional Chinese medicine (TCM) and also obtained degrees in the relevant medical fields. During the one-hour intake interview, he made some very quick diagnoses that became the basis for the treatment. Based on the color of my fingernails, he decided that I most likely had vitamin B12 deficiency and he recommended a special product (expensive) that he sold in his practice. Most striking, however, were the final phrases he articulated while I was in the process of leaving. He said that if the symptoms persisted despite taking the medication he had prescribed, I could return two weeks later for another half-hour visit, during which he could also provide me with a vitamin B12 injection.

I did purchase the recommended oral vitamin B12 supplement, but I did not return even though the symptoms did not abate. I made this decision not to return because there had been no difference with the regular medical field that I had experienced – a rapid diagnosis along one dimension without investigation of the person-in-his-setting, no inquiry into my lifestyle, no attempt to understand nutrition, exercise, and the person-environment interactions.

Although I had decided not to seek further help in the alternative medical field, two colleagues – she working in my faculty, he an internationally renowned scientist who often appears on TV – recommended another alternative health provider who apparently had assisted them with what had been a long-term ailment. I gave it another try. Here, the intake interview only cost $25 and led to a list of recommended testing procedures – which, as I later found out from the secretary, would have come to nearly $800 (to be born by the patient, as the insurances do not cover costs from alternative health providers). I told the secretary that I would consider first and noted some of the recommended tests for checking them out through online searches.

I had been immediately suspicious when the TCM practitioner expressed astonishment over the fact that I had gold crowns. For me, with graduate work in physical chemistry, the choice had been evident – gold is one of the least reactive materials and much better than the lead-based amalgamate fillings that contribute to heavy metal load in the body. In his opinion, the electrical potential between the crown and the cheek could be problematic to the health of a person. When I told my dentist about these claims, she only laughed and confirmed my suspicion that there was no (scientific) evidence that gold crowns were leading to problems, even though websites for alternative (holistic) health do claim allergies due to certain dental materials – generally amalgamates – as inducing health problems such as chronic fatigue and chronic inflammatory changes (rheumatoid arthritis, fibromyalgia, chronic neurological illness). I remained skeptical even though there appeared to be a link between the symptoms associated with the dental material and the possible diagnoses in the regular medical field.

The second test that I researched more closely concerned *Candida albicans.* In both regular and alternative health fields, this diploid fungus has been identified as a major concern (e.g. among immuno-compromised patients). Online, I found several questionnaires that are used to identify candida-related health symptoms and history. They all turned out negative. Thus, for example, on one questionnaire, my responses to nineteen out of twenty questions fell on the negative side so that there should have been little concern for an experienced health provider for pursuing this line of research – especially when the test to be conducted was to be one of the more expensive ones. My Internet research did not turn up the evidence required to reject the suspicions that there was little if any evidence that would have warranted the procedures and tests that this alternative health provider recommended.

... in Self-help and Changing Lifestyle

I had read on the Internet that there were individuals using marihuana to deal with the pain associated with chronic fatigue syndrome. At the time, this drug already was legal in Canada when prescribed by a health professional and was accessible through passion clubs. However, in the relevant culture, the officially grown plants are held to be less effective and helpful than the locally (sometimes illegally) grown variants. I did grow some plants, as there were no legal proceedings against individuals growing small numbers of plants grown for personal use. After a spring and summer in my greenhouse among tomato plants, I obtained what I needed to conduct my own tests. I found out that I did not like the effect that smoking had on my lungs, and did not think that it was compatible with my extended physical exercise. I also did not like the rapid effect it had on the mind, which made it impossible for me to do my academic work. On the positive side, the pain disappeared as anticipated. I experimented with ways of incorporating it into food materials (cookies). I found out that the active chemical in cannabis, tetrahydrocannabinol (THC), is fat- rather than water-soluble. The recommendations therefore include preparing extractions by placing powdered bud or leaf materials in heated butter prior to using it in cooking. After some experimenting with carefully weighed amounts, I found out the exact amount to be eaten to ease the pain without affecting my ability to do my regular work. There was a strange sensation of the pain disappearing and a prickling feeling, like heat, that was rising in the body right up to the earlobes while simultaneously leaving the forehead cool. I found out about the temporal lag between the two forms of taking: smoking affects the brain within minutes whereas the effects of ingested THC are noticeable only after several hours. It also constitutes an effective assistance to sleeping, because it led to better (deeper) sleep without any effects noticeable in the morning upon awaking and getting up. I told my physician. He was concerned because of the legal aspect of what I was doing; but he took note in my medical record that I was responding positively to this form of self-medication.

My continued research on the Internet and in databases of the regular medical literature (e.g. using databases such as Thompson ISI Web of Science) turned up positive study effects of dry sauna on symptoms associated with chronic fatigue syndrome, such as joint pain and muscle aches. In 2006, my wife and I decided to purchase a sauna. Within less than two weeks of daily sauna, the fatigue symptoms were easing and the joint pain was completely gone. I instantly stopped the self-medication with THC.

At the same time, my wife and I decided to go completely organic, in part because of the reports that autoimmune deficiencies may be associated with chronic fatigue syndrome, fibromyalgia, and other chronic illnesses. We expanded the summer-only garden into a year-round and permaculture installation and began to grow all vegetables and berries we eat and many of the fruit – a clear attempt to contribute to resilience, that is, the ability of animate systems to protect themselves and heal. In the process, I found out about environmental issues, growing conditions, requirements, and about the relative resistance of the plant to pests, allowing them to be grown without pesticides and herbicides. We also became members of an organization that fostered green corridors for different forms of wildlife – insects and birds in particular – to use during their migration.

... in the Standard Medical System – Take 2

Although the sauna regime had helped ease the problem, there was now an ebb and flow, with periods where the fatigue-related symptoms all but disappeared and periods characterized by more extensive fatigue. I returned to the physician to ask for assistance, which led to a new cycle of investigations. I first was sent to the neurologist, who conducted the same kinds of tests as before. I also was sent to the hospital to have my blood oxygen levels monitored over night using a clip fixed to a finger (pulse oximetry). Because of some confusion, I was not informed about the test results and my physician, who had received the results, had not red them and did not ask me for a consultation during which the results could be discussed. It turned out afterward that the results were negative (no apparent variations in blood oxygen levels) and would not have warranted the more advanced tests in the sleep clinic.

In the meantime, the neurologist had requested a session in the sleep clinic. On the eve when the tests were to be conducted, probes were attached to various parts of my body, especially to my head (Fig 7.2). The technician asked me to sleep in a way that the probes would not come off. As a result, I had to sleep on my back – which led to the most horrible night I had ever lived through, waking up more frequently than I normally do, with nightmares, sweating, and a lot of discomfort. I got up in the morning feeling having had any rest whatsoever. The thought came to my mind that the test conditions themselves had contributed to the results. How can you sleep wired up in a way that forces you into particular (even unnatural) body position? The diagnosis was that there were about twenty apnea episodes per hour, where the areal track was obstructed completely (e.g. because of a collapse of the structures in the back of the mouth) leading to a stop of breathing until the choked body came up for oxygen; there were forty such episodes during the REM period of sleep. As before, although I found the (multitude of) graphs interesting, as the processes involved in reading them, I could not see *myself* in the representations that displayed on the gigantic monitors in the control room. My bodily me was (made?) invisible in the technology-driven efforts of the sleep clinic. What can be seen in all the numbers and graphs on the monitor can be likened to the prints of feet on the forest floor, which never are the animate body that left them behind. But as a result of his interpretation of the graphs, which did not show the real *me*, the doctor listed three options that would *affect* my life: surgery, oral appliance (the U.S. FDA lists many different forms), and a device referred to as CPAP (continuous positive airway pressure). He advised against the first two and recommended the third option (here, too, sold in the associated store). He asked me for another session – which I believed to be another testing session to see whether a CPAP would change my sleep. I found out only after the test that the session was intended to fit the appropriate mask that I had not even agreed to purchase.

Fig 7.2 Means to register the manifestations of the animate body in the sleep clinic. a. The different probes attached to the body enter a data collection box ultimately connected to a computer. All over the body, there are probes and the wiring harness has to be kept in place by straps. A wonder if anyone can actually sleep under such conditions.

I had done considerable research on obstructive sleep apnea by the time I came for the second session. I was not convinced that a CPAP would improve our (my wife and my) quality of life. I did find two alternatives: (a) mouth exercises to strengthen the muscles in the back of the mouth, which prevents it from collapsing and (b) didgeridoo playing, which has the same effect. There were controlled medical studies on each of these methods with patients who had moderate levels of obstructive sleep apnea (about twenty episodes per hour). Both treatments had lowered, on average, the incidence from just over twenty to about eleven episodes per hour within three months. I left copies of the studies with the sleep clinic. The night was even worse, as all masks the technician tried on me gave me the sensation of drowning – as I could not breath against the minimum pressure. At midnight, I called the technician and offered him without alternative: to led me sleep without CPAP or I would drive home immediately. Because of legal implications if I were to have an accident, he led me sleep without CPAP. I returned for a final interview. The specialist's conclusion was that the device was not working for me and that I probably could live without one, because the apnea was considered moderate. He laughed off the possibility of the alternative treatments.

... *Becoming Chronic Fatigue*

Medical didgeridoos are available in Europe (Switzerland) where it is also possible to receive training in playing the instrument. With information again culled from the Internet I constructed a cheap alternative: a didgeridoo from black ABS plastic pipe. I also perused videotaped lessons from YouTube. I did the mouth exercises. In the course of the next three months, my sleep improved and I began to feel better. I later learned that when, for a variety of reasons, I did not get to do the mouth exercises for several weeks, the apnea episodes became noticeable and I repeatedly woke up at night with a racing heart, something I did not experience during periods with regular practice.

I had not stopped to look for information. Periodically I conducted researches on the Internet. In 2012, following a move to Australia and living without a house and garden to care for, I spent more time exercising. I had symptoms of fatigued muscles that did not recuperate. At that time, I made two discoveries: most of the same symptoms also were associated (a) with gluten intolerance and (b) lack of protein. I had repeatedly pointed out to my family physician something I had noted: A strong odor of ammonia after exercise, especially noticeable when I wore a rainproof jacket, which concentrated moisture from sweat on its inside. A further Internet research showed that a lack of protein in the food leads to the muscle protein to break down and to be consumed. In the process, ammonia is produced. Whereas it is normally passed out with urine, during heavy exercise it leaves the body with sweat and, because its levels increase in the body, it also leads to immediate fatigue because of effects on the brain and long-term fatigue because of the loss of protein in muscle.

I made two nutritional changes that had tremendous effects on life. I changed to a gluten-free diet, which led to almost immediate decrease of some symptoms (e.g. tremendous levels of bloating). I ate more regularly and supplemented my vegetarian diet with levels plant-derived (complementary) proteins at levels recommended for those on heavy exercise regimes. Within a few weeks, I was able to expand from the 100–150 km per week exercise regime to 450 km and more per week. The average speed on the tours increased to rates that were similar to those twenty years earlier, at an age of forty. Interestingly enough, a high quality of plant-based protein comes from hemp, the same plant that also produces the THC and that can be grown, because of its resilience, without pesticides and herbicides.

Together with these exercise-related changes, my capacities at work also increased. I was able again to work at the desk for eight to ten hours, as I had been able to do prior to the onset of the debilitating fatigue. At last, a sense had emerged of having conquered decade-old problem. I know that I have to continue the mouth exercises, because after having stopped or been slack about them, I experienced an increase in apnea – which I know to have occurred when I wake up with increased heart rates and less than the required sense of rest when I get up in the morning.

Pathos and Learning

In the preceding account, two kinds of data are presented. The first kind of data point to the incarnate experience of a chronic illness; because of its singularity, it cannot be shared. What does stand out and can be named and shared inherently is social and cultural by definition: any thing is a reality for two or it is nothing at all, a realization that L. S. Vygotsky writes in the final paragraphs of the last, posthumously published *Thinking and Speech*. But the source of the singularity is not some Self (identity). Instead, the source is the animate body, the aliveness of which is invisible. Whatever the various instruments and test results showed, are but manifestations (symptoms) of an animate (living) body, not the body, not life itself. Because biology only deals in manifestations, that is, in externalities, its very object escapes that science: life ('bio-'), which only manifests itself in rather than being the material body. In the same way, because psychology only studies externalities – whether manifestations of the psyche (mind) in some recording device or through verbal accounts of people involved in studies, it misses its phenomenon: the life of mind in the service of life.[6] The second point pertains to cultural practices related to different medical systems (standard, alternative, and self-help medicine). The purpose of the analysis is to extract from the accounts what is generalizable and independent of any purely singular experiences.

Pathos and its Relation to Knowing

From the preceding account we can learn that there exists a radically passive form of experience, something that transcends all knowledge and self-knowledge, all forms of 'I feel like …', 'This hurts …', or 'I know …'. Illness teaches us that we are exposed to the self-affections of the body prior to any conceptualization thereof and which manifest themselves in ways that we name illness, pain, or fatigue. Long before I became aware of yet another freckle in my face, my animate body had changed; and between my becoming aware and the diagnosis of melanoma in that spot, another two years had passed. It is only *after* we are already affected that a something comes to stand out as something to be articulated in words. It is only after having been affected that fatigue and pain become what they are, phenomena we can name; it is only after having been affected that I can name the melanoma-turned freckle. In what happened there to me was more passive than any passivity, any non-engagement I could think about and enact towards something by opting out or 'not doing a thing'. In that latter case I am still making a decision.

In and through the encounter with a chronic illness and the related analyses that followed, I came to understand (a) not only the role of pathos in illness but also (b) the foundational role of the pathic in all forms of knowing and (c) the point of breakdown of currently dominant (constructivist, structure / agency) epistemologies, which fail to account for the pathic. Prior to all knowledge and intention of an agential subject, an illness, as all pathic phenomena, is an event* that we are subject and subjected to. We are affected in dwelling prior to any conceptualization as such. Most importantly, in dwelling we are in relation with and thus affected by others before a separation can exist between the Other (being, object) and the Self (subject). Other and Self are the result of what has happened involving the relationship of two or more people in the ongoing event of life. Affection arrives prior to knowledge of causes, which, in the present instance, never were articulated with any certainty. Before he could comprehend what Fran had said, Graham already has been affected by what had been coming at him (see Fig 2.4, p. 26); before you will have been conscious of the orca, the light coming from that part of the page will have changed your retina (see Fig 3.2, p. 45); before Melissa could be aware of the mystery object to be a rectangular solid (rather than a cube), she already had been affected by the object; and before I could grasp the 'Indian temple' and even realize its nature as a road sign (Fig 6.2, p. 112, I had been affected in various ways. Any consciousness, any grasp of anything, presupposes having been affected, having been subject and subjected to specific conditions in which we always also are agential subjects.

Whereas it is possible to talk *about* pain – e.g. in the knee or shoulder joints – this talk is not the living phenomenon itself. The study shows that the pathic experience of the living thinking-body is inaccessible to the doctors. The sleep specialist has not had the experience of living with apnea or the rheumatologist of living with chronic pain in the joints. These doctors had only symbolic access: They knew *about* the symptoms but could not em*pathize* what it is to live (undergo) what I myself denote by the words pain and fatigue. I came to understand that they had only symbolic mastery: The doctors were talking about and attempting to treat something that they *literally* did not know. They only knew *about* living with these phenomena through the descriptions patients provided, who could use nothing but language to describe (more or less adequately) what stood out in their consciousness. This consciousness is tied to the language we have; the language is a manifestation of consciousness for others as for the self. The Aristotelian term *apophansis* points us to the relation between a perceived phenomenon and speech: As apophansis, logos allows that of which language speaks to reveal itself from itself. But that which does not stand out, the *living* body, inherently cannot be made thematic – thus the difficulties to communicate health-related issues or competent skills.

Although it might be impossible to describe in any unique way some taste or smell, we do recognize them and vividly remember living through related, specific situations – a result of the living body moving through the same series of sensations that it has undergone before. Indeed, we undergo again the smelling and tasting, and whatever stands out in our memories is tied to that re-living of the smells and tastes. Such a situation is described in a core scene of *Remembrance of Things Past*[7], a novel frequently cited in psychological works on how the implicit human memory works. In that famous passage, Marcel Proust notes that we could not ever *know* in the sense of (intellectually) grasp the senses and associated sense but only witness over and over again when we actually smell and taste – in his case the 'petite madeleine' dissolved in a spoon of tea. As hard as the author-protagonist tried, he could not remember the situation when and where he had undergone this particular smell and taste. Until, 'all of a sudden', memory *returned to him*. The author earlier had noted that it was not the madeleine and tea combination but something in him; at the same time, it was not his intellectual, archeological endeavor that was able to return to him the memory of the first time that the smell and taste had occurred to him. Unexpectedly, however, the memory returned, where the adverb 'unexpectedly' denotes the fact that his intellectual endeavors could not see (grasp) and foresee that memory. It is precisely that invisible body that eventually made it available again.

Doctors may talk about a particular form of pain and look for its causes without ever actually having been subjected to it. In this case, the doctors literally do not know *what* they are talking about, though they know the discourse for talking *about* the phenomena. The sociologist Pierre Bourdieu thus distinguishes between the two associated forms of mastery: symbolic and practical.[8] Symbolic mastery is related to observing, even when it occurs on the part of the practitioner; and practical mastery exists in the doing. This practical mastery and its recognition reside in a 'practical *sense*', the literal translation of Bourdieu's book title, which is a very different way of naming the issue than the Anglo-Saxon 'logic of practice'. The practical *sense* orients us to the way in which we sense and feel the world and what we do, which does not have to be *logical* at all. All of these considerations point us to the existence of forms of knowing that we cannot access by symbolic means precisely because they do not exist in the transcendental form and, therefore, cannot be talked about inherently. If we knew what the embodied knowing of a Tiger Woods or a Maria Sharapova consisted of or if 'bodily schema' were an appropriate representation thereof, we could teach it others. This bodily knowing, as pain and fatigue, are pathic modes given to us in our living, animate bodies. We can only know these by living them, and this is why they are the closest to us. These pathic modes of our lives are singular in and to our bodies, and, precisely for this reason, connect with us. The pathic modes are also the very foundation of empathy and sympathy, forms of affect that we are endowed with because of the pathic modes of living and which we cannot have without the pathic.

Science and Alienation

The presented case exemplifies how in seeking the causes of the illness, the different kinds of doctors – general practitioners, neurologists, allergists, rheumatologists, and alternative healthcare professionals (TCM, naturopathic) – focus on the material, objective and objectified body rather than on the larger context of an open, dynamic body in a dynamic environment. Characteristic of the approach in all cases is (a) a one-variable focus at any one time rather than a complex ecological approach of a dynamic, inherently open system; (b) a lack of allowing patient to participate, for example, by requesting a precise logging of food and exercise; (c) an absence of listening the whole range of symptoms and possible causes, failure to look at interactions of multiple variables; and (d) a failure to communicate

and thereby allow and enable the patient to become an integral part of the investigative process. That is, the members of each profession use a limited arsenal of
devices and approaches rather than studying the person-in-his-daily-environment.
In the end, the medical system, unable to locate the illness in the body, abandoned
(in my case) all attempts in finding a solution to the illness, leaving the patient to
figure out how to live in the face of pain and fatigue. Importantly, the one-factor-
at-a-time approach, while it may be scientifically appropriate, was associated with
an extended period of lack in quality of life, especially when the avenue pursued
turns out to be inappropriate – as in the case of the ferritin. Although the levels
were inappropriately low, it may have been a minor aspect in the range of causa-
tions.

The medical practices not only miss the living body but also, in singularly focusing on the objectified body *in itself*, also fail to investigate the body-in-the-
environment. All medical practices attempt to locate illness in the material body of
the person rather than taking a broader, environmental perspective. Thus, conditions and well-being related to environmental factors and transactions with the
environment, for example, in nature and quality of foods, thereby never can become facts to enter diagnosis and treatment. Especially those factors that could
pinpoint problems arising from the relations with the environment and those related to life-style-driven environmental conditions are not pursued. This is consistent
with the much publicized searches for treatments of cancer or obesity that affect
the individual body, which can then be treated by medication-based (quick) fixes.
This approach eschews and makes us blind to any attempt and political need to
find and address (possible) causes that arise from pesticide load in the environment, heavy metal load in certain foods, chemical contaminants, and so on. In a
broader perspective, it is possible to theorize an integral relation between environmental health and human health. 'Treatments', therefore, would begin with rigorous implementation of policies that decrease environmental factors that mediate
human health.

During the investigation, neither the doctors from the regular medical system
nor those practicing alternative medicine drew on what we might call the natural
expertise of people. Although environmental medicine emphasizes the need of
collaboration between patient and health practitioners, the patient is present in such
approaches only as an objectified body. The patient is not involved in the process
of finding out about the illness or in the collection of the relevant data. In my particular case, although there could have been a particular appeal to involve the person, because of my science and research backgrounds – e.g. by producing a dispassionate, precise protocol of nutrition and lifestyle – there was never an attempt to
bring about or encourage such collaboration. A log of all activities, all food intake,
and any other possibly factor in a log would have enabled an extensive examination of a range of factors.

In the course of living whatever the illness (and investigation), I learned about
science and its application, through the way in which it was individual doctors and
the (regular and alternative) medical field carried it out. There is perhaps a double
lack – one in the absence of more sophisticated approaches to dealing with com-

plex health issues that really affect people, physically and emotionally, two in the absence of scientific literacy in the sense of communicating with patients both the bodily and treatment sides. In the present case, we may notice a lack of consistency in some instances when an intervention appeared to work (although I had enacted in other cases rigorous experimentation typical of single-case studies). Thus, when an intervention was followed temporally by an improvement, I did not always engage in a process typical for single-case studies but was more concerned with remaining in a state of well-being rather than in trying to understand whether it was the intervention that *caused* the improvement. It turns out, however, that in the natural sciences, scientists act precisely in the same way when their equipment mysteriously works again after having stopped operating for a while. Even though the scientists I observed in a five-year ethnographic effort never figured out why some equipment had stopped working, they were satisfied to move on because it was working again without failing. Whereas controlled study of cause and effect may be appropriate for dispassionate investigation, the sense of well-being marked by positive affective tonality may override any interest in a dispassionate form of knowing.

There was a general absence of attempts to communicate specific aspects that entered investigation and diagnosis – e.g. the facts identified and their interpretation. That is, even though in this case both doctors and patient were highly trained, a *con*versation discussing the scientific basis and merits of the case and diagnosis never took place. We might conclude that those 'core practitioners' in the sciences, environment, and health fields more than the general public may have to be scientifically literate in the sense that they have to be capable and willing to communicate with others in a way that allows knowledge from their specialty field to inform relevant discussions. Health and environment individually seen but especially from their interrelation in ecological medicine should be a cooperative project involving patients and health practitioners, which, in the present case, has not occurred at any level. In fact, when the patient did provide information, then it was laughed off.

Knowledgeability and Debrouillardise

As a natural scientist with graduate and post-graduate experience in physics, physical chemistry, and biology, I have come in contact with and have learned a lot of scientific knowledge. However, in the case of my illness, none of the knowledge I had learned was applicable. We observe that despite tremendous background in science and science education, our symbolic knowledge still may be insufficient to cover those cases in real life that where science is really most relevant. I know that other people in my shoes might be more insistent ('agential'), but while undergoing the medical system I also knew myself as not doing well as a 'squeaky wheel'. If anything, we can extract from the preceding case study the presence of knowl*ability*, that is, the ability to acquire knowledge that might help solve the health problems. We also observe a certain level of making do with a situation and what it offers, an approach that has been termed *débrouillardise,* an orientation to life and problems arising therein. It was in the course of pursuing a relevant problem that I – in sustained inquiry – found out about and came to understand about health, diet and exercise, or physiology. I found out enough to be able to make scientifically informed decisions about changes in my life style.

After a lot of trying, abandoning, and retrying and only about six months before writing these lines, radical changes in diet – the very place where there is an interaction between environment and the personal body – led to equally radical changes in my well-being. Using approaches typical for single case (i.e. $N = 1$) designs, I eliminated and reintroduced certain foods, monitored the relationship between climate, exercise levels, and intake of liquids and minerals to arrive at a personal health that exceeded the state prior to the illness. In the course, I learned a lot of science, learned to eliminate medical studies the results of which may have been spurious or reported false cause–effect relations. All this science was literally personalized, motivated by the search of finding a solution to a problem that had touched me at the core. Those personalized practices included the growing of marihuana and preparation of TCH, the purchase and practice of sauna, and the dietary changes all *affected* me *directly* and without mediation.

Our Animate Bodies and School Learning

An important aspect of this chapter is the epistemological dimension, for the text articulates precisely what eschews explicit knowing and therefore anything that the constructivist metaphor can capture. But this chapter also has educational implications in the sense of tying together personal lives and the environment. In this chapter, we observe science, its content and nature, in the process of a chronic illness and the resultant pursuit of personal health and well-being. In the auto/biographical narrative, personal health and well-being are understood and treated to be irreducibly tied to environmental health, leading to changes in the home, immediate environment (garden), and types of food (organic, non-GMO). This concern for personal health and well-being also become an advocacy for environmental health and well-being in and through the practice of sustainable year-round permaculturing and the contribution to making wildlife corridors. Personal care and environmental care came to be integrally related. It is a way of nurturing the invisible animate body even though we can only know it through the ways in which it manifests itself to us (personally) and to the medical practitioners.

A central goal of education is for students to develop competencies required for making decisions about alternative actions in a politicized and political ethics of caring. This involves personal engagement in issues at a local level where these manifest themselves and are lived as relevant in the lives of those who are dwelling in a particular place. There is nothing more local than personal health, which affects us in an unmediated manner and despite any form of personal and collective knowledge. But personal health is tied irremediably to environmental health. That is, the politicized ethics of care first and foremost can be grounded in personal and environmental health. In the context of a public, politicized, and mediatized ethics of care allows students to work towards decisions about the way in which they lead their lives, the foods they want to eat and not eat because these contribute to a/n un/healthy lifestyle, the role of exercise in health and well-being. Lifestyle, health, and well-being are no longer symbolically accessed, as are almost all topics in present (science, health) curricula, which is why they touch, affect, interest, and engage students. Environmental and personal health, because these are close to and go under the skin, are ideal contexts for learning not only symbolically but also in flesh and blood and by modes inaccessible to language. Personal health questions are expandable to epidemiological studies, which could link children in any school to those in another other school within a country and with one or more schools in other countries wherever these are located in the world. There is a transactional relation interaction between the environments we create and inhabit, on the one hand, and our lives and the kinds of choices we make, on the other hand. It is well known that children will request candy if these are displayed in prominent places in the supermarket, such as the checkout counter, and where parents are less likely to engage in behaviors that would limit their children's access to the foods that lead to obesity. There therefore is a yet-to-be-explored potential for transforming the world through education, where any relevant subject matter plays one part in the bigger picture of education, though it no longer plays the exclusive domain from which to consider curriculum content and process.

In Tonga, where the obesity rates are the highest in the world, there are multiplier effects deriving from such efforts as operating gardens and commercial operations. Thus, the growing of vegetables integral to the nutrition objectives of educational programs addressing obesity. The most important goal was to enable to availability of vegetables for the community's own consumption. In so doing, the eating habits were to be improved. There are many examples around the world that show how children can be involved in the running of a garden and to learn sciences. In Tonga, in addition to the development of family gardens within the study communities, there was a multiplier effect that reached beyond the intervention. New gardens were established upon the initiatives of the locals. Interested groups from schools, churches, villages and youth groups have now formed committees (including representative of the Ministries of Health and Agriculture) to ensure the ongoing conduct of the program.

The case of Tonga shows that there is more to solving a health problem than teaching some specific subject in the school (e.g. science). In fact, if anything then we can learn that this health crisis needs to be thought from the plenitude of life, as educators have recently suggested and in terms of society as a whole, with its attendant division of labor and distributed forms of expertise. Any particular subject area then would take its place among many other forms of knowledge and relations that sustain and transform society – an approach that would clearly address the issue of diversity that is so central to an ecological approach to medicine. Economics and cultural traditions are just as important as knowing about how to optimize crops without fertilizers and in sustainable manner. Running a school garden not only produces vegetables but also comes with many opportunities to learn about the relationship between environmental and personal health and well-being. An organically run garden not only provides for nutritious and tasty foods but also can become part of a stewardship project – as I know from personal experience – and can lead to the establishment of corridors suitable for migrating wildlife. There is an increase in many species of wildlife, including pollinating species such as butterflies and different bee species. Students not only garden but also prepare and taste raw and cooked versions of what they have grown. It is even possible to sell the produce, which allows an expansion in the learning opportunities, for now economic factors enter the educational considerations.

Once educators decide that any content knowledge will fall short of what life requires, they can then focus on developing the ability to learn for life, knowledge-*ability*, and to cope with situations and complex (intractable) problems as they are encountered in real life, *débrouillardise*. Knowledgeability allow us to learn what is required when it is required and, exhibiting débrouillardise, thereby get ourselves out of trouble. As the case study shows, everyday life is not organized around a disciplinary field but around concerns and object / motives that orient societal activities. Many studies show that what makes people successful in schools is unrelated to success in everyday life affairs, even when investigators find structural equivalencies across situations – e.g. school mathematics and mathematics in the supermarket or workplace.

Most contemporary discourses in education are problematic in that they think education from within the disciplinary field rather than from within a larger perspective of life. One position emphasizes 'informed citizenship', but what science, mathematics, or social studies should informed citizens know and why they should know it? First, which concepts and processes are sufficiently general to be useful across contexts – even highly successful scientists have problems interpreting the graphs that appear in introductory college courses of their own field. Second, why should we not teach law (e.g., the legal status of marihuana in my case study) or finance and economy, areas that appear to have greater relevance in the everyday life of people? Much of our rethinking in education reform constitutes disciplinary navel gazing rather than looking at life more broadly and organizing knowing and learning as these play out in everyday life more generally – around the particular projects that we pick up from others, are deeply interested in, and investigate in a *sustained* manner. This flies in the face of the current organization of school life into subjects, which treats school life in the same way as a industrial production cycle determines not only what happens to a car-in-the-making but also how each human being involved in this making has opportunities to engage with the evolving product. Over the course of a third of a century of teaching science and research in education, I have come to the conclusion that the real problems derive from the institutional structures and the underlying epistemology. Thus, knowledge is such that it can be taught in disconnected, precisely timed units of time and in any place irrespective of the real person. Knowing and learning then are isolated from fullness of our everyday real lives, including the motives, interests, and needs that we live in and through our animate bodies; they are disconnected from the person who appears to us in flesh and blood.

The present chapter shows how, in everyday life, our knowledge pursuits are organized around projects and issues rather than by discipline. Whatever form of knowledge offers the potential to contribute to a solution enters the decision making, and sometimes it is not based and even contradictory to science (e.g. the complicated relation between marihuana, health, addiction, and law). Implementation will probably be less successful if traditional structures of schooling are maintained, which (a) interfere with the sustained level of uninterrupted engagement that any project in everyday life requires and which (b) in contrast to voluntary after- and out-of-school opportunities, force students to participate in tasks over which they do not have control in terms of structure, content, or evaluation. The structure of schools, as some educators have suggested, is itself the problem why education is perceived as having so little relevance to students' lives. In all but the fewest instances of the reform efforts and attempts to rethink science education, the structure of schooling appears to remain sacrosanct, although its main purpose contributes to the hierarchical structuring of a population with respect to their changes of accessing post-secondary institutions and professions). A much more radical interrogation of education and its nature may have to occur. Thus, just doing the same old things with a new topic – e.g. replacing science education by science | environment | health education – would not do the trick. In response to the question posed in the title of this article, one may say this: If science | environment | health were but a new driver in the same structure of schooling (new wine in an old bottle), then there would not be a real change. If this new topic and approach were to be one of the options, or one of the features that students would be able to pursue in an engaged and sustained manner, away from the traditional cycles, temporalities, and rhythms that currently characterize school life, then this is more of what I have in mind for a new form of education. The education I am interested in understands and theorizes itself from the whole of which it is a constitutive part – a resource in and to lifelong learning that promotes knowledgeability and débrouillardise.

The proposed approach is not a cure-all. We do know that doctors themselves often act against the spirit of the advice they give their patients. For example, some physicians advise their patients about maintaining appropriate levels of their diet and are overweight themselves; some doctors advise against smoking but continue to smoke themselves (a case in my extended family); a doctor may speak on public television against abortion but procures an abortion for his own wife (a case in my extended family); a Monsanto scientist who contributes to developing GMO crops only buys certified organic food for his own consumption (a fellow passenger of mine on a plane); or a beef farmer who eats beef only in countries where 'clean beef' is produced (no treatments during the life of the animals, no injection of chemicals after the animals' death). In all of these cases, there is a gap between what highly informed and trained individuals say ought to be done based on their knowledge (discursive action) and what they themselves do (practical action) to themselves and the environment. There is therefore never a guarantee that students who are involved in environmental activism will actually continue to engage in pro-environmental behavior or those involved in health-related initiatives will lead a healthy life. There is a relation between carcinogenic substances and comedogenic (acne-causing) activity. As acne literally goes 'under the skin', affecting teenagers physically and emotionally, an investigation of acne and environmental or cosmetic comedogenic substances may have greater impact on and directly changing student lives than the study of traditional school science topics in mechanics, the particulate nature of matter, or the Krebs cycle. But the students will develop the knowledgeability required to look up the particulate nature of matter or the Krebs cycle when these might expand their room to maneuver and range of options at hand.

Most importantly, this chapter contributes to a new epistemology in place of all forms of constructivism that have no means of theorizing the pathic knowing through the invisible animate body by their very nature focusing on representations of our bodies and the world. Addressing pathos, because it literally *affects* students physically and emotionally, means allowing them to engage according to their (passively) experienced and perceived needs. Students would be enabled to understand the relationship between our living selves and the representations thereof (e.g. in the X-rays of the rheumatologist or charts of the sleep specialist). In the context of the environment, they are enabled to understand a person as an abstraction from larger systems (ecologies) that are open rather than closed, where there is a continuous *flow* between what momentarily can be considered to be parts, each of which cannot be understood without the relation to the whole and, therefore, to all other parts. Students ought to be allowed to come to understand their own nature as an integral moment of the environment writ large, where there are continuous processes of exchange across open boundaries that are themselves subject to continuous change. The food they eat, the air they breathe, the (legal and illicit) drugs they consume, the exercises they do or do not engage in, or the chemical environments that they are in continuous exchange with – all of these phenomena will have their corresponding effects on how we feel and experience ourselves.

Notes

1 Bärbel Inhelder and Jean Piaget, *The Growth of Logical Thinking from Childhood to Adolescence* (New York: Basic Books, 1958), 309.

2 Maurice Merleau-Ponty, *Phénoménologie de la perception* (Paris: Gallimard, 1945), 108–109.

3 This idea of the three bodies is developed in Michel Henry, *Incarnation: Une philosophie de la chair* (Paris: Éditions du Seuil, 2000), 222–227.

4 Baruch Spinoza, 'Ethics', in *Complete Works* (Indianapolis: Hackett Publishing, 2002), 302.

5 See, e.g., Henry, *Incarnation*, 115–121. For Spinoza, substance, which is in and conceived through itself, manifests itself in attributes, 'which the intellect perceives of substances as constituting its essence'; substance is invisible and accessible only through attributes. See Spinoza, 'Ethics', 217. In a Spinozist Marxian conception, the '*thinking body*' of real, living man' manifests itself in 'two different and originally contrary objects of investigation', even though there is 'only *one single* object'; the thinking body thus is invisible, and what is visible are only manifestations. See Evald Il'enkov, *Dialectical Logic: Essays on Its History and Theory* (Moscow: Progress Publisher, 1977), 31.

6 This is a point made in Lev S. Vygotsky, 'Thinking and Speech', in *The Collected Works of L. S. Vygotsky, vol. 1*. (New York: Springer, 1987), 50.

[7] Marcel Proust, *À la recherché du temps perdu I: Du coté de chez Swann* (Paris: Gallimard, 1919), 65–69.

[8] Pierre Bourdieu, *Le sens pratique* (Paris: Seuil, 1980), 37.

8

Disappearance of the Subject

In 2007, I was invited to publish a book that presented a summary of my research career. It was aptly entitled *In Search of Meaning and Coherence* because throughout my scholarly life, I have attempted to make sense and bring into coherence the many existing theoretical approaches that I have become familiar with. But the coherence I was after concerned not only different theoretical frameworks but also the relationship between theory (e.g. some theory about knowing and learning) and my own life (e.g. my own knowing and learning). I had increasingly become aware of the fact that what many theories articulated was not what actually occurred in my own life. To give but one example, consider this. There is a lot of research on the 'construction' of identity. Yet my identity is never at stake; it never is in my consciousness while living my everyday life as a professor, shopper, client, patient, husband, and so on. I never have the sense of 'constructing' knowledge either and instead sense an increasing familiarity with and have an increasing capacity for doing certain things. Thus, even though I had been a fervent radical constructivist between 1988 and 1991, none of the discourses that I used with colleagues and in some of my writings actually described myself as a learner. Whatever the theory said was different from what I was aware of as a knower and learner. In the constructivist account, my subjectivity, my self, and my role as subject of activity had disappeared. This disappearance of the subject is the topic of the present chapter. But I am getting ahead of myself. In the following, I first articulate the relation between theory (e.g. of learning) and life (e.g. learning as it presents itself to us) and then move to showing how, in the very narration of events from an after-the-fact perspective, the nature of our subjectivity disappears.

On Theory and Its Relation to Life

After doing a Masters degree in physics, followed by a few years of teaching middle and high school science, I did a PhD focusing on the cognitive development of adults in the specific case of proportional reasoning. It was a quantitative study that

© KONINKLIJKE BRILL NV, LEIDEN, 2018 | DOI 10.1163/9789004377134_008

looked at the relationship between measures of short-term memory – i.e. visual and aural memory – and different dependent variables related to learning, such as the highest developmental level attained in a learning experiment and the amount of practice required to get there. The idea underlying the research was that the more short-term memory subjects have available, the more information they could process, the faster they could learn, and the higher the task difficulty level they could attain. Several articles from and related to my PhD thesis were later published in a leading (science) education journal, an indication that the study was judged to have been sound and that the research community accepted its results. However, when I returned to the secondary classroom two years later, I felt that the results of my thesis were irrelevant in the classroom, which was much too complex as to make my PhD work relevant. Students' real life in the classroom and at home was so much more important in learning than any relationship of learning to the short-term memory variables that I had used.

During the two years between completing the PhD and returning to the secondary school classroom, I had become familiar with and adopted constructivism as my epistemology. In lively discussions with colleagues at Indiana University where I taught for a while, I became convinced that constructivism provided better answers to how people learn *if they only wanted to learn*. But back in the classroom, I realized that the individualistic approach to constructivism could not be the answer, for the social aspects of classroom life were so much more important than anything individual that one might theorize. Following the video-recording of students after school and in class while doing one of the standard tasks that I was using in my teaching – concept mapping, sometimes also called mind mapping – I wrote the first article ever in the discipline of science education on the 'social construction of scientific concepts'. I was writing about how students 'collaboratively constructed concepts', how the 'used adversarial exchanges,' and how they 'formed temporary alliances'.[1] I had also noted that there was something like an evolution of their language, which I could see in other contexts too. Upon further reflection on the data, it occurred to me that there was no evidence that students were consciously 'constructing' anything. They were just talking their way through the task; and their linguistic expressions evolved in the pursuit of the task not because they intended to change the expressions. This evolution rather than the intentional construction of language was so important and pervasive that only a year or two later, I was turning away from social constructivism as a viable theory and began focusing on the role of language in knowing and learning.

The perhaps most important period for coming to understand that theories of knowing and learning do not describe what we actually attend to and do was associated with a three-month stay at research center in northern Germany. Colleagues from a nearby university had provided me with a data set from a teaching–learning experiment in a tenth-grade physics class, the same class in which Birgit from chapter 6 was a student. As part of watching and analyzing the videotapes, I was completing the same tasks that the students had been assigned to do. Lo and behold, I found myself doing and noting some of the same things that students were doing.[2] But my colleagues already had expressed themselves negatively about some of these students, attributing to them low motivation or low ability. Moreover, in discussions with these colleagues, I was told that my observations and my experiences could not be true because they were incommensurable with the radical constructivist and enactivist theory they were developing.

Over the years, I made a few more theoretical turns but increasingly realized that educational research was not attending to the 'view from within' and to the 'view from the shop floor of the social world'. As a research community, we were not attending to what the classroom looks like if things do not make sense or if you are handicapped in some way. More than once I was thinking about my own childhood. In fifth grade, living in a boarding home to attend grammar school, I was on the way to turning deaf. But nobody noticed it, including myself – I was apparently lip reading. The teachers thought that I was a dumb country boy and, for this reason, failed to answer their questions – especially those they asked standing behind me. When my hearing problem due to a painless inner-ear infection was finally discovered, the oto-rhino-laryngologist said that I was less than two weeks away from permanent deafness. I did not do well that school year and repeated it. Over thirty years later I began asking myself: What does the world of such a clueless kid look like, who not only has trouble in school but who does not even know that he does not hear? Beginning with the latter part of the 1990s, one strand of my research was concerned with learning as seen from within and through the eye of the learner.

One of the things I realized was that not only quantitative research methods but also qualitative research methods do not attend to the view from within. They do not attend to the fact that persons act rationally and based on what appears to be the most reasonable way to act at the time. There was one situation in particular that drove the point home when I began to reflect about it. As part of a research program on coteaching – teachers learning to teach while teaching at the elbow of another – I was teaching with a novice teacher (Natalie) who was doing an internship at the time prior to receiving her certification. At one point, there was an issue with a student, Stacey, whom Natalie had reprimanded even though, as I had seen from where I was standing, it was not Stacey who was at the origin of the commotion. Before I had any time to reflect, a thought had taken up place in my mind: This is stupid, how could Natalie act in this way? But right as I tried to find an answer to the question, I found myself thinking: 'If she acted in this way, then it likely was the most reasonable thing to do then and there otherwise she would have acted differently'. I was embarrassed in the privacy of my own thoughts for having found her actions stupid before trying to understand how the situation looked to *her*. I realized that to comprehend my teaching partner, I needed to look into her lifeworld. I needed to find out the particulars of this lifeworld. Even before having had the time to think this all through I was sure that once I knew Natalie's lifeworld with all the things and relations that populated it, then her action was the most rational thing to do at the time. Indeed, that same afternoon, when we had time to talk about the event, Natalie explained that she called out Stacey and asked her to sit elsewhere in the classroom because she did not want to appear as 'picking on' Derek, who 'generally started the problems'.

The entire event had not been very long. The issue got settled and we were continuing to teach. But my professional life had been changed forever. I became increasingly convinced that in not considering the view from within – the individual, the group – research in effect is erasing the subject; it is erasing the subjectivity of the individual, which research then has to reconstruct through its special methods that need to be described because they are different from what we do in our everyday lives. With these erasures, the subject in effect disappeared – even from qualitative research that nevertheless claims to be about the 'meaning' people 'construct' in relevant situations. But in the case of Natalie, there was no evidence that she constructed anything. She did not construct a situation but *saw* a particular constellation and acted upon it – just as I saw the situation in a different way so that her action did not *make sense to me.* There is no evidence that Natalie constructed a 'teacher identity', just as I did not construct my 'researcher (-teacher) identity' – I just witnessed Natalie acting during this lesson that we taught together. She also did not construct the identity of the students, Stacey and Derek. She acted to get the perceived problem go away and to get everyone back to work. It made sense to her as well to act as she did – this is why she acted in this rather than another way. Indeed, the sense of her action derived from what it was to achieve a little into the future, that is, from its *in-order-to*-motive: to have everyone back at work without Derek feeling picked upon. This is different from the *because*-motive that she may be provided ex post facto. When asked afterward about the incident, Natalie said something like 'I did this *because* …'. Because Natalie did not construct meaning or an identity, researchers have to do so. They use special methods to extract it from the data precisely because it was not directly made available in Natalie's action. These special methods of researchers are different from those that we use to produce and make visible the different facts of our social worlds. Research, too, builds on the because-motives, which always already is an ex-post-facto perspective rather than the view of a person confronted with an open future, where any next action makes sense in the face of the pertinent in-order-to-motive.

The subject and subjectivity also get erased because researchers – quantitative and qualitative alike – do not attend to the fact that we not only act but also are subject and subjected to a situation. As teachers, we *undergo* classroom life as much as contributing to it through our actions. As shown in chapter 2, we are not even in control over our own actions (speech), because we grasp our doings with any precision only afterward, that is, after seeing the effect that these have had from the actions of others. We experience this lack of control every time we fail to do what we intended (thought) to do. The model of the translocutional nature of speech (Fig 2.4, p. 26) allows us to understand that although Natalie had called out Stacey, asking her to move to a different seat, the student let her and everyone else know that the teacher had picked on her. Even though Natalie had not intended to pick on Stacey – her in-order-to-motive was to stop the problem and get the students back to work – she now was confronted with the fact that she had picked on Stacey. This was the new reality; and Natalie acted upon it by explaining to Stacey: 'everyone is doing more work, that's why I think you need a better environment, a better place to be'. That is, Natalie was not in control over her action, for its sense turned out to be 'picking on Stacey'. Because this chapter is about the disappearance of the subject, I return to these issues in chapter 9 where I articulate different dimensions that are required for better understanding the subject and subjectivity.

Increasingly I also became aware that there is something about the research methods that is not quite right. How could something be relevant to the lives of the persons research is writing about when it takes *special* methods to uncover it from the data? Both quantitative and qualitative research methods are described in research articles, where they are considered to be a distinctive feature that separates (social) science from what ordinary folks do. The three – Natalie, Stacey, and Derek – pulled off the situation *together* in a way recognizable to everyone who happened to witness it. Not only Stacey but other students as well could see the teacher Natalie picking on the student. Stacey let Natalie know – and, because the talk was public, she let everyone else in the classroom know as well – that she felt picked on even though 'she had done nothing (wrong)'. What all bystanders at the time could witness was a familiar happening of the type 'a-teacher-picking-on-a-student-who-had-done-nothing-but-who-has-to-bear-the-consequences'. Thus, the participants not only produce the situation but also make it visible to one another and to every bystander as well. All such everyday doings disappear from theory, which, thus completely obliterates our subject positions in life. But such doings also disappear in our own mundane narratives by the very way in which these stories are structured. Thus, the transactional dimension of life, which also characterizes the double perspective of the subject, disappears. I begin by retelling some memorable moments of classroom life, which I then subject to an extended analysis.

Memorable Moments of Classroom Life

From 1982 to 1986, I was living in a town in Newfoundland where the unemployment rate among 18–25-year adults was round 75 percent. The fishery from which the people in town and the surrounding villages lived was in decline; and the forests that once had provided an income to people in nearby lumber mills also were gone, taking too long to regrow to harvestable size in a reasonable number of years. In this town, I taught in the local high school attended by the students from the town and the surrounding villages that were too small to have their own school. But young people had little incentive to attend school. Duane, the student appearing in the narrative below, today describes the life back then to have been tough. In an email in early 2017, he wrote about the perception of young people and their parents of the teachers at my high school: they presumably had gotten into the profession because it was an easy way of getting a job for those more academically inclined. I know that many of my colleagues did not prepare for class, merely opening the textbook where they had left a bookmark at the end of the preceding lesson. Duane concluded that it was a surprise that any student managed to get an education. Duane and I came to be connected again after other students from the school had invited me to become a member of a Facebook page.

I had never forgotten Duane. Over the thirty-one years that have passed since we were teacher and student to each other, I have time and again retold in relevant contexts two stories in particular that involved him. It turns out that Duane, too, remembered certain events pertaining to our relation.

After taking up contact, Duane and I exchanged a few emails. He wrote about how school faculty and others expected him and me 'to be like lithium and water: The no-nonsense German teacher vs. the smart-assed local punk'. Among others, I was teaching computer science, open for tenth- to twelfth-grade students but limited to a total number of twelve because there were only three computers. In his email, Duane described how he was advised to stay out of computer science to avoid the unavoidable clash with me, the only person in the school certified to teach that course. But, he added, 'it didn't quite work that way', that is, he never found himself in a situation of clash with me. As if supporting his assessment, Duane provided two stories involving the two of us.

The first story went like this: 'I hadn't been to your class for a few days. The principal caught me in the hallway and was pleased that now he had me – he knew I was supposed to be in your class at that time so now he had an excuse to expel me. All he had to do was get you on side. Knocked on your classroom door, explained the situation, and you said, "No, I just excused Duane five minutes ago to visit the restroom. There's no problem". Hahaha, the look on his face was gold!'

His second story, which immediately followed the comment that there was no clash between him and me, captures an aspect of our last face-to-face meeting before I headed off to pursue a PhD and, in its course, decided not to return. Duane wrote: 'I remember the last words you said to me before you headed to Mississippi, "Never compromise your ideals, for nothing and nobody"'. He added, 'And I haven't!' Duane summarized and concluded, 'You certainly made a mark on my life'.

The stories Duane told and that captured what he remembered more than thirty years later describe events that I had forgotten. In fact, as hard as I tried, I could not remember these events even though they sound probable. It makes sense to me today that I might have acted and spoken in the way he described.

For me, there were other things that I continue to remember to the present day. I do vaguely recall that my colleagues had warned me: Duane is going to be a nightmare. Everyone knew about him, walking the hallways, being kicked out of his classes, and every now and then being suspended from attending school by the principal. I already had taught his brother, who had been, as the colloquialism goes, 'a pain in the neck', always disrupting class and challenging the teacher. My fellow teachers said that Duane was worse. But it never turned out this way. There are three events related to Duane that I remember to the present day.

First, one day Duane had come to class apparently having smoked a joint. He giggled and laughed together with another student who also appeared to be on a high. I remember talking to Duane: 'I hope you are having a good time'. I then reminded him that because he, as everyone else, worked on a contract basis, he could organize his work as he wished as long as it was handed in on the contracted date. But, I insisted, he could not keep others from working. I suggested that he go to the washroom to sleep or to the library to work. And so he did. He never bothered anyone during this or indeed any computer science lesson.

The second event that stands out to the present day pertains to the single two-week period at the end of which – i.e. on a Friday afternoon – he had not submitted the deliverables of his contract. After the last class of the day, I called up his father letting him know about the leeway I had given his son, who had failed to deliver. I then went home for the weekend. The next morning, stepping out of my house, I found Duane's work on my doorsteps. On my part, there were no reprisals, no late penalties. We never talked about it any more. It never happened again.

The third story that I have been telling in relevant circumstances concerned the fact that Duane started coming to the computer science room after school. At that time, he was virtually guaranteed access to one of the three computers. He not only worked on achieving the goals he had stated in his contract for computer science but also began using the computers in other ways. I assisted him in learning how to use a word processor; and he began to type out all his assignments for other courses as well. I showed him how to (and helped him) edit his texts prior to printing them out for submitting them to the relevant teacher. He was beginning to hand in all assignments in a readable form, which had not been the case before (his handwriting was atrocious). In the end, he did well not only in computer science: To the surprise of all teachers and the principal, he ended up with the third highest grade point average of the entire graduating year.

At this point, readers might begin to wonder. Was there not a promise in the title and the opening paragraphs of this chapter to address the disappearance of the subject and subjectivity? All these stories – Duane's and my own – do these not reflect his and my subjectivity at the time? The answer is that while manifesting aspects of subjectivity, they do so only partially and one-sidedly. More importantly, research that extracts from these stories structures of experience and particular lessons to be learned make the subjects and their subjectivities completely disappear. One reason for this arises from the fact that the stories inherently are told after the original events*, here over thirty years later, rather than presenting life from the inside, both inside the person and from the inside of the situation. This is the distinction between inchoate life – which we produce and witness in the heat of the moment without knowing what will have happened next when we are able to turn back and look at what has happened – and *an* experience – which is something completed and which we recount in view of knowing how some situation has ended. I now turn to work out some of the pertinent issues.

Inchoate Living vs. *An* Experience

In both sets of stories, what had happened is described from an ex-post-facto perspective. Each story is about a complete unit, with a definite beginning and ending; it may therefore serve to draw some lesson. Thus, for example, Duane described the condition – not having been in the classroom where he was normally scheduled to be. It is the antecedent condition and the because-motive for the fact that the principal (who had caught him roaming the hallways) and he were standing in the doorway to the computer science lab. The description of the instant is provided, where the principal speaks to the teacher, which, in the story, is to provide the reason for expelling the student. But the story ends with a dramatic resolution: the teacher legitimized Duane's presence in the hallway. More so, Duane reports a facial expression on the part of the principal, noting it to have been 'gold'. At this point, the story also contains a marker of a gleeful laughter ('hahaha'). The whole event has been standing out for Duane from all the other things that may have occurred on that day and everything else that has happened since but that have been forgotten. The story is complete, with a definite beginning and, for Duane, a happy ending that also featured a thwarting of the principal's – i.e. his perpetual opponent's – scheme. As such, it is the account of '*an* experience' in the sense it 'has a unity that gives it its name'.[3] In this case, the name may be something like, 'The day I didn't get expelled' or 'The day you saved my ass'. In the second instant, the name might be 'the most important advice I received from you'. More importantly, they are part of a bigger story, which Duane names at the end: You certainly made a mark on my life. We do not know what he might tell a researcher interested in finding out more about our (his and mine) relation and how it left a mark. Duane might talk about how I acted differently toward him, did not judge him, and perhaps even how I colluded with him, protecting him when he was exposed to the threat of being suspended from attending school. In my case, too, the stories are complete and, thus may be named, which might include something like this: 'What you do when a student is stoned' and 'The day a student submitted his work on a Saturday'.

In pragmatic philosophy, the term *experience* appears, sometimes in the formulation '*an* experience' to mark an event that stands out from the flow of life. There is no longer a happening witnessed by those who are in the situation, who act by doing something or nothing and thereby contribute to the recognizable constitution of the unfolding order of social life. Instead, a form of closure has occurred and participants now may look back and grasp it. They may grasp it precisely because closure has been achieved – a shot in football (soccer) is a 'winning shot' only once we know how the game has ended. That is, once a form of closure has been achieved, effects are known: it is *this* shot that won the game. In Duane's story, it was my statement ('No, I just excused Duane five minutes ago to visit the restroom. There's no problem') that made his day, preventing suspension and giving him an opportunity to glee in the face of an opponent 'who was pleased that now he had [Duane]'. Because the event captured in the story is complete, those aspects of the now-grasped event may be picked out that contributed in a causal way to the outcome. In the football (soccer) example, it was *that* (memorable) goal that won the game; in Duane's story, it was my reply to the principal that provided a perhaps unanticipated resolution to his precarious position. In this way, causes may be attributed. This goal is the cause for winning the game – rather than the others that only contributed to a draw; and it was the statement attributed to me that brought about the release of Duane.

We now see how a cause is invented after the fact to provide an explanation. Whether some act causes a particular outcome cannot be known, as we see from the story in Natalie's classroom. She had intended asking Stacey to move to a different desk, and to a certain extend achieved this goal. But more importantly, she had been seen to be 'picking on' Stacey, who had done nothing (wrong). After the fact, Stacey's complaint ('Why do I have to move, I didn't do anything') makes sense in the face of an occasion of having been picked on. This effect emerged and was not anticipated.

Life is *emergent*, that is, it unpredictably leads to new forms. Causes thus are imputed based on the knowledge of how things have turned out.[4] That is, the causal structure and analysis in terms of separate elements is the result of an ex post facto account. Life thereby becomes intelligible in terms of cause–effect relations. But philosophers such as Friedrich Nietzsche, Maurice Merleau-Ponty, Mikhail Bakhtin, or George Herbert Mead all strongly argued against the intellectualization of the world that we not merely inhabit but actually live. We are subject to life before grasping what actually has happened to us. For us to grasp a part of the stream of life as forming a unity, this bit of the stream has to have an end. Afterwards, the parts of the now-completed event make up a whole without leaving their place. But the particular nature of the event emerges with and from its end. While we are in the midst of it, what happens is at best an event-in-the-making or *event**, where the asterisk marks that the particular nature of what is happening is not yet given. Any story thus precisely misses to account for the sense of the happening at that instant – e.g. while the three of us were standing in the doorway and before the principal opened his mouth to inquire about Duane's absence from the classroom. In one of my stories, it is the fact that I found the contracted work for the preceding two weeks on my home's doorstep on Saturday morning that made this aspect of my life stand out. To this standing out belongs that there had not been (noticeable) negative consequences. Duane and I carried on. The issue was resolved and did not warrant further talk. But we know that life is not a finished and predetermined story. On Friday afternoon, I did not know what would happen next. I could not foresee that the work would be delivered by the next day; and I could not know that Duane was not going to mess up classroom life during the following week in revenge for my call. It was really only after the year had ended that both of us could talk about our relation and the things that happened to us and that we made happen in the way that these are described in our stories. That is, the particular significance of these events is tied to the way that the year as a whole had turned out: there had not been a single clash.

In English, the term 'experience' is used to categorize what is captured in our stories. It may be said that both Duane and I reported different cases of having had *an* experience. But the English term experience is confusing, being employed in very different, sometimes inconsistent, and thus confusing ways.[5] Thus, researchers might report on how Duane 'experienced' the situation, especially if they had asked about what had gone through his mind at that instant when the principal knocked on the door to the computer science lab and how he had felt at the time. Here, the verb form is used to invoke aspects of a situation as viewed from within

– while generally not noticing that Duane would not be able to go back to the instant in the doorway and thus inherently would tell his story after there was some form of closure to the situation. In other languages, there are different words to refer to the historically different perspectives. Thus, the German language denotes the equivalent to Dewey's 'an experience' as *Erfahrung*, something we have gone through, which stands out, and from which we have learned something. The French call this *expérience*, a word that also translates the English 'experiment'. The German language distinguishes this phenomenon from another one, which is how an unfinished happening appears to us while we are in the midst of it: *Erleben* literally denotes how we live – witness and feel – what is going on without having a grasp of it. *Erleben* is a verb employed as noun (like Heidegger's *Sein* [Being], which is the noun form of *sein*, to be). *Erlebnis* is an alternative word, but, because it is a pure noun, also denotes something as a completed thing, as a process rather than as an ongoing inchoate happening under way. Some translators choose the expression 'lived-experience' to denote these two German words. Because this English expression also is a noun, the same problems exist as with the German noun only word. French philosophers use the term *vécu* as an equivalent, which may be translated as 'that which is lived'. But the term is a little bit confusing, as it is a noun form built on the past tense of the verb *vivre*, to live. In the past tense form, its use is confronted with the same problems that come from connoting something that has occurred in the past and has come to an end.

To avoid such confusions, which enter and define the nature of the subject and subjectivity, analysts position themselves better if they denote the inner reflection of a situation as *going through* or as *being lived*. We might want to add, 'being lived and felt' or imply that saying a situation is 'being lived' implies that it is felt. Indeed, shortly before his death, the Russian psychologist Lev S. Vygotsky proposed *perezhivanie*, which translates the English words experience and feeling. He thought of it as an equivalent to the German *Erlebnis* and *Erleben*. I also use the verb 'to witness' because it does not imply the knowledge that comes with closure that turns something happening into a definite event. We may witness something without knowing what it turns out to have been – like the Las Vegas shooting on October 1, 2017 where 58 people got killed, when many of those present talked about not having had a clue about what was going on. Thus, Duane was in some way living the situation at the door and before my reply without knowing what type of event it will have been at the end of the day. The French philosopher Maurice Merleau-Ponty describes the result of clearly distinguishing between an experience and living-through: 'When an event is considered at close quarters, at the moment when it is lived through, everything seems subject to chance: one man's ambition, some lucky encounter, some local circumstance or other appears to have been decisive'; but after the fact, 'chance happenings offset each other, and facts in their multiplicity coalesce and show up a certain way of taking a stand in relation to the human situation, reveal in fact an event which has its definite outline and about which we can talk'.[6]

With this distinction in place, our task becomes one of thinking about and theorizing the subject and subjectivity *in ongoing life* rather than in the narratives –

even in those that the actors themselves provide after the fact. To understand my actions at a particular point in time, and thus my subjectivity, researchers must not look at and analyze the ex-post-facto accounts thereof, which are always construed after the fact in the light of the outcomes. But in real life, we do not know where the ends of significant stretches of living are until some form of closure actually has occurred – which itself can be established only after the fact (e.g. the 'game-winning' goal). That ending, according to Dewey, is part and defining of what makes *an* experience. The unity of *an* experience in this sense is the availability of the end. Already in the nineteenth century, Friedrich Nietzsche warned his readers of the danger of using historically later events and outcomes to explain patterns in what happened earlier: 'the pattern only proves that one and the same happening is not also another happening. Only because we have interpretively imputed subjects, "*agents*" into things the impression is created that everything happening is the consequence of a force / constraint that a subject exerts – who exerts? Again by an "agent". Cause and effect – a dangerous concept when we think of a *something* that *causes* and a something *affected* by it'.[7] We avoid Monday-morning quarterbacking when we clearly distinguish between *in-order-to-motives*, representing motives viewed *before* acting, and the *because-motives*, which may be attributed only *after* having acted.

In-order-to-motives are associated with another form of unity, one relating to the way in which we live and live through times of our lives that then become specific experiences. Thus unity is correlative with how we, in our animate bodies, are caught up in life and before some happening is grasped and thought as *an* experience. As the situation at the entrance to the computer science room unfolded, and prior to what I had said, everything was out in the open. Neither the principal nor Duane could know what I was going to say, and, thus, what the conclusion of that happening and thus the event* would be. In fact, even I could not know what I will have said when I ended speaking; and nobody at that instant could know its effect – until after the principal told Duane to continue and after he went back to his office. Nobody could know whether my saying would bring about some conclusion. The same, of course, also pertains to me. When there was a knock on the door, I could not know who was outside and what was going to happen. The reply to the principal's initiation was provided, face-to-face with the two individuals and without the benefit of a time out for considering any possible implications. I replied without making up a full reply in my mind, evaluating its full content and how it might affect the game in play – like chess players cogitate the consequences of a move for what could happened next. Certainly, it would have been impossible to understand or predict the long ranging impact that this instant in our lives would have on Duane for the remainder of the year and for his personal development. I could have never anticipated that the statement would become part of *an* experience – i.e. a memorable one – that defined Duane's life. As can be seen from the fact that I have completely forgotten the situation, it likely was but an integral part of the stream of my life, unremarkable thus unremarked and unmarked on my part.

Most definitely, the event was not a construction of Duane. He, just as the principal and I, was subject and subjected to the situation. It is the associated aspect of passibility – the capacity for suffering and sensation – that is an integral part of being caught up in live, of being part of life. It is precisely this part that constructivist (and cognitivist) approaches exclude from thematization and thus obliterate in their theories of the subject and subjectivity.[8] The real subjects and their subjectivities disappear. What was happening at the entry to the computer science lab happened to us – the principal, Duane, and me – as much as we contributed in making what it was. We all were shaped in the process. In popular language, one might want to say that Duane's fate at that instant depended on my reply. He knew that he had not been to class for some time, and so he might have anticipated to be suspended for a few days from attending school. The principal in turn might have anticipated suspending the student. In his actions, he makes known that he required knowing more, to be certain about the illegitimacy of Duane's absence from class, for he would not have needed to check with the teacher first.

It is apparent from the preceding, that *an* experience can be *had* only after the fact; only then is it a whole that can be grasped. The situation is very different when we position ourselves within the unfolding situation. This situation cannot be called *an event*, for such a thing must have an end. In the absence of the end, it may at best be an event-in-the-making or an event* for short. As can be seen from dramatic situations – e.g. the fateful day at Columbine High School or being on 9/11 (2001) in the World Trade Center – just before the tragedy arrived, most of those presents in the sites may have thought something like 'just another day in the office'. Nobody of those affected would have thought about 'history in the making'. Similarly, when the principal had 'caught' Duane in the hallway, the student did not know what kind of event he was in. 'Being caught' could have been part of the cause of a suspension if things had turned out that way: Duane was suspended *because* he had skipped class and thus had no excuse for not being in the lab (which was to be ascertained by asking the teacher). If a researcher had prompted Duane right at this instant for a description of his present 'experience', Duane might have said, 'I'm in shit'. Duane would not have been able to know what will have happened until he was in a position to look back. The principal and I were in the same situation. From within what was happening – i.e. from within what after the fact will have been an event* – not one of the three protagonists could know how everything will have turned out once they looked back on the day. That is, nobody had an idea about how *what* he was witnessing later was part of a definitive event – an *Event* – that Duane later recalled in the way he did in the email to me. That aspect of our subjectivities inherently disappears when we tell stories after the fact.

From John Dewey's reflections on the nature of '*an* experience' and even more from the French novelist Marcel Proust's analysis of the difference between voluntary and involuntary memory we may surmise that the presence or absence of affect (emotions) plays an important role in the disappearance of the subject. The latter suggests that voluntary memory, with its appearance in words ('intelligence'), conserves nothing of the remembered – we might say that there are just words.[9] What the memory of intelligence provides is but a story, which inherently appears in the language that we have in common with other members of society.

As a result, what is captured in the words is dead for the person. This is precisely what I observed among pilots, who, following a four-hour examination, are debriefed. There were many situations where pilots did not recall actions or situations in which they were part. Even though flight examiners retold what had happened, the events remained dead for the pilots who had forgotten what had happened. This situation is very different when we are led to relive a situation – e.g. the madeleine dissolved in tea in Proust's novel, the flashback that takes a soldier back into combat, or the various less-dramatic flashbacks that are part of our everyday lives. Reliving means that we are back in the situation, undergoing again the associated affects, and, thus, in (approximately) the same subject position. The subject thus has not disappeared.

In the end, Duane rejoiced and told the event with a marker of glee ('Hahaha'). But things could have turned out differently. Having forgotten about that exchange at the entrance to the computer science lab, I do not know what went on in my mind at the time. If an educational researcher had asked me at the end of the day, I might have remembered – but in any case I would have given an answer in light of the fact that Duane had spent the rest of the lesson in the computer science lab. Had I said something differently, the principal might have rejoiced for a while finally having caught Duane in an act that warranted suspension. On my part, I might have wondered what was going on when the two were at the entrance to the computer science lab. Accordingly, any account of how we *lived* and *lived through* the situation – i.e. what we were aware of and how / what we felt – cannot be thought in terms of cause–effect relations. This is so because it is in principle unknown and what a cause will have been attributable only after everything has come to an end. The upshot of these considerations is that the *sense* of the performed (lived) act can be obtained only *from within* this act, but not from the theoretical transcription thereof. That is, 'it is only from within the actually performed act, which is once-occurrent, integral, and unitary in its answerability, that we can find an approach to unitary and once-occurrent Being in its concrete actuality'.[10] Instead of 'Being', we might as well have said 'dwelling', and Being always is the Being of a subject. This is consistent with the suggestion by Karl Marx and Friedrich Engels that individuals are how they express their lives, and what individuals are depends on the material conditions of their expressions (productions).[11] In retelling something that has happened to them, even the protagonists are not the same subjects, and in each case the subject has disappeared.

The difference between the open-ended, inchoate instant of life witnessed from within and the finished, ex-post-facto perspective also is apparent in Duane's second story. Whenever we last met – I do not specifically remember that event – I may have indeed uttered those very words that he now quotes me to have said. If he had heard the statement as advice, it could not have been more than an instruction for his future actions. It could have not been more than the verbalized form of an in-order-to-motive for his life. However, we know from research that the relation between instructions (stating in-order-to-motives) and actual situated action that follow is inherently open. Even the most competent engineers and scientists may intend doing something only to find out at a later point that they were doing something else or they might find out that they cannot do it (like constructing a second version of a machine that was successfully working for their clients). Thus, it is only after the fact that Duane can say with any certainty that he never did compromise his ideals. At the time he may have indeed *intended* living his life without compromising. But it is only now over thirty years later that he could use it for explaining why the relation with me had such an impact on his life as seen in the fact that he never did compromise. The problem of most research consists in the confusion of these two, very different forms of motives and thus in the way the subjects and their subjectivities are constituted. The living subject disappears when open-ended in-order-to-motives are replaced by because-motives that always only are attributable after the fact and with hindsight. That is, there are changes when we go from living and witnessing life to retelling something that has happened. The narration makes previous moments in our life present again – it literally is a re-presentation or *re*presentation. Even if a protagonist produces a narration, it still is a representation not the real thing – which is why Proust may have referred to it as a past that is dead. The narrative is a form of mimesis, a copy of life that is nevertheless part of life. The disappearance of the subject and subjectivity – e.g. those pertaining to each of the three participants at the entry to the computer science laboratory – is tied to the shift from a happening to its representation as an event*, that is, as an event-in-the-making, which can be told only once the event is given after closure has been achieved and the happening has ended. This is so in everyday life and even more so when the narrations of participants come to be theorized.

Life and Its Mimesis

The narratives from school life presented above are ex-post-facto accounts of events rather than the inchoate dwelling, the living and living through of being-there (e.g. being a participant at the computer science lab door). When such narratives become part of research, the events are further transposed by means of theoretical discourses available – e.g. the discourses about the construction of identities, resistance, psychological personalities, or school and classroom management. To show how the subject and subjectivity disappear, I revisit one of the preceding stories, the incident at the door to the computer science lab.

The story as Duane told it in his email is made up of clearly identifiable elements. There are three actors: the principal, a no-nonsense German teaching computer science, and a student who after-the-fact describes his former Self as 'smart-assed local punk'. The three individuals are involved in a dramatic event. It is dramatic because the story is told for a particular purpose: it is to show something, exhibit a particular message, or have a point. In this case, the point is dramatic, for something unexpected arises. The story begins with articulating the situation before the main plot: Duane had not been to class for a few days. In the theory of dramatic structure, this phase is referred to as *exposition*. This structural phase is followed by that called *rising action*, where the story builds to the point of interest and tension. In Duane's narrative, this corresponds to the account of being caught in the hallway. There are markers of a historical antagonism, such as when the story states that the principal 'now had the student'. For whatever unaccounted-for reason, the story positions the principal as the guy wanting to 'expel' Duane. Having been caught in the hallway is a reason for the suspension. The narrative builds to the *climax*, the third phase of dramatic structure, as another person is introduced: the teacher. The principal's success and Duane's fate now were in the hands of the teacher, whom the principal had to get on his side. In the *falling action*, the conflict between the main actors – protagonist Duane, antagonist principal – unravels when the teacher provides a legitimate reason for Duane's presence in the hallway. The final phase, *dénouement*, is represented in the last phrase. In that phase, the protagonist is better off than he was before, and the antagonist not only is marked as having lost but also recognizing this loss, a recognition that is marked by 'the look on his face', which, to Duane, 'was gold'.

In the story, there are recognizable actions that are attributed to the individual participants – including the main figures, the protagonist (Duane) and antagonist (principal). The student *has failed* to be in class. The principal *caught* the student, *knocked* on the door, and *explained* the situation. The third person, the teacher *speaks*, and in so doing helps the protagonist get out of a difficult and potentially calamitous situation. Even though actions are ascribed to individuals, the logical sequence between pairs of actions is implied. Thus, some form of interaction is present – e.g. the principal explains the situation and the teacher makes a statement in reply.

The main point of the narrative lies in its final two parts (falling action, dénouement). By providing a legitimate reason for Duane to be in the hallway even though he has been skipping class, the teacher has helped him out (colloquially speaking, has 'saved his ass'). The story provides an example for the earlier statement that the teacher and the student did not clash, as many predicted, and that life turned out differently. Not only did the computer science teacher and trouble student fail to clash, but also the former helped the latter even in a situation where the opponent was higher up than both in the institutional hierarchy. In toto, the teacher has had a great impact on Duane's life.

Narrative is intelligible because of its form. Duane did not just provide some (utterly) subjective account of an event, but he does retell the situation using a common language and employing a familiar plot structure. Everything thus is designed for intelligibility – though storytellers mostly do so without being consciously aware thereof. Being designed for intelligibility means being designed for the generalized other. That is, the story cannot be ascribed to Duane alone. It is social through and through. The particulars are indexed to some actual situation in his (and my) life. But the language and the emplotment, the actors, actions, and processes all imply the other.

Duane provided a story of a now-mythical *Event** some thirty-one years earlier that had involved both of us. This brief analysis of the narrative shows how the narrated event is built up of actors and actions. Even though Duane, a participant, retells the situation through his eyes, something has been lost such that the original subjectivity has disappeared – and with it, the nature of the subject. This is even

more so as soon as research begins to fold theoretical terms into the story. For example, researchers interested in the topic of *identity* may use such stories to make a
case how identities 'get constructed'; and researchers interested in power structures
may retell the story in terms of power-over – the principal as in power-over teacher
and student, the teacher in power-over the student. Why all such approaches miss
the subject and subjectivity as these appeared in the original *Event** requires us to
return to it with an intention to relive it from a first-time-through perspective. That
is, we need to resituate ourselves, place ourselves in the shoes of the participants,
and see what is happening without taking recourse to things that have happened
later – even in that same *Event**.

The data as provided in the ex-post-facto narratives do not give us access to the
instant that the participants were living and living through, a happening inherently
inchoate until some point afterward when closure has been recognizably achieved.
Everything in the different stories is told and analyzed from a perspective of hindsight. To see what is happening from a different perspective requires following the
actors from within the happening and prior to their grasping what will have happened to them. Moreover, to fully understand all forms of actions also requires
emphasizing the actions of the recipients of communicative action. A first step is
achieved in the following transcription of the conversation as it might have happened at the door to the computer science lab.

1 Principal: Isn't Duane supposed to be in your computer science class?
2 Teacher: No, I just excused Duane five minutes ago to visit the restroom.
                There is no problem.
3 Principal: Oh, okay. (*to Duane*) Okay, go to class then.

The transcription is of a type that readers are familiar with. All words that can
be heard on a video- or audiotape are transcribed; and they are attributed to the
person who has articulated them. What we thereby obtain is a sequence of statements each attributed to a speaker, who thereby is shown to have taken turn. Each
action thereby is ascribed to an individual to whom is attributed a speaking intention and a form of thought that precedes the speech act. These *self-actions* are said
to be connected because every subsequent turn takes into account an earlier one,
whereby the respondent first interprets what has been said and then replies. We
thereby get something generally referred to as *interaction*. Such analyses often
point out differences in the 'meanings' that individual participants 'construct'.
With such a manner of proceeding, researchers already analyze *inter*actions, where
the action of some second speaker follows the action of a first speaker: a completed action follows a completed action. Although this is the common and predomi-
nant approach to transcription and the role of language, it is a misrepresentation of
life. This is so because life does not unfold as a sequence of individual actions,
which are generated and expressing forms of pre-existing thoughts.

Real life is different. It does not occur in an on–off fashion, where one actor is
turned on to do something while a second actor is turned off waiting until the preceding one has finished only to begin acting on whatever has been done before.
This on–off approach clearly is represented in the preceding transcription, where

the teacher is put in off-mode while the principal is speaking and put into on-mode when it is his turn. Although invisible, forms of mental processes – interpretation, meaning making – surreptitiously are inserted between the two speaking turns by implying that what has ultimately been said (the *Said*) is an externalization of an internal state. We know that real life is different because we are never in off-mode. This is made apparent in chapter 2, where a transactional (translocutional) model of a conversation is presented (see Fig 2.4, p. 26). I return to this model for the present purpose. Thus, for example, when the principal's vocal cords and mouth move to produce what we transcribe as 'Isn't Duane ...' then the parts of the teacher's inner ear also resonate to yield 'Isn't Duane ...'. Those same words simultaneously are in the mouth of the principal and in the ears of the teacher (and Duane, of course, and in the audio part of the recording equipment that researchers would have used). The words, therefore, not only belong to the principal but also to the teacher. More so, to be able to reply at all, the teacher has to actively listen and, in so doing, receive without knowing what it is going to be. Even speakers, unless they read off a script or reproduce a rehearsed speech, do not know in advance the exact text that they will have said when once having finished their turn. We may therefore minimally augment the preceding transcription by also including the concurrent actions of the non-speaking individual (Fig 8.1). Whereas this still does not represent the *Event** in its totality, as it actually was lived and lived through at the time (always once-occurrent and thus unattainable for ever), it is at least a starting point for our considerations that yields some surprising results.

The revised transcription features actions that not only co-occur with speaking but also are required for a conversation to be possible in the first place. Thus, for example, the first turn not only places the words into the mouth of the principal but also into the ears of the teacher. As seen in chapter 2, what happens literally is a form of *corresponding* (Fig 8.1) in both senses of the word. The two participants are corresponding in the sense of communicating with one another. An old, now largely obsolete sense of the verb included 'holding intercourse with one another', that is, relating to one another. The second sense of corresponding is captured in the ensemble of 'agreeing with' and 'being similar or analogous to'. Thus, the words exist for both – or we do not have a communicative relation at all. The revised transcription (Fig 8.1) allows us to see that corresponding consists of two actions, involving two people. *Corresponding* thus is a social act, a transaction. It involves a going (in turn 1 from the perspective of the principal) and a coming (in turn 1, from the perspective of the teacher). Corresponding is not something individuals can do on their own. It is something that people do together. There is a unity, corresponding, and only within this unity do subjects take their place with particular forms of subjectivity. It is within this unity that we have to address the ethics of an act. Moreover, because corresponding is happening, it occurs in and produces time. Anything we might want to say about the subject or subjectivity while the talking occurs is possible only after the fact and when the Saying has ended. But this is only part of the story.

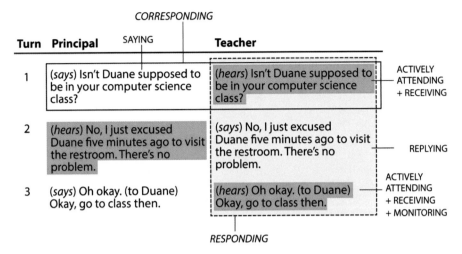

Fig 8.1 A more complete transcription of the *Event* at the computer science classroom door and the different dynamic forms that can be witnessed from within.

    The teacher is not in off-mode while the principal is speaking. Instead, the teacher, to be able to reply at all, must have been actively attending and receiving what is coming at him. He cannot know what is coming, placing him in a condition that is the focus of chapter 9, that is, as potentially vulnerable because exposed to the unseen thus unforeseeable and unforeseen. From everyday conversations, we know that we live in the speaking of others. We do not have to interpret our neighbor's statement 'What a nice day today' but immediately reply, which, on occasion, might be something like 'Sunny, but a bit on the cool side'. There is research suggesting that the maximum pause between two speakers is of the order of one second. Would that be enough to represent in mind what the previous speaker has said, interpret it, and then produce a reply? Research in the cognitive sciences suggests that this is not possible. Even in the case of an unpretentious computer game, such as Tetris, mentally rotating a simply object consisting of less than five squares in a single configuration (e.g. forming an L-shape), interpreting it, and initiating an action would take way more than one second. In this case, the player is already seeing what is there, whereas in speaking situations, the recipient, such as the teacher in the transcription, does not know what is currently coming at him. But we know from everyday talk that our replies are forming while the other person is speaking – we often start replying while the Other still is speaking and therefore has not finished the phrase which alone makes for its 'meaning'. That is, our replies begin to form before we know what will have been said and before knowing what we have received and what has happened to and affected us. Thus, stating that the teacher has interpreted 'the message' and externalized the interpretation in the reply fails to capture real life. To understand the subject and subjectivity we have to be more inclusive than focusing on the reply. We need to take into account that in that original *Event**, the teacher is active while the principal is speaking;

and this activity is pertinent to the *Event**, for it is generative in the responses as a whole. Together, the active listening, receiving of words, and replying are parts of *responding*. But because we cannot know how our actions – here the *saying* of the said – affect the environment generally and the recipient of our talk specifically, what we have done is available only after we have seen what we have done and how this has affected others. In conversations, the effect of our actions tends to be available in the reply of the other. We thus conceive of a movement that begins with actively attending and receiving, goes through replying, and ends when we will have seen (heard) what we did. This movement, we refer to as *responding* (Fig 8.1). From the perspective of the teacher in this particular case, responding consists of a coming (words from the principal), a going (words to the principal), and a coming (words from the principal). This action of responding, therefore, consists of a continuity of concurrent comings and goings.

To understand the subject and subjectivity, we may now consider what generally is referred to as 'thinking'. Here, thinking is taken to mean whatever happens in the brain whether we are conscious thereof or not. It is immediately apparent that thinking also is a movement co-extensive with what I term *responding*. Thinking therefore is co-existent with and dependent on the same coming and going. It begins with something on and from the outside, deals with issues arising on the inside, and ends by attending to what is occurring on the outside. The immediate consequence is that thinking cannot be attributed to the person alone. Thinking is a function of the relation between two people or between a person and the environment. Thinking is a characteristic of the person–environment relation rather than of the person alone. When it pertains to communication, therefore, thinking has characteristics of a person and the interlocutor. The result is serious: thinking is not individual at all, it is social through and through. Subjectivity is not individual, it is social; and the subject is not a self-sufficient entity warded off from everything else. The subject is social through and through. Once we arrive here with our analysis, what might be the cryptic phrase of a philosopher far removed from the world all of a sudden makes sense:

There is nothing *other* for us from the outset that would not be our *own. For the very existence of the mind is possible only at the borderline where there is a continual coming and going of one into the other,* at their dynamic interface, as it were – an interface that is defined not by the fact of their difference (in other words, not by a difference in outward [discernible by the subject] states between what is psychologically *self* and what is *other,* the stuff of natural science, as it were), but by a single process of their mutual generation and mutual determination.[12]

The subject and subjectivity, therefore, can be understood only at this interface of a continual coming and going; the Self and its Other are the mutually generated products of the overarching movement of life. To resist giving oneself to the ideology of the independent monad curled up upon itself, who at best is able to 'construct' the Other and the social internally, Gregory Bateson recommends to us viewing attributes of individuals as the result of two persons in relation. Rather than thinking about a relationship as the result of putting two elemental subjects together, he suggests 'thinking of the two parties to the interaction as two eyes, each giving a monocular view of what goes on and, together, giving a binocular view in depth. This double view *is* the relationship'.[13] This double view actually is represented in our revised transcription (Fig 8.1), here referred to as *corresponding*. Attributes that are commonly used to demarcate the subject, to characterize its subjectivity, really are forms of relations that then are attributed to one part of the relation. In the present, the attributes 'smart-assed local punk' and 'no-nonsense German teacher' are but characteristics of relations with others that are then, in a process of reduction, attributed to one member of a relation. Whereas the real subject and subjectivity live in relations, ascriptions and narratives decompose complex worlds and situations in characteristic forms (agents, actions, causes, effects, etc.). The relationship is first and *precedes* the identification of parts, especially the parts as independent of the relation. Otherwise we end up with circular forms of reasoning. As a result, 'only if you hold on tight to the primacy and priority of relationship can you avoid dormitive explanations', and Bateson elaborates saying that humans do not contain an aggressive instinct in the same way that opium contains a dormitive principle.[14]

The revised transcription (Fig 8.1) makes salient how the words that sound in the mouth of the principal simultaneously ring in the ears of the teacher (and Duane, who later is retelling them). There is one phenomenon, the sound, which is common to and thus integrates all participants and witnesses. Together, they constitute a binocular view that is in depth and constitutes the relation. The principal and the teacher are but parts of and defined by their relation. Through the words, the two *live in* the consciousness of the other. Language – as philosophers (e.g. Karl Marx, George Mead, and Ludwig Wittgenstein) and psychologists (e.g. George Mead and Lev Vygotsky) suspected long ago – is but practical consciousness simultaneously existing for the Other and the Self. The horizontal dimension of the transcription, manifesting simultaneity, reflects the sociological aspect of the communicative exchange (Fig 8.1).

Scholars interested in the subject and subjectivity thus have to return to and investigate the inchoate living through (witnessing and feeling) characteristic of real life. Otherwise we end up having to attribute characteristics of relations to individuals and, thereby initiate the disappearance of the subject and subjectivity. Focusing on transactions means that we bring into view how the people of interest to research are caught up in the world that is partially of their own making. Transaction means a continued flow from one actor to another, each acting as for the purpose of being intelligible to the Other and producing a response to which s/he can react in turn. This leads to the fact that the nature of individual actions can be established only *after* the fact but not before or in the act.

The living universe and everything we find therein is transactional. The subject and its subjectivity exist in and arise from a transactional world. As soon as we make some 'final attribution to "elements" or other presumptively detachable or independent "entities", "essences", or "realities", and presumptively detachable "relations" from such detachable "elements"'[15], the subject caught up in the real world and its subjectivity have disappeared. Of course, any 'discourse of action is itself a part of the situation of transaction that flows from one agent to another, exactly as spoken language remains caught in the process of interlocution, or, if we may use the term, of translocution'.[16] Action thus becomes an object for the social sciences through a form of objectification that is similar to the act of fixation of verbal discourse into written text. This reduction turns a transaction into the action of individuals, one taking the turn after another. The subject of the action (discourse) no longer is the subject of the happening after the fact conceptualized as the *event**. In the happening, the subject only exists as *subject**, that is, a subject-in-the-making – where we need to keep in mind that in both expressions the 'subject' really is available only after the fact.

Concrete Human Psychology

This chapter is a contribution to the debate about the subject in and of (educational, sociological, or psychological) research. It shows that the subject disappears as a result of the transposition that occurs in the construction of data, which are analyzed by formal analysis that requires special method for making the psychological and sociological orders of the world appear. This disappearance of the subject is the manifestation of a phenomenon that also realizes itself in the gap between theory (mimesis$_2$) and the everyday praxis of people (mimesis$_1$). When teachers and other practitioners complain that theory does not pertain to their world, it is because they cannot find their subjectivity in the latter. This also makes it difficult to see how theory could transform praxis (mimesis$_3$). In the preceding sections, I show how the transposition reduces a fundamentally relation (transactional) world into a textual world where agents, actions, things, and events are the basic elements of descriptive and explanatory narratives. The textual world is one of things, processes, and external forces; it is not a dynamic one, not one of relations and continuous flow. This is what Martin Heidegger made thematic in the difference between Being (*Sein*), which always means being-alive and thus becoming, and beings (*Seiendes*), fixed stuffs and processes. Educational and psychological research, as all the other formal analytic sciences and whatever method applied, take as their object actions that have undergone a process of fixation, become things attributed to individuals. Research thus constitutes the disappearance of life from its narratives, and, with it, the disappearance of the subject and subjectivity. Both, subject and its subjectivity are relational, as life in general. As things, they are the product of relations that are available only after the fact. With the disappearance of the relational (transactional) aspects of social life goes the disappearance of the subject and its subjectivity.

In this chapter, I describe how the subject disappears in the transposition from living life to a narration thereof. Narration indeed is part of life, but this itself needs to be analyzed in the way I suggest in the preceding section, by means of a first-time-through analysis. A first difference between the subject in life and the subject in narrative exists in the fact that in everyday face-to-face encounters, dis-

coursing means understanding, whereas the language of narration (as in texts) requires interpretation. This is so because the Self and its psychological Other live
through happenings together, in a world that is common to them. The principal and
the teacher did not require explications; they did not need to interpret the Other but
immediately grasped the situation that was of their own making. Each Self lived
not only grasping the acts of the others but also lived *in* the acts of understanding
the other. This makes the speaking of each intelligible; what the Other says immediately makes sense. It allows the principal to address the teacher in a manner to be
able to get what he needs – a statement that affords deciding whether Duane was
(not) legitimately in the hallway. In each instance, the Other and the sense of the
ongoing life are not only accessible, open to interpretation, but they are given immediately. In contrast, narrators of events no longer live in the situation; the social
scientist lives there even less. Instead, social scientists retell events for the purpose
of thinking about and theorizing the actions of individuals. The consequence is that
we attempt to access others' living consciousness only as objects of thought rather
than as directly given in the relation. That is, each form of retelling constitutes a
transposition that brings about an abstraction from the relation where the subject
has taken its part in producing stereovision.

Both Duane's and my account manifest how in everyday life, future relations
between people are predicted based on analysis by elements. Both Duane's in-
formants and my colleagues were predicting a troublesome relation between the
student ('smart-assed local punk') and his teacher ('non-nonsense German') based
on characteristics that were attributed to them. What is here apparent as an everyday, commonsense method also is characteristic of scientific and interpretive psy-
chologies. The question then is how might we fix this situation? How can we bring
the subject back into our educational and psychological studies of teaching and
learning? To this question, Maurice Merleau-Ponty already had an answer. He
suggested a need to 'return to the lived world that is prior to the objective world,
since it is in it that we shall be able to grasp the prerogative as much as the limits
of that objective world'.[17] That is, educational and psychological research can be
made relevant when it becomes concrete, that is, deals with the phenomena of everyday life rather than with abstractions. If life is relational, then only a relational
ontology will get us closer to how we live, witness, and feel life. Quantitative and
qualitative researches alike have to recognize their crude error that occurs in the
transcription of life and shift to accounting for and theorizing life as it is led and
felt from within. How might this shift in the epistemic project of education and
psychology be brought about? How does science become concrete?

Historically there already has been a proposal for such a change in psychology.
Thus, a 'concrete psychology does not put itself in the place of anyone; it analyzes
the drama and explicates the drama by that which it is effectively explicated qua
drama, that is all'.[18] The preceding narratives from school life were indeed in terms
of drama: the unsuspected turn that life takes at the door to the computer science
laboratory, the advice during a last encounter that becomes descriptive of an entire
life, the orientation of a teacher that respects the individuality of a student, who,
again unsuspectedly, turned out to be among the highest achievers of his graduat-

ing class. When teachers provide each other with advice, it is in these and similar ways rather than in the form of abstract concepts (including those from qualitative research). But such narratives do not go far enough, for they tend to decompose what has happened into individual actions rather than on the inherent social actions of which what the individual does is an integral part.

A concrete science takes the real drama of life as its subject. The preceding allows us to anticipate a contradiction: Is a dramatic description not also a transcription? This is indeed the case. The difference comes about in the change of analysis. It needs to recapture the double view that *is* the relationship. Politzer recommends analyzing drama *in terms of drama* rather than in terms of isolated elements, including agents, actions, causes, and effects. Our research narratives need to heed the advice that the relationship comes first and, pertaining to the subject and subjectivity, these are the results. Relationship also means openness to the future. We therefore need to return to the unfinalized and transactional nature of life. The minimal unit of analysis is one that itself is drama, a transaction. This is quite apparent in the revised transcription (Fig 8.1), where transaction is made visible in the concurrence of speaking and attentive listening that make each turn a part of the conversational exchange: each turn belongs to two people or it is not a turn in the exchange. In other words, there is not even an exchange unless the word belongs to. The dramatic world is transactional, and its analysis requires retaining units that are themselves transactional. In that world, human beings are not ratiocinating subjects, who apply a priori and experiential concepts to life, but are subject and subjected to the conditions that they contribute to creating: the subject is an *advenant* to whom things advene (see chapter 9). In unfolding life, these subjects witness what is happening, which they grasp as a whole only when everything has been said and done. This subject does not merely construct its world (or itself) but is given a world – the subject as *the gifted* – and affected by itself and others – the subject as *patient*.

The revised view of the human subject – always caught up in an unfinished world where the effects of its own actions are as unknown as any other aspect of the future – has implications not only for the subject of social science research but also for its place in society. It is a view of a human being who competently copes with the challenges of living in a once-occurrent world that never repeats itself. This concrete social science is not oriented toward control but toward freedom. The discipline could then work on making a positive contribution to the world that acknowledges the fallibility of the subject in morally constituting the world to which it is itself subject and subjected in the immediate and distant future.

Most discourses in the social sciences are unsuitable for understanding and explaining how such open and unexpectedly ending events as the principal catching Duane have on the formation of an individual in the narrower and larger sense does not deserve the denotation to be a science ('-logy') of the psyche. These social sciences have no means to theorize the *dynamic nature* of *events** – because the theories are in terms of entities externally related by means of the exchange of symbols internally processed to produce interpretations. The relational aspect of life, and thus the relational nature of the subject have disappeared. There is therefore no way of somehow grasping the nature of subjectivity, for 'all attempts to force one's way from inside the theoretical world and into actual Being-as-event are quite hopeless'.[19] In a relational approach – which is something that I realized during the last several years working at the high school level – teachers or principals are not in (complete) control. They never uniquely determine what happens in their schools or classrooms. Concerning the latter, teacher and students together bring the curriculum to life in a dialogical fashion. On the other hand, traditional psychological advice would have been unhelpful for dealing with Duane. Given the warnings I had received from my fellow teachers, I should have thought about control, for example, by considering offering small rewards for good behavior or by paying more attention to well-behaved students. Troublemakers ought to be given less attention or ignored altogether. As I was a relatively new kid (teacher) on the block, educational psychologists may have advised me to consult with my peers or ask the principal for advice and assistance. I *did* speak to other teachers but if I had followed their practices, I would have had to expel Duane from class as my colleagues did, or ask him to see the principal, who might have then suspended him from attending school for a few days. It is only when we return to the ways in which we really live our lives, caught up in some current field, that we come to understand the nature of the subject and its invisibility in educational research.

Notes

[1] Wolff-Michael Roth and Anita Roychoudhury, 'The Social Construction of Scientific Concepts or The Concept Map as Conscription Device and Tool for Social Thinking in High School Science', *Science Education,* vol. 76 (1992), 537.

[2] My extended study of learning through the eyes of the learner and from the perspective of the shop floor of social reality was published as Wolff-Michael Roth, *Learning Science: A Singular Plural Perspective* (Rotterdam: Sense Publishers, 2006).

[3] John Dewey, *The Later Works, 1925–1953. Volume 10: 1934. Art as Experience* (Carbondale: Southern Illinois University Press, 2008), 44.

[4] See, for example, Alfred Schütz, *Der sinnhafte Aufbau der sozialen Welt* (Vienna: Julius Springer, 1932), 100; and Lucy Suchman, *Human-Machine Reconfigurations: Plans and Situated Actions* (Cambridge: Cambridge University Press, 2007), 72.

[5] Pragmatic philosophers suggest restraint when it comes to using the term 'experience': 'As a general thing it would be well to use such words as *concern, affairs,* etc., where now the word experience is used. They are specific where the latter word is general in the sense of vague'. It be a good term, however, 'when a name is wanted to emphasize the interconnectedness of all concerns, affairs, pursuits, etc., and it is made clear that *experience* is used in that way'. See John Dewey and Arthur F. Bentley, 'Knowing and the Known', in Rollo Handy and E. C. Harwood (eds.), *Useful Procedures of Inquiry* (Great Barrington: Behavioral Research Council, 1999), 187n1.

[6] Maurice Merleau-Ponty, *Phénoménologie de la perception* (Paris: Gallimard, 1945), xii.

[7] Friedrich Nietzsche, *Werke Band 3* (Munich: Hanser, 1954), 539.

[8] An extended description and discussion of the challenge that passibility provides to all constructivist epistemologies is provided in Wolff-Michael Roth, *Passibility: At the Limit of the Constructivist Metaphor* (Dordrecht: Springer, 2011).

[9] Marcel Proust, *À la recherché du temps perdu I: Du coté de chez Swann* (Paris: Gallimard, 1919), 64.

[10] Mikhail M. Bakhtin, *Toward a Philosophy of the Act* (Austin: University of Texas Press, 1993), 28.

[11] Karl Marx and Friedrich Engels, *Werke Band 3* (Berlin: Dietz, 1978), 21.

[12] Felix T. Mikhailov, 'The "Other Within" for the Psychologist', *Journal of Russian and East European Psychology*, vol. 39 no. 1 (2001), 20–21.

[13] Gregory Bateson, *Mind and Nature: A Necessary Unity* (New York: E. P. Dutton, 1979), 133.

[14] Bateson, *Mind and Nature*, 133.

[15] Dewey and Bentley, 'Knowing and the Known', 133.

[16] Paul Ricœur, *Du texte à l'action: Essais d'herméneutique II* (Paris: Éditions du Seuil, 1986), 190.

[17] Merleau-Ponty, *Phénoménologie*, 69.

[18] Georges Politzer, 'Les fondements de la psychologie: Psychologie mythologique et psychologie scientifique', *La Revue de la Psychologie Concrète, 1* (1929), 56.

[19] Bakhtin, *Act*, 12.

9

The Subject-in-the-Making

Karl Marx and Friedrich Engels assert that not consciousness determines life, as idealist (constructivist) philosophers tend to take for granted, but that instead life determines consciousness.[1] The constructivist metaphor posits the subject and then explains life in terms of the various constructions that the subject achieves alone and in collaboration with others. The constructivist metaphor thereby constitutes a position that Marx and Engels denounced to be an outmoded philosophical take. These authors also critique the idea that individuals construct their identities asserting 'that the individuals do indeed make *one another*, physically and spiritually, but do not make themselves, not in the nonsense of Saint Bruno, nor in the sense of the "unique", the "made" man'.[2] Coming from a very different tradition, the American pragmatic philosopher George Herbert Mead takes a similar position when he writes that 'the self appears in the social act and is a derivative of the gesture, that is, the indication by one individual in a co-operative act to another of some thing or character which is of mutual interest'.[3] In Mead's analysis, the Other is a social object in my action if I, in addressing the Other, also address myself and in so doing maintain both attitudes. The Self will have appeared when the indicating event is associated with the Other, that is, the social object. I exhibit the machinery of this double perspective in the case of pain and illness (chapter 7).

In the present book, all considerations concerning knowing, learning, and education begin with *dwelling*. After birth, and before building and thinking, we always already are dwelling, integral part of social relations with others. These social relations change, and so do we – as infant and, importantly, as parent. The subject therefore never *is* a thing as such; instead it always becomes. The subject therefore can be grasped and determined only after the fact, after a happening has concluded and become an event. At any instant, we can speak only of who the subject *will have been* once we are able to look back. In the unfolding, therefore, we have to take the 'subject' as provisional, a fact that I mark by adding an asterisk: *subject** is a shorthand for subject-in-the-making assuming that the definitive content of the term 'subject' is available only after the fact. The characteristics are attributed to that *subject** are not his/her own. This has led the American anthropologist and

© KONINKLIJKE BRILL NV, LEIDEN, 2018 | DOI 10.1163/9789004377134_009

philosopher Gregory Bateson to state that it is nonsense to talk about individuals in terms of 'their' dependency, aggressiveness, pride, courage, passive-aggressive behavior, fatalism and so on. Instead, 'all characterological adjectives are to be reduced or expanded to derive their definitions from patterns of interchange, i.e., from combinations of double description'.[4] It is for this reason that in different approaches to social psychology, and based on different philosophical traditions, *personality* is theorized in terms of the ensemble of social – Marx and Engels suggest 'societal' – relations. But an interchange, a relationship, is not a thing and is not a determinable process: it is a continuous flow-like happening inherently open and unsettled toward the future. The 'subject' as a definitive entity, therefore, always already is an entity of the past, the stuff of narratives as we see in chapter 8. At any now point, we have a subject*; and there may indeed be something like an 'in-order-to-identity', some inherently open project the subject* is working toward so that after the fact that individual had a specific identity as a goal. As with any plan, recipe, or instruction, however, there is no determinate, causal relation with what will have been achieved. Thus, for example, chapter 8 shows how irrelevant the constituted (past) subject may be for the future, as apparent in the irrelevance of the characterizations attributed to Duane ('smart-assed local punk') and me (no-nonsense German teacher'). Neither term was appropriate for describing the actual relation we produced for one another and that we underwent. In fact, had the exchange at the door to the computer science lab turned out different, Duane might have referred to his teacher as 'an asshole'. Instead, he recounted the event over thirty years later in support of the description that I, his teacher, have had a tremendous impact on his life.

There are problem with the going conceptions of the subject, thought as agent who constructs him/herself (i.e. Self and identity) and who engages with others to construct and negotiate the social world. In other approaches, such as the social psychology of Lev Vygotsky, activity theory originating in the work of Alexei Leont'ev, the pragmatist psychology of George Mead, and the ethnomethodological take of Eric Livingston, there is a primacy of the social. The distinction between *Self* and (social, material) *Other* is possible only (and premised by) the social relation that existed among our (animal) forebears. These relations give rise to larger entities, which, for Bateson, achieve a process that is aptly named *practice*. Bateson describes a number of such higher order systems that are appropriately described at the systems level rather than in a reductionist manner as a composition from elements – e.g. dog–rabbit, gibbon–dog, or human–dolphin. Such systems evolve and create ever higher-order patterns of behavior merely based on information created within the system, as a result of the relation. But in this relation, information about one part is made available to another part. That is, *the system* behaves in a way to maintain itself. Each part (individual) behaves in such a manner that it maintains the conditions for behaving in this way, including the conditions required for changing the behavior. Once approached from a systemic perspective, self-knowledge is not necessary at all. Indeed, in everyday situations we tend to act without seeking recourse to a notion of Self. *Dwelling* does not require a Self. The Self, if it becomes thematic to a person, is the result of building and thinking that are possible only because we are already dwelling, inhabiting an inherently social and material world (see chapter 2). Bateson uses the analogy of switching on the light: 'When the hand ("my" hand?) touched the switch, the necessary information about *relationship* between hand and switch was created; and turning on the switch became possible without collateral information about me, my hand, or the switch'.[5]

Once we approach the question of the subject from the perspective of the relation – rather than postulating the subject to be the self-sufficient element on which everything else including the relation is built ('constructed') – then we come much closer to how we live and undergo life and, thus, how we feel and what is in our minds, including the sense of Self that we have. I begin the rethinking of the subject by considering the fact that we are not only agents, who act, but also patients, who are subject and subjected to the present conditions, including those of our own making.

The Subject* as Patient

To investigate the phenomenon of the subject, I return to the situation on the doorstep to the computer science laboratory, where the principal together with the student whom he had 'caught' in the hallways showed up, knocked, and addressed the teacher. Although the exchange was never recorded, we may assume for the moment that it unfolded in the way described in chapter 8 – the details do not actually matter for the type of analysis that I conduct.

Turn	Principal	Teacher
1	(*says*) Isn't Duane supposed to be in your computer science class?	(*hears*) Isn't Duane supposed to be in your computer science class?
2	(*hears*) No, I just excused Duane five minutes ago to visit the restroom. There's no problem.	(*says*) No, I just excused Duane five minutes ago to visit the restroom. There's no problem.
3	(*says*) Oh, okay. (*to Duane*) Okay, go to class then.	(*hears*) Oh, okay. (*to Duane*) Okay, go to class then.

There is an aspect in the unfolding of talk that has not yet been considered (chapter 8). As the first sounds emerge from the principal's mouth ('Isn't Duane supposed to be …'), the teacher does not know what is coming at him. Yet to have any hope in appropriately replying, he has to actively attend to the talk. He has to open up to be able to receive. He has to accept the gift of the word and thereby share in it. But attending to the talk of another, in opening up, recipients also expose themselves, become vulnerable, and eventually may feel insulted, attacked, hurt, or accused. Indeed, it is easily conceivable that in that instant, the teacher might have the sense of an accusation that is coming. Duane was supposed to be in that classroom for which the teacher is responsible. The accusation might be that a student is wandering in the hallways though he should be supervised, that is, the teacher might be accused of not fulfilling his supervisory duties. Whereas some readers may think that this is farfetched, I have indeed been subject to such a situation in another school, where the assistant head master entered my classroom and began accusing me for something in front of the students. In that incident, the students stood up for me, and the head master apologized and then left again. But let us return to the computer science classroom door. While the teacher is actively orienting and listening to the words from the principal – i.e. he is an active subject* of action – he also 'undergoes the actions of another'. Undergoing the actions of another is the definition of the word *patient*. We are thus not only agents but also patients in the unfolding of life. It is not that we are sometimes patients, such as when we go to a healthcare provider, as I had to do when a mysterious illness struck me (chapter 7). Instead, we are subject and subjected to the (verbal) actions of another while *actively attending* to and *receiving* the words of the other; and we are subject and subjected to the ever-changing world surrounding us and to which we adapt in the process. In the philosophical literature this has led to the notions of the subject* as 'the gifted [*l'adonné*]' or 'the advenant', that is, the subject* to whom events advene.

It does not require a lot of analysis to see that already in the case of moving my body, it resists that intention – as noted repeatedly in preceding chapters. An effort needs to be mobilized to overcome this resistance. Within the animate body, there are thus two tendencies that operate simultaneously: one agential, the other patient (i.e. enduring pain, affliction). Instead of the adjective patient, we may also use an equivalent adjective deriving from ancient Greek: pathic.

The analysis here starts off by looking at the teacher actively listening to the school principal and, in so doing, being affected by something that he cannot grasp (know) until such a point that this something will have been completed and thus a something of the past. That very same phenomenon can be observed in the context of other bodily senses as well. Thus, for example, when Melissa sticks her hand and explores the mystery object to find its shape, she is active; and she is actively setting herself to be affected by the object. She is patient while she is agent. When we touch something to know how it feels, the agential and pathic dimensions are present simultaneously – manifestations of the same animate body. While the hand and fingers go out to explore, touching simultaneously means being touched by what is there. The fingers are affected all the while being intentioned to find out the surface texture of something within our reach. We do not know what is coming, for otherwise there is no need to explore by means of touch. If in the process we get cut or pricked then the source of that action is the something: we do not say 'I cut / pricked myself' when we get hurt while exploring. In some instances, we actually learn to be cautious in touching, such as when the surfaces might be hot. In such instances, if the learned response were not to approach such surfaces or areas cautiously, our attempt to learn would lead to being heavily burned. Many children learn this lesson early: they are affected in the attempt to actively explore and find out. Those readers who have taken a chemistry class (or had a chemistry-oriented unit in general sciences) know that in the (active) attempt to learn by means of the sense of smell, one can be seriously affected. Thus, (chemistry, general science) teachers tend to ask their students to waft above the test tube or beaker and to take but a whiff to capture the essence of the smell without getting hurt (notice again the passive tense). In all those situations, sensing means that we are affected. We are subject and subjected to whatever is coming at us and that we can know only in and through the encounter. In all of these situations, there is a coming and going; in other words, there are afferent and efferent flows. In the previous chapter I quote Felix Mikhailov, who wrote that the very existence of mind is possible only at that dynamic interface created by the coming and going. In the same vein, Bateson does not consider 'inside' and 'outside' to be 'appropriate metaphors for inclusion and exclusion when we are speaking of the self'.[6]

The preceding analysis shows how the recipients of talk, those who actively listen, also expose themselves to the unknown to which they are subject and subjected. The teacher cannot know what is coming at him, and we thus cannot know the nature of the subject. The teacher may be an *informant* in the case against Duane; he may be the *accused*; or he may function in various other ways that novelists imagine in the course of creating interesting drama. The teacher's *subject** position is open until sometime later, when the *Event** can be considered to have come to an end, has become graspable as '*an* event'.

The principal, too, is in the position of patient. First, and consistent with the preceding analysis, every agency is accompanied by pathos: to speak means to expend effort as the animate body works against itself (its own resistance) to produce the sound. But there is a second way in which the principal is in the position of the patient. He, too, in speaking, is exposing himself. This is so because he cannot know with any precision what he is doing until he knows the effect that his Saying will have had. (The *Said** always is in the making until the *Saying* has ended.) That is, the principal is not in control over how the Saying affects the situation generally and the teacher specifically until after this effect manifests itself in the relation. But when the effect has manifested itself, the event of *affecting** already has come to a close. Bateson expressed this in the proposition that a first human player 'proposes' and the recipient 'disposes'. The teacher 'disposes' of the action that the principal 'proposes'; the principal thus is subject and subjected to the sense of this action, which he does not (completely) control but which he – the relation – has to take into account subsequently.

Some readers initially might find this thought strange. But consider a situation where you intend asking a question or refuse to tell something difficult to a teenager, who lets you know that s/he feels insulted – e.g. by saying, 'don't mother me' or 'don't treat me like a child'. That is, the Said in this instant has the sense of an offense or insult. This is and has to be dealt with in further actions, such as when you explain that your real intent was to ask a question or to protect the person rather than to insult him/her. In other instances one person makes a statement and the other responds by saying, 'You are asking me a question?' In such situation, the intended effect and the actual effect diverge, and it is the latter that now has to be addressed and resolved.

In the situation at the doorsteps to the computer science lab, the part of the exchange (turn 2) treats ('disposes of') the preceding phrase as a question concerning the legitimacy of Duane's presence in the hallway. Thus, as we move away from thinking about a conversation as the result of two individuals adding independently to a relational (social) approach, we find that there is *one* (inherently social) transaction rather than two independent but connected actions. In chapter 8, we see that a single turn constitutes a unit of *corresponding*, and this unit simultaneously involves a going (from the perspective of the principal) and a coming (from the perspective of the teacher). The same can be said about the second turn. But from the relational perspective, the two turns constitute one social action, one transaction, one exchange. Indeed, the exchange is not unlike an economic exchange of two goods, one of which functions as measure of value (exchange value), the other one as a measure of use (use value). The transaction of corresponding thus involves two double movements, two movements of coming and going. Because 'coming' inherently means being affected and 'going' inherently means acting and affecting, both the principal and the teacher, in those two turns, simultaneously are agents and patients.

The result of this analysis then is that who each person can be is a function of the relation. It is not up to one or the other person to construct their identity, as we can find the situation described in so many publications. Saying that I construct my identity is in fact completely effacing the nature of the *subject** and her subjectivity. As *subjects** we are in a relationship with others. There is therefore always a double description defining the relationship as a whole and, when analytically isolated, the two (or more) subjects constitute, and are constituted in and by, the relation.

The *subject** is continuously in the making as patient, because s/he is exposed to the unknown, the actions of the generalized other, which may have their origin in the natural world (e.g. when we get burned) or social world (e.g. when we get hurt because insulted). But we are also patients with respect to our own actions, because doing something repeatedly tends to makes us better at doing it. Indeed, in such cases as language learning, we come to master a language when we speak and write it – and not merely by listening to or reading others. It is therefore not surprising to discover that subject and subjectivity have been defined in terms of the pathos that comes from exposure: 'the subjectivity of the subject is vulnerability, an irrecuperable time, un-assemblable dia-chrony of patience, exposure always to be exposed, exposure to expressing, and thus to saying, thus to giving'.[7] Exposure to giving leads us to the above-noted notion of the subject* as the gifted [*l'adonné*], and it leads us to conceiving of the notion of the advenant, that is, the subject as product of *what happens to them* (advenes).

L'Interloqué

In very different traditions of thought, there is recognition that the Self cannot be the origin of the subject and subjectivity. There cannot be self-consciousness as the origin of collective consciousness. Both Mead and Bateson tie consciousness to the existence of double vision, making it the condition for consciousness to emerge. Marx and Engels, later quoted by Vygotsky, also note that language is consciousness for others and the Self. The term consciousness itself marks this double origin, as it literally means knowing (Lat. *scīre*) together (Lat. *co[n]-*). In this section, I begin by articulating the problem of the genesis of the subject and then return to the event on the doorsteps to the computer science classroom to work out some aspects of the solution to the problem.

The Problem of the Genesis of the Subject

The problem of the subject and subjectivity poses itself when we consider that originally – on both evolutionary-historical and ontogenetic grounds – there was neither subject nor subjectivity. There is no ego (*I*) or me; there is no Self that distinguishes itself from the generalized Other (things, species members). There is no subject that could have constructed for itself a model of its Other or its Self – on what would the subject base such a model? How would the subject know that the model is the model of something else? But this is precisely the position of constructivism, as one of its foremost theorists Ernst von Glaser articulated it: 'constructivism ... holds that insofar as we *know* these Others, they are models that we ourselves construct'.[8] The models are externalized and treated as if they existed outside and independent of ourselves. In the same way, we 'construct a model of the entity that we call our "self" and externalize it so that it ends up as a "thing among other things"'.[9] But, it may be ask asked, 'Who are the *we* or who is the *I* that constructs the models, of the Others, world, and its Self?' This question indeed remains unanswered. In developing theories of knowing and learning, we need to look at the evolution of the human species and the ontogenesis of the child and ask whether any explanatory concept that we appeal to can and does exist as a phenomenon at a given stage. Immanuel Kant was unable to deal with time and space and thus made them *a priori* conditions that precede any experience. Constructivism, as seen in the preceding quotations, posits the subject who constructs models of the Other, world, and its own Self.

To make his case, von Glasersfeld takes what he calls an infant's discovery of the difference between two movements across its visual field. When the hand of a parent moves across this field, the infant may have the visual experience of some moving shape. When the infant moves its own hand, its sensory experiences from the arm come to be correlated to the visual experience. Later, the difference between the two experiences is accentuated when the child can reliably generate the second form of experience but not the first. Here, the load of the explication is placed on the notion of experience. The notion remains unexplained, as much as the phenomenon of the *who* of that experience. Constructivism does not provide an answer to the question of how development can emerge from within the originary solipsistic entity.

A very different approach is offered in the social psychology of Mead. Here, the genesis of the Self and subjectivity advances from the periphery to the body of the infant. Mead recognizes the difficulties in traditional psychology that presupposes the Self as an entity antecedent to the social process, which then explains communication, and, as others, supposes the Self as the product of social process and communicative exchange. Thus, 'if you presuppose the existence of mind at the start, as explaining or making possible the social process of experience, then the origin of mind and the interaction among minds become mysteries'.[10] That vision cannot be the origin of the Self; the earliest forms of consciousness arise from contact. When the infant is in contact with the world, 'the object arouses in the organism the action of the object upon the organism, and so becomes endowed with that inner nature of pressure which constitutes the inside of the physical thing'.[11] As a result, the object acquires an inside for the organism (infant). It is the object that stimulates the organism to act in the same way as the object acts upon the organism. That is, the origin of the Self does not lie within it; instead, the origin of the Self lies in the response to the appeal from the object. But there is not yet an object in itself. Initially, the effort (e.g. of the hand) is continuous with the resistance of the object. Thus, for example, for a cyclist the same sensation may arise from tired muscles (inside) or a rising contour of the road (outside) – other senses (e.g. vision) and other information (e.g. knowledge about how long one has been riding) are required to make the attribution. In the ontogenesis of the infant, these sensations of effort and resistance necessarily appear before the infant can have a sense of its Self as an entity. The resistance, the effort within the object, has to appear before the infant can identify an effort of its own. That resistance is active, not passive – therefore it cannot be a physical object appearing before and as separate from the subject unless such an active resistance exists. Against the constructivist attitude, Mead is adamant that the infant does not project its own inner content onto the world. The just-noted 'response from an inside must come from the organism and not from the physical thing outside it, but it cannot be located within the organism until the organism *has been defined by its interrelations* with other things'.[12] The organism, the animal, the infant *responds* to the surrounding world, and, in sensing its own actions, responds to itself as well. The double perspective has begun to occur at the heart of the individual's perspective, which thus is both its own and that of the generalized Other. Marx arrives at a similar conclusion based on his analysis that the object can be a human object only under the condition that it is a societal object. The individual thus becomes a subject as a societal being, which is reflected in the societal object.[13]

In the social psychology of Mead, consciousness emerges when the organism responds to the responses to its own actions. This first happens in social situations before it happens with objects. This has occurred, for example, when the infant produces a hand movement in anticipation of a parent reaching the object that lies in the linear extension of that movement. At that point, the infant addresses in his own actions the response of the Other. It produces the hand movement in anticipation of a specific response. At that point, its behavior includes the behavior of the other. The infant thus is taking the attitude of the Other towards its own actions, which take their particular form in anticipation of the preferred response. Some readers might all too quickly jump to the conclusion that I merely described a pointing gesture, assuming that there is nothing to the infant pointing to the wanted object. But this is not so. Lev S. Vygotsky actually uses the example of pointing to show that its genetic origin lies in the relation. Initially there is a movement on the part of the infant; the mother takes the movement to be a failed attempt at grasping the object in the extension of the movement and hands the object to the infant; and finally, the infant begins to point.[14] Exactly the same kind of emergence of new patterns of behavior has been observed among bonobo, where the infants come to reproduce a particular body movement that is part of a pick-up sequence in which the mother picks them up. Again, first there is the movement and then the body position that freezes an instant of the movement serving as the stimulus that initiates an actual pick-up sequence. In both cases, the relation is first. It is the origin of an infant's responding to a response by anticipating the latter in its action that stimulates the response. When the infant does something to get another person to act in a particular way, then this doing takes into account the other's perspective.

L'Interloqué as the Answer

From within the event* unfolding on the doorsteps to the computer science laboratory, the principal is addressing the teacher, who, as the addressee, also is the one appealed to. The teacher grammatically appears in the accusative form, that is, he is the direct object of the transitive verb 'to appeal' or 'to address'. The principal appeals to (addresses) *him*, the teacher. In turn 1, the teacher is the appellee (addressee) – from Fr. *appeler*, to call, appeal. The teacher, in the principal's orientation, is the designated interlocutor. Readers notice that here, too, the teacher is in the position of the patient – he has been selected as respondent, he is the one to answer (and thus also answerable). As the one who is called upon, the teacher is the *interloqué*, the adjectival equivalent of which includes the senses of being baffled, stupefied, bewildered, amazed, astonished, and taken aback. Even though the teacher, as interlocutor, is in an active position, as *interloqué* he is in the position of recipient, he is being done to and done by. In Latin, *loqui* is a deponent verb: a verb that is active in use but takes its form from the passive (or middle) voice. In the French language in which the concept was developed, the verb is transitive, such as when saying that 'the principal's question has taken him aback [l'a interloqué]'. Here the question is the subject that acts upon the teacher. But in French, the verb *interloquer* tends to be used in the passive form, as when saying 'the teacher was taken aback by the question'. It also appears in statements where the person appears in the accusative case, such as in the phrase 'the principal's gaze bewildered him [the teacher]'. Even in the reflexive use, *s'interloquer de (quelque chose)* (to forbid, to be astonished by), the verb mobilizes active and passive voices simultaneously. The concept of the subject as the *interloqué* thus works together with the preceding analysis of the subject as patient and agent.

This word choice has consequences, because the *interloqué* no longer is the autonomous constructivist subject constituting reality as a solipsistic monad curled up upon itself. The constructivist subject has available only the 'meanings' that it constructs itself, based on experiences in the social and material world, which in turn are a function of preceding 'experiences'. The constructivist subject is thus running in circles, locked in an infinite regress as to its origins. The discourse developed here includes the subject as patient, who is subject to and shaped by the world as much as it is moving about in and shaping the world. As *interloqué*, the subject is baffled, stupefied, bewildered, and amazed not only as the result of the actions of others but also in and as the result of its own behavior. Don't people sometimes say, 'I can't believe I said this'? As *interloqué*, the computer science teacher 'finds himself the derivative pole of a relation in which he no longer has any of the (autonomous, autarkic) substantiality implied by event he least subjecti(vi)ty'.[15] Because he cannot know what is coming at him in the saying he now is attending to, he is also surprised – the verb to surprise in the senses of to implicate, capture, assail, to take hold of, to affect with. Surprise actually is a marker that something else, from the outside, has taken hold of the *interloqué*, who therefore cannot be (at) the origin of that which s/he came to know. Surprise, in the same way as bewilderment, stupefaction, or astonishment, thus dispossesses the *interloqué*, who as a consequence cannot be the originary pole of its own – as the constructivist metaphor holds. We also can understand the *interloqué* in juridical terms, as the one subject to the interlocutor, an order of a court signed by the judge making or pronouncing an order. As such, the concept of the *interloqué* makes all questions of the subject questions that concern the *who?* It makes the question of its rights subject to another question that precedes the former: *which fact?*

The *interloqué* does not know what is coming at him/her, and, thus is surprised by something that can be grasped only after the fact. The summons and surprise institute the *interloqué* 'without defining him in any other way than by his status as *interloqué*. For before I am anything, before in me *I* exists or *I* invent, the possibility of being a subject or a *Dasein*, surprise must indeed summon me, *interloqué*'.[16] As a result, 'I identify myself as *interloqué before* being aware not only of my subjectivity but also of what or who leaves me *interloqué*'.[17] This notion of the *interloqué* provides for a link to a pragmatic ethics and philosophy of the act.

In the preceding section, we observe two sides to a (social) act. One the one hand, there is the real act of the teacher's speaking. But the speaking does not have its origin in the teacher. Instead, the teacher, qua *interloqué*, answers to an appeal from another (the principal). The being of the act thus is the result of the reply. But the content / sense of the act (i.e. turn 2) cannot be derived from that being but has its genetic origin in the reply of the principal. The act can be understood only when both dimensions are recognized to be manifestations of a single unity. These dimensions constitute a two-sided answerability: the answerability for its being and the answerability for its sense must be part of the same unity.[18] There is indeed a double responsibility (answerability) on both parts of the relation – the principal and the teacher. This (only) initially is a strange thought: the one subject and subjected to the address, a victim of sorts, is co-responsible for being a victim. But this is the immediate consequence for our understanding of the subject – which would also arise from taking seriously Michel Foucault's idea of power-knowledge to be an effect of a relation. If it is an effect of a *relation*, then one (e.g. the principal) is not inherently in power over another (e.g. the teacher). The principal is not in control over the sense of the statement in turn 1. Instead, whatever the teacher qua *interloqué* replies contributes to determining the sense of the preceding turn; and it constitutes the new state of the situation as a whole. In replying with 'Oh, okay, go to class then', the principal submits to this new state as the condition for continuing. The principal now accepts that Duane legitimately was in the hallway rather than skipping class; and we observe no further contest over the fact that this is the state of affairs.

The subject as *interloqué* highlights the ethical dimension: answerability. The Kantian constructivist ethics is epitomized in the imperative that we act upon others as we would act upon ourselves. In this approach, answerability is tied to my intended act, the conception of the act in the mind. The preceding analysis emphasizes something else: the fact that the patient of the act also is answerable for its shape. This is a direct consequence that each act has two sides. It is therefore absolutely impossible to claim a non-alibi in Being, as Bakhtin suggests. But I am going further than Bakhtin, who writes about answerability of the individual. It is an issue that is spread across our relations and thus goes beyond my whole once-occurrent life, which always already is a life in common with others. Each deed is not just mine but ours. The constructivist position thus misses practical ethics twice: first in failing to recognize that theoretical cognition never penetrates practical life because it misses the living deed, as Bakhtin describes it; and second because practical life is transactional, which means that we jointly produce the social act and that we are jointly responsible for it. Thus, in addressing the teacher, the principal is affecting the teacher in anticipation of the preferred reply. The teacher, however, is not innocent, is not merely the recipient of an action: in replying, he also (temporarily) concludes the ongoing social action, ultimately constituting the sense of what the principal has said (which in fact might be further reconstituted in subsequent instances of the relation). The same of course is the case for the teacher, who, with his reply, is affecting the principal; and the principal in turn attests the effect of the reply that preceded it. Because the reply in each case also constitutes the sense (content) of the preceding address, the one affected, *interloqué*, cannot abrogate his responsibility.

Although the concept of *interloqué* has been developed in (phenomenological) philosophy, there are clear developmental psychological implications. In cases of seeing something we have not seen before, such as the orca emerging from a black and white field (Fig 3.2, p. 45), the figure is giving itself to be seen. We do not construct it in the way we construct a house from Lego blocks following a more or less diffuse image in our mind of the thing; we do not conceive of the orca and then see it. In becoming aware, we respond to something that appeals to us and to which we respond; the movement of our eyes that leads to perception is the result of an entrainment, inherently a relational (i.e. transactional) phenomenon. In the course of our early lives, we find ourselves aware of something that we have not constructed but which corresponds to a new level of awareness standing against our previous level of awareness that appears to be more childlike, more uninformed, even more innocent. In responding, the *interloqué* discovers him/herself subject and subjected to a relation. As a consequence, the *interloqué* is very different from the constructivist subject, who is the source of all his/her knowing, identity, and affects. Indeed, the *interloqué* allows us to renounce the self-constitution of the constructivist *I* (Self). In this way, 'the *interloqué* finds himself the derivative pole of a relation in which he no longer has any of the (autonomous, autarkic) substantiality implied by even the least subjecti(vi)ty'.[19]

Marx and Engels note that individuals are what they express and how they express it. Thus, who the teacher is (i.e. as a person) is attributable only once the reply is available as a whole. There is a possible contradiction between Duane's statement that he had not been to class for a few days and the teacher's statement that he had given Duane the permission to go to the washroom. This might have led some researchers to infer that the teacher lied. In this situation, the teacher then would be 'a liar'. The subject position is that of a person who does not speak the truth. Apart from the fact that this is pure speculation typical of qualitative as much as that of quantitative research, the form of the argument is based on the work in which the nature of the subject is constituted. It is an attribution based on the action. The individual, however, is not the genetic origin of the reply. The reply is the act of an *interloqué*, the one to whom an appeal has been made. From the perspective of the *interloqué*, the appeal has come from elsewhere. The *interloqué* therefore also is in the position of the *advenant*, the one at whom something advenes, the one defined by the coming of something.

Both concepts – *interloqué* and *advenant* – make salient that the project of the subject is never finished. We are always *subjects**, that is, subjects-in-the-making. It did not come as a surprise to me that a recent British study found personality to change throughout the lifespan (between the age of 14 and 77), as there was no stability in any of the six characteristics researchers had investigated.[20] Moreover, the *subject** is not in charge of its own destiny, for both the initial appeal to act and the effect (sense) of its act lie outside of the boundaries of its animate body. Moreover, that exchange with the principal also became a defining moment for the relation of teacher and student, as seen from the perspective of the latter as recounted more than 30 years later. It becomes constitutive of their relation, which, in Duane's own words, has left a mark on his life as a whole.

The Death of *Auto*poiesis

The idea that the subject constructs itself – i.e. as the product of a self-creative act or *autopoiesis* – not only is at the heart of von Glasersfeld's radical constructivism but also the core of the enactivist approach generally credited to Humberto Maturana and Francis Varela. In this chapter I articulate some of the dimensions that are part of an overall argument for why autopoiesis – whether that of the subject, subjectivity, or its knowledge (the Self's knowledge and its self-knowledge) – never can get us to the *subject**. *Auto*poiesis is impossible both on evolutionary-historical and ontogenetic grounds. A perfect case of this and the viability of the alternate approach outlined here are exemplified in the results of the work of Alexander Meshcheryakov, a Russian social psychologist who worked with deaf-blind children in the Soviet Union.

Meshcheryakov notes that the children in his ward for the deaf-blind do not display exploratory intention, such as it would be ascribed to them in the various constructivist traditions. Instead, the terms 'vegetable' and 'vegetative life' are invoked in his as in the writings of others. The children do not inherently try to walk, feed themselves, or find out about the world surrounding them. They do not exhibit intentions such as the intention to explore, that is, they are not 'naturally' curious, as it is often said about children. In sum, they do not act in a typically *human* manner. Vygotsky had previously noted that any higher psychological function of a human being *was* a social relation first. Marx and Engels do indeed articulate a developmental perspective in noting that humans appropriate their typically human behavior in acting as *human* beings. But they can act in a typically *human* manner – i.e. distinct from other animals including their closest relatives – as a consequence of their social relations. Thus, 'each of his *human* relations to the world – seeing, hearing, smelling, tasting, touching, thinking, gazing, feeling, willing, being-active, loving, short, all organs of his individuality … are in their *objective* behavior or in their *behavior toward the object* the appropriation of the object. The appropriation of the *human* reality, their behavior toward the object, is the *enactment of the human reality*'.[21] The authors add a point referred to in chapter 2, which very important in the present book, 'human *activity* and human *suffering*, for suffering, humanly understood, is a form of self-enjoyment of man'. Human relations – rather than the individual autopoietic subject – therefore are the condition for the specifically human relations to the world. Meshcheryakov, who quotes this passage from the works of Marx and Engels, bases the entire educational program for the deaf-blind on these and related insights. He takes the child's mind to be shaped as it relates to other people, and, in the course, relating to things and the world that has been shaped through human labor – thus is social (cultural) through and through. It amounts to acknowledging the genesis of the specifically *human* subject in and as of human relations. Thus, assuming deaf-blind children would learn by manipulating objects alone, a constructivist assumption, is a blind alley. Concretely, this genesis included the following.

Meshcheryakov notes that prior to being instructed deaf-blind children do not exhibit the need to explore the world around them; they do not exhibit any skills in navigating the surrounding world and the things they encounter therein. When given some thing to play with or use, they simply drop it. They do not display a 'natural' curiosity and neither are nor become interested in exploring things and environments unknown to them – as so often stated about children in various contexts, including Piaget's works on the cognitive development. The objects and things that children encounter become significant and of interest when they are part of sense-bearing and affective relations with others.

In the institution for the deaf-blind, tools were introduced in the course of meeting the children's want for food – need, as a specifically human (psychological) reality did not exist initially. An adult would hold a child's hand in which a spoon has been placed, guiding the latter in the movement from the plate to the mouth. Initially, the child simply dropped the 'instrument'. Adults were not only assisting and guiding the child to feed herself but also explored the instrument to allow the thing to stand out in its functional quality on the way to food. The food, satisfying the want, was allowed to emerge for the child as the object / motive of the activity, which always already took place at a table and after having taken a seat. It is therefore out of this sense totality that individual things come to stand out in their significance: the object is born in human relations. In Meshcheryakov's words, 'orientative-investigatory activity emerges as activity directed towards knowledge of an object that has previously figured in a "practical" activity. The result of this activity is the actualization of the image of a thing with the help of which the child satisfied an organic need'.[22] That image of the thing toward which the child's actions are oriented in the course of the activity – e.g. eating a meal – is the object / motive (in activity theory), in other words, the *in-order-to-motive*. It is not just an individual object / motive. The object / motive, being social through and through, is tied to and conditioned by the relationship. It thus is a *societal* – i.e. typically human – object / motive. As such, it first exists *as* the relation with another human being.

The observations made in the institution for the deaf-blind children reveal that until they receive training by relating to objects while relating to other people, the 'world of the deaf-blind child is empty and pointless'.[23] This, of course, undermines all the presuppositions made in the various forms of constructivism, especially those of the radical and enactivist kind. There is a primacy of the social in the development of the typically *human* individual. The child becomes a subject and develops subjectivity in the relation with others. Indeed, the distinction of the object as a thing in its own right, standing over and against the individual, is a result of the social relation. The human individual does not construct his/herself. There is no *auto*poiesis in the sense of the self-made human. In the history of thought, the idea of the isolated individual (mind) that builds its world and begins to think about it, engaging in exchanges with other individuals once these are encountered, this idea has been referred to as *Robinsonade* – e.g. by Karl Marx and Max Weber. *Robinsonade* names the idea that action is independent of acting socially and consentiently. Autopoiesis is a myth that does not hold water upon closer investigation. The subject and subjectivity – always only ex-post-facto available outcomes of social relations – are thus social through and through.

The subject*, in the same way as its subjectivity*, never *is*; and when it *is* then it does so only in the past tense: there *was* a subject. In the present, the subject can only be a project, something like a plan. It has an *in-order-to* orientation. It is only with hindsight that we can get at that something, which, with Dewey, we might call '*a* subject', a complete unit with beginning and ending. Thus, we can only get at the *subject* and her subjectivity as something closed when the then happening (i.e. the mythical *Event**) lies in the past and has achieved a form of closure.

Notes

[1] Karl Marx and Friedrich Engels, *Werke Band 3* (Berlin: Dietz, 1978), 27.

[2] Marx and Engels, *Werke 3*, 37. St. Bruno is a reference to Marx's first mentor, the German philosopher and history Bruno Bauer, himself a student of Georg F. W. Hegel.

[3] George Herbert Mead, *Philosophy of the Act* (Chicago: University of Chicago Press, 1938), 75.

[4] Gregory Bateson, *Mind and Nature: A Necessary Unity* (New York: E. P. Dutton, 1979), 133.

[5] Bateson, *Mind and Nature,* 136.

[6] Bateson, *Mind and Nature*, 132.

[7] Emmanuel Levinas, *Autrement qu'être ou au-delà de l'essence* (The Hague: Martinus Nijhoff, 1978), 85.

[8] Ernst von Glasersfeld, 'Facts and the Self from a Constructivist Point of View', *Poetics*, vol. 18 (1989), 444.

[9] von Glasersfeld, 'Facts and the Self', 445–446.

[10] George Herbert Mead, *Mind, Self, and Society* (Chicago: University of Chicago Press, 1972), 50.

[11] George Herbert Mead, *Philosophy of the Present* (Chicago: University of Chicago Press, 1932), 122.

[12] Mead, *Present*, 135.

[13] Karl Marx and Friedrich Engels, *Werke Band 40* (Berlin: Dietz, 1968), 541.

[14] Lev S. Vygotsky, 'Concrete Human Psychology', *Soviet Psychology*, vol. 27 no. 2 (1989), 56.

[15] Jena-Luc Marion, 'L'Interloqué', *Topoi,* vol. 7 (1988), 179. The English text does not translate this French word.

[16] Marion, 'L'Interloqué', 180.

[17] Marion, 'L'Interloqué', 180.

[18] Mikhail M. Bakhtin, *Toward a Philosophy of the Act* (Austin: University of Texas Press, 1993), 28.

[19] Marion, 'L'Interloqué', 179.

[20] See Matthew A. Harris, Caroline E. Brett, Wendy Johnson, and Ian J. Deary, 'Personality Stability from Age 14 to Age 77 Years', *Psychology of Aging*, vol. 31 (2016), 862–874,

[21] Marx and Engels, *Band 40*, 539–540.

[22] Alexander I. Meshcheryakov, *Slepogluxonemje deti: razvitie psixiki v processe formirovanija povedenija* (Moscow: Pedagogika, 1974), 79.

[23] Meshcheryakov, *Slepogluxonemje*, 75.

10

There is (a) Life after Constructivism

Constructivism, in various forms and guises, constitutes the form of thought about cognition and consciousness that dominates education and psychology. Its fundamental supposition is the informationally closed organism, which 'constructs' its own descriptions, concepts, conceptual frameworks, theories, and view of the world. The building blocks with which the organism operates are the results of the organism's own activity. They are the result of a cognitive method by means of which the organism abstracts patterns from its own experience. In these suppositions, (radical) constructivism agrees with an enactivist position, which formulates the ways in which the organism 'constructs' itself and its cognitive apparatus – a process termed *autopoiesis*. Knowledge thus is the self-generated result of an active organism. Because the organism is theorized as informationally closed, it cannot ever ascertain the truth of its knowledge. Instead, the organisms can at best test its viability by engaging in experiences (experiments). In the enactivist approach, cognition is thus reduced to the biological organism. But philosophers and psychologists since at least the Dutch philosopher Baruch Spinoza (1632–1677) have emphasized that we cannot get from biology to the whole, living person – in flesh and blood, so to speak – that appears in behavior as a *thinking body*. In the same manner, we cannot get to the whole person and its behavior when take thought as our starting point. Moreover, there is no possible way to get from thinking to the material body and vice versa. This is so, as Spinoza suggested, because thought and body are two manifestations of one and the same substance. The different manifestations, however, do not constitute the phenomenon. They are external to and estranged from it. Any relation between such manifestations thus is accidental, a point that the German philosopher Georg Wilhelm Friedrich Hegel (1770–1831) elaborated and demonstrated.

One of the dominant concepts in constructivism is that of 'meaning'. The focus on meaning leads researchers immediately back to the solipsist position, for 'it is easy to show that meanings do not travel through space and must under all circum-

© KONINKLIJKE BRILL NV, LEIDEN, 2018 | DOI 10.1163/9789004377134_010

stances be constructed in the heads of the language users. … There is no doubt that these subjective meanings get modified, honed and adapted throughout the course of social interaction. But this adaptation does not and cannot change the fact that the material these means are composed of can be taken only from the individual language user's subjective experience'.[1] Here, the social appears only in a weak sense, as a dimension of the environment where the viability of subjectively constructed knowledge and meaning is tested. It is thus not surprising to find in many research articles analyses of the negotiation of meaning, identity, self, and whatever else lies in the researcher's interest. There is no discussion of where and how meaning can exist when there are no words – infants to not come to this world with words; and how would they know that particular sounds correspond to the same world despite large variations in sound quality, speed, intensity, prosody, prosodic variation, and so on? A word, indeed any sign, operates on the condition that it is a feature common to and constitutive of a relation. It is not an individual's thing that can be offered up in social interaction.

I know that (many of) those with commitments to constructivism get upset when someone says that our intellectual worlds could have never come about if human evolution had depended on the mind beginning to process meanings. There are many careful analyses – e.g. on the parts of George Herbert Mead, Edmund Husserl, and others – that show the Other's perspective always already is presupposed in our own. The generalized Other always already is within ourselves and does not first have to be constructed – as constructivists suggest. It was Mead in particular who showed that our notion of the object as something standing out to be touched or otherwise operated upon at some later time is a *result* of always already existing social relations. Relations exist through exchange, the simultaneous giving and taking that exists on the parts of all. Thus, in chapter 5, I quote the Russian philosopher of psychology, Felix T. Mikhailov, who wrote that '*a relation generative of man is nothing other than the affective, sense-giving relation of our animal forebears, in the first instance, toward one another*'.[2] Here, 'generative of man' means generative of everything that is specifically human, including the human psyche, behavior, language, thinking, and so on.

While writing these lines, I am foreseeing two reactions on the part of the reader. The first is the one I already refer to above. It is rejection and a reassertion of the fundamental tenets of constructivism without considering whether these tenets hold scrutiny. In my own life, the close reading of the data I collected in real classrooms – while I was still a teacher – showed to me first that there are problems with radical constructivism in the face of the apparent social events that were at work when my students were doing whatever they were assigned to do. This initially led me to articulate a social constructivist perspective on the 'social construction of scientific knowledge' – in the very first papers taking such a stance in the field of science education. But in that very first paper presenting a social constructivist perspective, I had sown the seed for a pragmatic approach to language. Thus, some aspects of what happened are described as an evolution and stabilization of statements. But such an evolution is not constructed, as the students making concept maps could not know what they were making. Once they had made a concept map, they were then in a position to rationalize why they had made it in the way they had done. But it is apparent from closely looking at what is happening that there are surprising twists and turns in the course mapping right up to the point when whatever existed – the map of scientific concepts – was taken as the final thing. At that point, a temporary closure had been achieved, and the students could now look back and talk about '*an* experience', attributing some specific beginning and ending, articulating cause (e.g. 'I/we did this because …'). During the year that this paper was published (1992), I also wrote another article entitled 'The Co-evolution of Situated Language and Physics Knowing'. Based on the analytic work I had conducted, I came to the conclusion that language and the things it makes stand out cannot be separated. That any word is different for you and me is inherent to the word not to our individual constructions of its personally relevant meaning. As described above, each thing standing out and its corresponding name(s) implies a double vision that indeed creates depth – mind and consciousness. Students have this language in common, though they may use it differently. The individual thus is not generative of the language, or the things that it refers to; and the process cannot be described in analogy to the builder constructing a house. By that time my analyses had moved me away from both radical and social constructivism.

The second reaction that I anticipate can be articulated in the form of questions: 'But what do we put in place of (radical, social) constructivism?' 'Can there be a life after constructivism?' The answer to these and similar questions is implicit in the preceding paragraph. For me, there has been a quite exciting life after constructivism. There is a life after (radical and social) constructivism; and mine is but a manifestation of this possibility. For me, all the changes that I have undergone in the course of my scholarly life were the results of working with people in the field – e.g. with Natalie, who appears in chapter 8 – or of working with the videotaped materials that I collected as part of doing research. Perhaps because I did not seek to confirm theory, I opened myself up to be affected by the data and by how people in real life produce and make visible any relevant structure (see chapter 9). By opening up to be affected, I also exposed myself to vulnerability, to having to change because what I had been seeing and describing with respect to cognition and the human psyche no longer fit. I was active and receptive, active and passive in my own transformation as a scholar. I thus allowed myself to continuously *become* at the risk of having to abandon previous beliefs and being confronted with the unknown.

In this book, I articulate an alternative to the constructivist perspective. This alternative begins by recognizing that there is a primacy to dwelling over building ('constructing') and thinking, and dwelling always already involves social relations. Indeed, these social relations are the genetic origins of anything that is specifically *human* – like (a) the higher psychological functions, personality, and mind that Lev S. Vygotsky and his student Alexei N. Leont'ev were concerned with based on their reading of Karl Marx and Friedrich Engels; (b) the Self and mind that George Herbert Mead investigated; or (c) the personal characteristics and mind as the English anthropologist and philosopher Gregory Bateson suggested.

Over the course of chapters 2 through 4, I develop the idea of dwelling as the ground for building and thinking. It is because of our dwelling that we are rooted. But, as shown in chapter 3, we are uprooted when we are made to acquire arbitrary, decontextualized materials to be regurgitated on demand with the excuse that this is to be good for our education. On the other hand, there are ways that we may expand our capabilities based on the very familiarity with the world that we have already acquired. Under the appropriate conditions – such as shown in the case of the Bill Nye video – the dwelling-related common sense and basic familiarity of those engaging with educational materials are validated as the very ground of any cultural acquisition. This common sense is validated in the face of the fact that the common sense is overturned. During the cultivation of culture, we produce again and reproduce the intellectual revolutions that the first scientists also underwent; and, in the same movement, we come to reproduce understanding and understand again what has been attributed the cultural pioneers as their innovation and gift to culture.

Many a teacher, educational researcher, or psychologist has experienced how difficult it is for students to move away from the commonsense ways of talking about certain phenomena. As seen in chapter 5, it is not that we construct that common sense and fail to construct a scientific sense. Instead, that initial sense is given to us – in the way that the cube is given to and sensed by Melissa. The thing in the shoebox *feels* like a cube, it *feels* like having three equal orthogonal sides, making it rational to say that it is a cube. Even though we may look at something over and over again – like Melissa, who is touching the thing over and over again – what we feel does not change (lightly). That initial sense comes to be overturned as the consequence of an instruction that has emerged in the activity of the group in which Melissa is one member. It is in the process of touching the thing again that the same movement of her hand leads to a different feel. There is pregnance to the movement, which gives birth to a new form. All of a sudden – and to Melissa's great surprise – the thing feels like a rectangular prism. Here again, movement in an unfamiliar terrain – the unknown insides of the shoebox – is the ground of the image that arises. Her grasping is an analogy for the searching movements of the eyes gazing at the ink plots that may eventually reveal a hidden orca / killer whale (Fig 3.2, p. 45). In that chapter we also observe the importance of the social relation, which here takes the form of an instruction between students – instruction both in the sense of teaching and in the sense of providing a recipe for what to do.

In the description of the time when Melissa feels a rectangular prism in her hand rather than a cube, it appears as if there is a 'sudden' insight, as if something were 'suddenly' revealed or 'suddenly' entered the clearing to be seen. But awareness is not sudden. There is a movement from non-awareness to awareness; and there is a particular structure to it as well. This movement is the focus of chapter 6, where I describe the emergence of something that is not yet tangible – something not unlike an indefinite shadow in the twilight of an early morning. That something is there without our doing; it is given to us prior to any interpretive effort. Interpretation may begin only when something has taken shape, whereof we may ask questions or begin to wonder – as in the case of the Indian temple the existence of which I had been unaware.

This chapter on becoming aware provides us with insights on how our familiar worlds, filled with a range of things, comes to be populated with additional things that – after the fact – we postulate as having pre-existed our awareness of them. The increase in the articulation of the world – which thereby comes to have more and more parts – is not the result of an intention or a construction. Instead, the additional object is given; and it is only because it is given to me that I can begin to interpret it. But if it is given to me then it can also be given to others – though their positions and thus their perspectives cannot ever be exactly mine. In this phenomenon, we already see evidence for the need to change the widespread constructivist conception of the subject. The world is not (entirely) of our making: as the recipients of things given, we are the gifted; as the recipients of acts, we are patients; and as the recipients of an appeal, we are *interloqués*. All of these aspects of the subject, dimensions of subjectivity and life as it appears to and is felt by us, are developed in chapter 9.

In chapters 5 and 6 particularly, I describe the role of movement to the emergence of objects in conscious awareness. The movement is not some abstract thing or concept but a characteristic of the body. But the *thinking body* that feels and is affected is not the one theorized in current theoretical approaches. In the enactivist take on constructivism, there is a biological, material body. That body cannot get us to consciousness. All attempts to do so will fail because we cannot get from the manifestation of something to the real thing or to a second manifestation (i.e. thought). The constructivist take, which gives primacy to thought is but a rebirth of idealism in educational and psychological thought, an idealism that many post-Kantian and post-Hegelian philosophers have debunked. The idealism continues to reign even though it was rejected by authors – including L. S. Vygotsky or J. Dewey – who appear in the lists of references of present-day scholarly works. That thinking body is captured neither in the third-person entity of science – or medicine, as described in chapter 7 – nor in the first-person body of our conscious experience, where something stands out as pain. It is precisely the being-alive of the thinking body that is invisible. It is that body that resists and feels resistance prior to the conceptualization of Self and object, the two sources of resistance – as seen in the works of G. H. Mead or P. Maine de Biran (1766–1824).

The separation of the two and the emergence of the object in the consciousness of persons is the consequence of social relations where the relationship between two actions in the form of cause (precedent) and effect (antecedent) first is established. It is in the relation that what comes to be the subject anticipates and orients to what comes to be another's action; and the emergence of the anticipation (orientation) is the genetic origin of mind. This anticipation (orientation) is not private but displayed for the other, who, in his / her behavior, displays an orientation to the same field of behavior and future action. The living body is invisible to the subject, who, for example, has no access to the source of what comes to stand out and manifests itself as pain. I can interpret ('construct') something as 'muscle fatigue' only because the something already stands out motivating the use of the expression.

Whatever stands out is given to me, my consciousness. Who is giving it to me? The answer is: my own living body, which, in its movements, is affecting itself. The medical system, thus, has a double challenge in that it has no access to my subjectively felt body; and it has even less to the invisible body, which it cannot conceive because the field only deals with manifestations (symptoms).

The living body is invisible and remains unarticulated in constructivist theory. But the subject* also disappears because important dimensions of life remain unattended. This disappearance is responsible for the fact that we do not recognize ourselves in the pages of the scholarly literature and for the lived and living difference between theory and practice. More so, the disappearance of the subject* begins in the mundane stories of and from our lives in which the transactional nature of life is reduced to sequences of actions attributed to different individuals. The result is at best an *inter*actional picture of social life and at worse a *self*-actional picture. Both pictures lend their support to the constructivist perspective, which is based on the idea of life as the consequence of our individual thinking. In the *trans*actional perspective, however, every action goes both ways – it is social through and through, such as when the communicative act consists of saying (one person) and actively attending / receiving (another person). That communicative act, manifesting itself in the word (sign), simultaneously is in the mouth (signing hand) of one person and in the ear (eye) of another. This double vision *is* mind. This double vision also means that mind only exists as a continuous coming and going. That coming and going – recognized by philosophers of very different intellectual heritage, such as G. H. Mead and F. T. Mikhailov – is the origin of any boundary between Self and Other (things and selves). This coming and going – e.g. actively attending / receiving the voice of the Other and speaking for the Other – 'creates the borderline situation in which the alien is identical with one's own and one's own exists as an experienced reality of Other'.[3]

The position I present in this book is the result of phenomenological investigations. But the phenomenological view is not a subjectivist (solipsistic) take. Instead, readers can see that the position is fully grounded in the way we live life, that it, it is fully grounded in dwelling and the common sense that comes with it. But this life is subject to rigorous analysis. This analysis importantly shows what is hiding itself from being seen – especially our Greco-Roman, individualized (Americanized) way of seeing and thinking about the world: it is a relational world that conditions everything that I (my Self) can be. This has radical consequences for how to think about students or teachers as much as about all the others who appear in and co-constitute our lives. In the classroom, I am what the relation allows me to be; any one of my students is what our relation allows him / her to be. That relation is outside of our control and manipulations even though we do contribute to its existence: the relation is both constitutive of who we become and itself an emergent accomplishment. Just as I undergo my osteoarthritis or my cancer, I undergo a relation as much as I contribute to its existence. But actions never are completely mine because whatever I do is only part of what we do together. What we do together is not under my control – as seen in the simplest example of intending to make a joke that is received and marked as an insult, which now requires a lot of joint work to deal with the insult. This fact, in most cases, cannot simply be talked away. It has been felt and has emotionally affected another person, and, in the aftermath, has consequences for the joint emoting and thinking of the relation.

In the course of this book, we thus have moved far away from constructivist ideas about knowing, doing, and learning. Yet despite the phenomenological bent of this inquiry, we are equally far from the solipsistic take of so-called 'phenomenological' studies that perhaps are more deservedly classified under 'woe is me' type understandings of how the world works. Everything we relate to and within ourselves from the moment we are born, all these things are given to us 'not as an ensemble of mediators between [ourselves] and nature, but, in fact, as subjectively [our] own: for all of these things are subjectively "everyone's"'.[4] These things initially include everyday objects, sound-words (which themselves are things) concerning these things, and the different forms of adult subjectivity. All these things are part of our con-sensual world rather things ('meanings', 'interpretations', 'constructions') of our own making. These things first are jointly sensed, in joint activity, jointly (though not identically) thought and felt.

The preceding paragraphs show that this life after constructivism is one that we share with others and that we jointly achieve rather than one where we are caught in the prisons of our private (solipsistic) minds. It is a world of affective relations with others, where we affect one another, which is reflected in the individually and jointly felt affects (emotions). It is a world in which we are dwelling together, and which emerges as a world in consciousness – our joint knowing – only as a consequence of our social relations.

The view articulated here ultimately leads to the recognition that life is not about *me*. It is not even about us. We all are mortals. But life continues; and so does society. Life and society reproduce themselves in and through me, you, us. The appropriate analytical unit and category for understanding human behavior, psychological and sociological aspects, are life and society. I am what life and society – through the societal relations that produce and reproduce it – allow me to be. Life gives us cancer, arthritis, or Alzheimer's. Society gives us places where we can be educators, masons, businesspersons, presidents, or hairdressers. We may be better off accepting our lot by recognizing that life and society not only re/produce themselves but also become aware of themselves in and through us. We are thus gifted with a world rather than the autonomous (autocratic) creators of the world inside and outside of the mind.

Notes

[1] Ernst von Glasersfeld, 'Facts and the Self from a Constructivist Point of View', *Poetics*, vol. 18 (1989), 444.

[2] Felix T. Mikhailov, 'The "Other Within" for the Psychologist', *Journal of Russian and East European Psychology*, vol. 39 no. 1 (2001), 26.

[3] Mikhailov, 'Other Within', 26.

[4] Mikhailov, 'Other Within', 27.

Index